THE
ROADS
THAT
LED
TO
ROME

BY
VICTOR W. VON HAGEN

Director, Roman Road Expedition

WITH PHOTOGRAPHS BY
ADOLFO TOMEUCCI

THE WORLD PUBLISHING
COMPANY
CLEVELAND AND NEW YORK

THE
ROADS
THAT
LED
TO
ROME

For my three daughters Adriana, Bettina and Victoria, who have been part of this long expedition to search out the roads that led to Rome.

ACKNOWLEDGEMENTS

All the photographs except those listed below were taken by Adolfo Tomeucci. The author and publishers would like to express their thanks to him and to the individuals and institutions mentioned for permission to reproduce them.

Keith Richmond: pp. 145, 146, 153, 157

The Ministry of Public Building and Works: pp. 215, 220, 221, 227

The Joint Library of the Hellenic & Roman Societies: pp. 216, 217

Aerofilms Ltd: p. 224

The map on pp. 18–19 was drawn by Tom Stalker-Miller.

CONTENTS

EMPERORS

FULL NAME	KNOWN AS	EMPERORSHIP
Gaius Julius Caesar Octavianus Augustus	Augustus	27 BC – 14 AD
Tiberius Claudius Nero Caesar	Tiberius	14–37
Gaius Caesar Augustus Germanicus	Caligula	37–41
Tiberius Claudius Drusus Nero Germanicus	Claudius	41–54
Nero Claudius Caesar Drusus Germanicus	Nero	54–68
Servius Sulpicius Galba	Galba	68–69
Marcus Salvius Otho	Otho	69–69
Aulus Vitellius	Vitellius	69–69
Titus Flavius Sabinus Vespasianus	Vespasian	69–79
Titus Flavius Sabinus Vespasianus	Titus	79–81
Titus Flavius Domitianus Augustus	Domitian	81–96
Marcus Cocceius Nerva	Nerva	96–98
Marcus Ulpius Nerva Trajanus	Trajan	98–117
Publius Aelius Hadrianus	Hadrian	117–138
Titus Aurelius Fulvius Boionius Arrius Antoninus Pius	Antoninus Pius	138–161
Marcus Aurelius Antoninus (Marcus Annius Verus before)	Marcus Aurelius	161–180
L. Verus	Verus	161–169
Lucius Aurelius Commodus	Commodus	180–193
Publius Helvius Pertinax	Pertinax	193–193
	Didius Julianus	193–193
Lucius Septimius Severus	Septimius Severus	193–211
Marcus Aurelius Antoninus Bassianus Caracalla	Caracalla	211–217
Publius Septimius Antoninus Geta	Geta	211–212
	Macrinus	217–218
Varius Avitus Bassianus	Elagabalus (Heliogabalus)	218–222
	Alexander Severus	222–235
	Maximinus	238–238
Marcus Antonius Gordianus	Gordian I	238–238
Marcus Antonius Gordianus	Gordian II	238–238
	Balbinus	238–238

	Pupienus	238–238
Marcus Antonius Gordianus	Gordian III (Gordianus Pius)	238–244
	Philip	244–249
Caius Messius Quintus Trajanus	Decius	249–251
	Trebonianus	251–253
	Aemilianus	253–253
Publius Licinius Valerianus	Valerianus	253–260
Publius Licinius Gallienus	Gallienus	253–268
	Claudius Gothicus	268–270
Lucius Domitius Aurelianus	Aurelian	270–275
	Tacitus	275–276
	Florianus	276–276
Marcus Aurelius Probus	Probus	276–282
	Carus	282–283
	Carinus	283–285
	Numerianus	283–284
Gaius Aurelius Valerius Diocletianus Iovius	Diocletian	284–305
	Maximian	286–305
Constantius Chlorus	Constantius	292–306
	Galerius	293–311
	Licinius	311–323
Flavius Valerius Aurelius Constantinus	Constantine the Great	306–337
Constantinus II	Constantine II	337–340
Flavius Julius Constans	Constans	337–350
	Constantius	337–361
Flavius Claudius Julianus	Julian	361–363
	Jovian	363–364
	Valentinian	364–375
	Valens	364–378
Augustus Gratianus	Gratian	375–383
	Theodosius	379–395
	Arcadius	395–408
Flavius Honorius	Honorius	395–423

I · THE MONUMENT

The most enduring monuments of Rome are not the ruins of empire that even now lie scattered over much of Europe and Asia, nor are they those imposing remains, saturated with history, which mutely stand in Rome's Forum. The most enduring monuments are those ubiquitous, those overwhelming Roman roads. It is the massive grandeur of these stone-laid highways which lead out to the most remote horizons which is Rome's monument. Those Roman *viae* – each like a gigantic thread weaving together all the then-known world, stitching city to city – moved unerringly across mountains, over marshes and into the Sahara to link up with the fortresses guarding the *limes* of North Africa.

These were not mere highways of laminated strata indifferently constructed, but highways precisely laid – inlaid, as it were, with pavements of massive stones, the underside of which was shaped like a diamond, truncated so as to be set into a yielding bed of gravel-sand. Each polygonally shaped stone, though massive and heavy, was cut to a jeweller's precision, set and interlocked so that the road surface would be as solid and unyielding as Roman virtue, and so constructed that it was expected to endure a century without repair.

It is not possible to overrate the value of these great *viae* in the history of man's development. Rome became a mobile civilisation and the mistress of the world because of her systematic control of world-space through her roads. From out of the Forum, from the 'Golden Milestone' on which distances were recorded, paved roads led to every province. These continuous, well-engineered public roads went to the Rhine and the Danube, they flowed into the lands of the Scythians huddling around the edge of the Black Sea, to the Euphrates, to Africa, to Arabia and even along the outside edge of India, that great wedge of subcontinent. Twenty roads issued from Rome. These twenty developed, throwing out sideroads and laterals growing and multiplying in space and time, until during the reign of Diocletian, Rome was administrating 372 distinct roads. These 53,000 miles of communications were taut strings of civilisation, great life-lines that went off to the edge of every horizon.

Italy was traversed by roads and its provinces pervaded. The Roman

Outside Rome the old Via Flaminia, its stones worn smooth by centuries of traffic, runs alongside the modern highway

engineers did not evade nature, they conquered her; if they met a river it was bridged, if a marsh intervened the road became a causeway. The road zig-zagged over the Alps but when rock became dominant it was tunnelled. Water was outwitted by the elementary technique of avoidance. The Romans made sure that it was not there. Thus road building went on for eight hundred years until, as it must for all empires, the end came.

By that time Rome had paved the world.

In two thousand years, there have been only five attempts to present the Roman road system in its entirety.

Early descriptions of Roman road system

In 44 BC Julius Caesar and Mark Anthony initiated a survey of Italy. It took the Greek geographers Zenodoxus, Theodotus, and Polyclitus more than twenty-five years to compile the information with a map of the network of roads. Later Agrippa, under Augustus, mapped Holland and France. The result of these studies was a huge sculptured chart that was set up near the Pantheon. It is presumably from this that the Roman itineraries were compiled. Later, Vespasian made a large map of the fourteen quarters of Rome.

In AD 217, the Antonine Itinerary (*Itinerarium Provinciarum Antonini Augusti*) was compiled. It was a route book, indicating military routes in the time of Caracalla, the Emperor M. Aurelius Antoninus. It listed cities and way-stops and the distances between them. It was first printed in 1521, and reprinted not much later in Leland's *Itinerary*. Roger Gale published those parts which relate to Britain in 1709, followed by Morsley in 1732, who printed the itinerary – iter by iter. An edition was published in Latin by Parthey and Pinder (Berlin, 1848) and still another in 1921, which may be considered definitive, by Cuntz. The number of times it has been printed suggests the importance attached to it by scholars.

Dating from AD 250 is the *Tabula Peutingeriana*, known as the Peutinger Tablum after the German humanist Konrad Peutinger, who discovered it. The itinerary is the Roman world in the flat. The Ptolemaic projection results in a severe topographical distortion. However, the map covers the Roman empire from India to Britain, with cities, way-stops, roads, and distances. The map, which is preserved in the Nationalbibliothek, Vienna, is a twelfth-century copy of a third-century original Roman itinerary. It is 22 feet 5 inches in length and $13\frac{1}{2}$ inches in height. It has been continuously published since 1587, most recently in 1962.

Nicolas Bergier's *Histoire des Grands Chemins de l'Empire Romain*, Paris, 1622, is an attempt, through the close reading of classical literature and a study of the then-known Latin inscriptions, to tell the whole history of the Roman roads.

Konrad Miller's *Itineraria Romana*, Stuttgart, 1916, is a detailed and analytical study of the Peutinger Tablum and other Roman itineraries, plus a study of the classical literature as well as the results of modern archaeological investigations. It is massive, technical, and incomplete.

That the Romans themselves needed a more particularised knowledge

A glimpse of the Roman Forum and the Via Sacra, along which the victorious emperors returned with booty from foreign lands. In the background is the Arch of Titus

of their road system and the distances involved in its traverse became evident in Caesarian times; itineraries and travel tables became common and could be obtained from booksellers in Rome. But archaeologists are now forced to collate laboriously the information from a myriad of sources on the direction of Roman roads, while once this information was common knowledge. It took Rome centuries to build its thousands of miles of all-weather roads – roads that stretched from Hadrian's Wall in Scotland to the Persian Gulf, from Spain to the Caucasus, from the sand-seas of Libya to the gloomy forests of the Teutobergerwald in Germany. Fifty-three thousand miles of roads spreading into what are now thirty-four countries – only Ireland and the Scandinavian countries escaped the attention of the Roman road-builders.

Fifty-three thousand miles of roads

For anyone merely to cover all the distances and all the congeries of terrain into which Roman roads enter is quite a feat in itself. So it may be that the extent alone of the subject has deterred a systematic study of the Roman roads as a whole. This network of roads which helped to provide a unity that, wrote one Roman, 'gave to all the world a shared law . . . and intertwined them under a single name . . . in regions most diverse', never has, strangely enough, except for these given exceptions, been studied in a general and systematic fashion.

Many are the classical allusions to this wonder of the world, which certainly surpassed the other seven, but the references are scattered over a wide range of authors, both Greek and Roman, and they say little or nothing about construction or the road system as a whole. Strabo and Polybius, both Greeks in the service of the Romans and historians, have left considerable information. Pliny the Elder, whose insatiable curiosity led him to his death in the eruption that engulfed Pompeii, has left us many descriptions in his *Natural History*. Livy, in his accounts of Roman history, stops his breathless flow of the past, although not too often, to speak of roads – 'Aemilius . . . put a road [the Via Aemilia] from Placentia to Ariminum in order to make a junction with the Via Flaminia . . . .' Pausanias, in his *Description of Greece*, writes of the roads through the Greek states; Tacitus deigns occasionally to speak of bridges and ways; Procopius, the Greek-speaking secretary of Count Belisarius (the reconqueror of Rome), stops long enough in his narrative of that depressing sixth century to pause and look at the Via Appia and recall that it was built eight centuries before and still was in good condition; orators and dictators, generals and classical tourists leave their impressions now and then. Poets are more generous; Horace in his satire on a journey to Brindisi is a veritable Baedeker. The poet Statius, forced to give sycophantic praise to his master, the Emperor Domitian, still was able to give a poetic, step-by-step description of the building of the Via Domitiana: 'First comes the task of preparing ditches, making the borders as deep as needed.'

The bibliographical references relating to the Roman road system in one form or another – articles, monographs and passing references – are

The Roman Forum from the Temple of Saturn. Located between the Capitol and the Palatine, the area was first used as a market place, but it soon was used as a public centre

This Roman tombstone was found on the Via Appia near Capua.

so vast in number and content and so dispersed that no bibliographer has attempted to set them down. And the physical exploration of the roads, the traversing of them through sand, marsh, plain, and Alps is an immense undertaking.

To effect a study of Roman roads in the twentieth century, however, one has scarcely to begin *ab ovo*, as did Monsieur Nicolas Bergier in the seventeenth century, when he asked himself rhetorically why no one had ever written a history of the Roman roads. When Bergier, Avocat au Siège Présidial de Rheims, began his inquiry into the origin of the Roman roads system, in 1617 he was surprised at the prevailing ignorance on the subject – '. . . albeit these great Roman roads lie right before our eyes, in fact under our very feet, we ourselves behave towards them as do the peasants who attribute them as the work of demons, giants, and fairies using magic arts. . . . Even in our day (this year of grace, 1622) many stand amazed at the great extension of the Roman roads, the manner in which they have been paved and the audacity of their ways which cross our great provinces in France.'

Rheims – the ancient Durocortorum – in the time of Nicolas Bergier still preserved its Roman arch of triumph. The city had been an important Roman road junction, so that the ancient paving-stones over which Bergier moved on his daily walk to the courts of Rheims were a constant reminder of the presence of the past.

A chance remark Bergier made to Conde du Lis, adviser to the youthful monarch Louis XIII, about the method of collecting road tolls on the 'high roads' and the manner in which the Roman *curatores* had handled the matter of road financing led to royal interest and a demand that Bergier set down on paper these observations. No sooner had the king's counsellor read the abbreviated account than Bergier was ordered in the king's name to extend his study of Roman roads to all of France and even beyond, in fact, to the whole classical world. Since neither ancient nor modern scholars had attempted it, being doubtless put off by the sheer magnitude of research, the subject was therefore a worthy project for a French savant.

Bergier was ordered to assemble all the aspects of the Roman roads and 'render its image as a whole'. Moreover, the book was to be written in French 'for the benefit of a wider reading public'.

The final study, *Histoire des Grands Chemins de l'Empire Romain*, a closely printed two-volume book of more than a thousand pages, took the better part of five years to complete. Its importance, even now, lies in its careful gleaning of classical literature for descriptions of the construction, direction, finance, and administration of the Roman roads. The subsequent editions of *Histoire des Grands Chemins* – for there were many – further enhanced its worth, since Bergier's attention was called to an itinerarium, a Roman road chart, of which the original existed in Vienna. The new editions featured a remarkably fine engraving of this Tabula Peutingeriana, the map of the Roman road system. Edward Gibbon used this edition for his *Decline and Fall of the Roman Empire*. The work of Bergier had widespread influence.

Nicolas Bergier's account of 1622

Since Nicolas Bergier's *Histoire* there has been a widespread although uncoordinated investigation of Roman roads. Britain has been studied so often that it seems incredible that new roads should still be found. One scholar investigated the Roman road system along the Rhine, another the roads through the Alpine passes, and in Syria during the French occupancy French archaeologists (immensely helped by aerial photography) did a fine survey of military roads leading to the old Roman *limes* frontier forts. Algerian roads were studied in detail, yet neither Tunisia nor France itself has received attention. In Italy, while there are many slender pamphlets on individual roads, there is surprisingly no complete book on Roman roads. Roman and pre-Roman log roads in Belgium, Holland, and Germany have been widely studied, and two centuries of inquiry have produced an impressive bibliography on those countries. But still all this literature on Roman roads is widely scattered and a mere compilation of all these sources would be no small labour.

Excavations of Roman sites throughout the world have been extensive during the last century. Archaeologists have found sections of Roman roads leading to or out of many of these covered sites; a compilation of these details has given important aid to the search for roads since these paved city streets indicated the direction of a given Roman road when it disappeared. Small sections of paved Roman road appear at almost every excavated site; recent excavations at Elea, a city of Magna Graecia, have revealed the earliest use of the arch and one of the first known pre-Roman roads in Italy. When Italian road-builders were constructing the new

Left: Nicolas Bergier produced in 1622 an account of the Roman road system.
Right: The beginning of the *Tabula Peutingeriana*, the oldest itinerarium of the Roman world.

coastal highway between Terracina and Naples they uncovered the small Via Flacca, which had never been mentioned in the itineraries. A section of one of the oldest Roman roads, a lateral that connected the Via Tiberina with the Flaminia through Capena, was recently found buried under twelve feet of soil. The Via Traiana Nova, which connects Bolsena – one of the lakes north of Rome in the Etruscan country – with the Via Cassia never appeared in the literature until a very recent survey found the road with its milestones. The Via Julia Augusta, which runs out of ancient Aquileia, the famed Roman port of the Upper Adriatic, was found on excavation to be completely intact with its stone kerbing. One of the last consular roads to be built, the Via Severiana, which connected Terracina with the port of Rome, was uncovered at the point where it entered Ostia. Detailed studies of relatively short sections of road in many countries are being incorporated in the enormous undertaking known as the *Tabula Imperii Romani*. When completed it will be no less than a compendium of the Roman roads all over the known Roman world. It is drawn to a scale of 1 : 1,000,000. Its editors make use of all available reports, ancient and modern, to lay down the exact direction of the Roman roads as well as the position of cities, villages, ports, temples, aqueducts – in short, every phenomenon of the Roman world. This Tabula, first proposed by Dr

The Tabula Imperii Romani *begun in 1928*

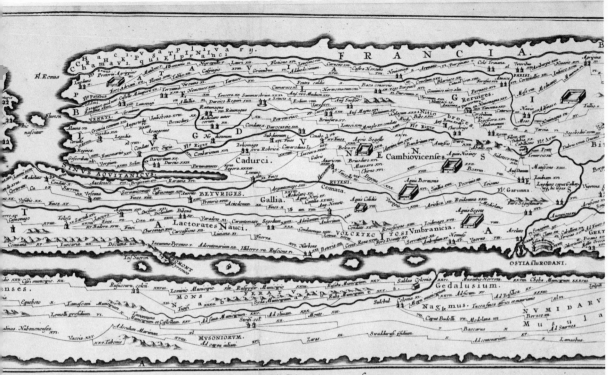

ERIANÆ. SEGMENTVM PRIMVM, ab oftiis Rheni bonnam vſque.

O. G. S. Crawford in 1928, led to the formation of an international committee to carry out the work, but it had scarcely begun to function when war interrupted the whole programme. Only eleven sheets of the great map have been published.

In addition to the itineraries already mentioned and the classical allusions to roads and builders there are other clues that help in the search for the Roman roads. One such clue is provided by the silver cups of Cadiz. In 1852, when workmen were digging the foundations for a house in what was once the Baths of Vicarello at Bracciano, a large lake north of Rome, they found four large silver beakers made in the form of milestones. On these were engraved the names and distances of way-stops between Gades (Cadiz) and Rome. These lists confirmed the itineraries and even included additional towns, some of which are not immediately identifiable.

In southern Italy workmen dug up a fragment of stone on which was sculptured the itinerary of the coastal road on the Tyrrhenian side of Italy, the Via Popilia that went from Capua – the first terminus of the Via Appia – to the Straits of Messina. This discovery partially solved the mystery of where that road (built in 132 BC) actually went.

In the silver mining district of north-eastern Spain, Spanish archaeologists recovered four inscribed clay tablets – *tesserae* – which once served as

Archaeological finds

The roads of the Romans

guide-posts to travellers on the roads, giving the names of towns and the distances between them. These *tesserae asturianae* were prepared, according to the inscription, by C. Lepidus Maximus.

In the Roman provinces of what was once Cappadocia – now part of Turkey – an archaeologist found another piece of a sculptured road itinerary that gave information on the Via Sebaste – a road over which St Paul once walked. Such is the nature of some of the archaeological clues.

And then there is the vital information to be gleaned from the *miliaria*, the milestones, which were erected every 1,000 paces or Roman mile on all Roman roads after 123 BC. A massive cylindrical stone, over six feet in height and weighing two or more tons, the miliarium generally gave the distance from the town where the road originated, and name and titles of the emperor under whose auspices the road was built, sometimes the names of those who built it ('. . . Legio III Augusta built this road') and sometimes the date when it was finished. In addition the miliarium generally specified whether the road was repaired (*restituit*) or built at the emperor's own expense (*pecunia sua*) and whether it was a gravel road (*via glarea*) or a paved road (*via strata*). Such information, provided by miliaria and other Latin inscriptions, is incorporated in the collection of inscriptions, the *Corpus Inscriptionum Latinarum*. A miliarium found *in situ* is evidence that the road passed there, even when the road itself no longer exists. However, thousands of miliaria have been removed; many are found to have been used in building houses, churches, and foundations, while others have been moved to museums and with no record made of their precise provenance.

Thus armed with ancient Roman itineraries, details from the classical writers, and voluminous studies of the Roman roads one sets out to find physical evidence of a given section of road. However, two thousand years can change a landscape: rivers have risen, the road may have been buried under deep layers of detritus, and very often a city has retained its ancient name but changed its locality, as happened in coastal Italy during the Middle Ages when marauding Moors caused the people to take to the hills. In such ways the direction of the original Roman road may be lost.

Communications existed many centuries before the Romans. Throughout history men have made their way to markets. Early traffic was a luxury traffic. Men travelled a thousand miles, for example, to reach the Baltic Sea to obtain amber, a light and easily transportable item, cheap at the source, costly at the market.

The appearance of wheeled transport revolutionised the movement of goods. Since the first known appearance of the wheel was in Mesopotamia in 3500 BC it is to this area that we must look for the first formal roads, for with the wheel were introduced prepared roads and bridges.

Persia excelled in roads. The Persian kings tried to make an empire out of their conquered lands. Darius began the road-building, and one of his roads, joining Susa to Persepolis, can still be seen.

The Persian Royal Road went out from Susa, crossed the Tigris above the ancient city of Arbela, moved into mountainous Armenia, crossed the Upper Euphrates into the vastness of Cappadocia, passed through Ancyra (mod. Ankara), and ended near Sardis at the edge of Greek-held Lydia. Later it was extended to Ephesus. It had post stations attended by grooms and itineraries for travellers – maps drawn on papyrus that gave distances between way-stops. It was a true highway. Parts of the track system may even have been paved, although Xenophon mentions that in one of the Greek wars with the Persians the Greek chariots were mired in the mud. Nonetheless the roads as well as the bridges were maintained.

The Susa–Sardis road was 1,677 miles in length and divided by 111 post-stations. According to a Greek historian, caravans took 90 days to traverse it from end to end, although royal couriers, changing horses at each post station, could cover the distance in seven days. Herodotus, who apparently saw the couriers in action, marvelled at their speed and wrote of them, 'Neither wind nor storm nor rain can halt them in making their appointed rounds'.

Although Egypt's principal route was the Nile river road, several auxiliary roads were also developed in that country. Ancient routes lay along the dry, open valleys of the desert; they were traversed by traders and police, travelling along a route of organised posts. The Egyptians even had a hieroglyphic for 'road'; it represented a causeway bordered on both sides by towering papyrus.

Five routes of varying importance went to the Egyptian gold mines, for gold-bearing quartz was plenteous in the eastern and south-eastern mountains.

Of the five principal routes in Egypt, one went toward Libya, one to Palestine along the Mediterranean, the third crossed the Sinai peninsula to Aqaba, the fourth went up the Nile to Nubia, and the fifth crossed the high, broken mountains between the Nile and the Red Sea, beginning at Coptos close upon Thebes and terminating at Berenice, a natural port on the Red Sea. All these were later systematised and extended by the Romans, who needed only to enlarge, repair, and in some instances pave these ancient ways.

The Greeks contributed little to the techniques of road building. Greek roads were at best *hamaxitoi*, footpaths, while directions were indicated by piles of stones to which each traveller added. Moreover, Greek tracks usually lacked water and hospices, a fact which Aristophanes ridicules in his *Clouds*, writing that '. . . roads without inns are no better than life without holidays. . . .'

A good road system can only be developed within a framework of political order, and the Greek roads reflected the turbulent politics of Greece as well as its complicated topography. Greece had to wait for Roman occupation before it acquired all-weather roads. In areas controlled by Mycenae, however, there were several roads, in all probability

Overleaf: The *Tabula Peutingeriana* is 22 feet 5 inches long and 13¼ inches high. This portion shows the city of Rome.

21

ellaca. XIII.   Lusomana. XII.   aquinco.   XIIII.   Vetusallo.   XXV.   annamatia.   XV.   Lusione. X.   ditari

Bonista. XII.   Piretis. XI.   Luntulis. VIII.   Iovia. X.   Sirotis   X.   Bolentio   X.   Mariniams. VIII.   Ser
ad p

P ad fines   XX.   Siscia.
Haur Re ab Haure.   Burnomilla
XII.
N aserie.
Yebino.   Sardona.   XI.   V

XX.

flu. Tinna. Castello firmani.   Eupra Maritima.   XII.   Castro trentino
Bolentia   Misiu.   Sacrata. VI. flusor. R. Tinna.   XII.   N   V   amite
firmo viceno.   X. sisternas. III.   Crulos. VII.   Pitinum. XII.   Priserno. XII.
XV.   Intervenio.   aque cutilie   Reate. XVI.   ad nouas. VIII.   Homento.   VIII.
rpicano.   ad marti.   Palacrinus. III. forveen. XII.   VII.   Creto. XIII.
Inter mamaria XII.   de uo Falsico. XII.   fanfar.   fidenis
a. ad marti.   via Saura
Palacrinus. III.   ad ponte
Interamno. VI.   aqua uiua.   VII.   ad duocesinu.   ad rubras. VI.
ne Recine XI.   Interamno. VI.   ad sextum.   via clodia. III.   Ponte Adriani
VIIII.   Veios.   VI.   ad sextum   via clodia. III.   Pontecco.   saiis   via la
Careias   VIII.   ad Sco. Pe   bauon
VIII.   Turres.   Bebiana   Iorio. XII.   via aurelia
VI.   Pyrgos.   X.   alsium. VI.   VIII.

Gallum Gallinarum.   XV.   Thartagine colon
XVI.   Thuburbiminus.   III.   Thuraria.   XV.   Cicisa. XVIII.   thun
IIII.   Sicilibba.   XIII.   Inuca. II.   ad mercurium. III.   ad pertusa. XIII.   XV.   Vthica.   Bibar
TH VR RIS   X. durta.   XII. Tuburbomaiu.   XV.   Onellana.   XVI.
sea. XII.   Veggo.   X.   Auila.   VII.   autipsidam.   VI.   Vhappa.
XVIII.   Thasarte.   ad thasartho.   Si z es v a   Mi l i a.
thiges.   XXV.
thusuros

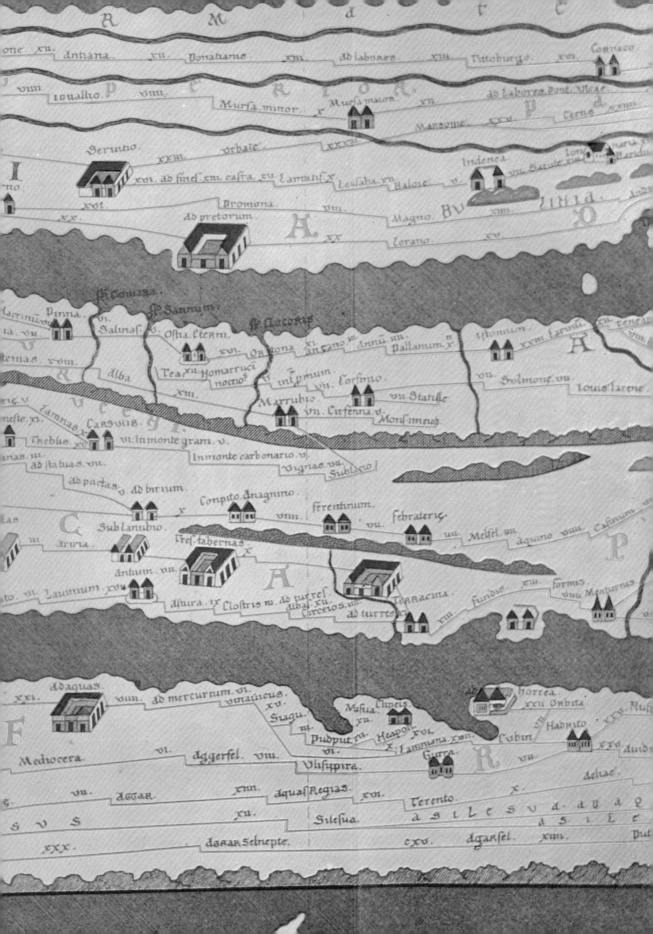

processional roads. These were built of cyclopean slabs of rock, polygonal in shape. Although Homer speaks of bridges as if they were common in Greece, an ancient Greek bridge has rarely, if ever, been seen.

It was in search of sapphires and other things that the Macedonian invasion followed the caravan routes to India. When Alexander the Great invaded that immense wedge of land he found that roads already existed in India. Although he had travelled through all the Middle East empires, he had seen no such roads as these. They were built of burnt brick, baked and polished. The roads were wide enough to take pedestrian as well as mule-caravan traffic; they were built as step roads with treads low enough to allow the easy passage of laden mules, and they were lined with 'all manner of trees bearing yellow fruits'.

China's roads were plentifully supplied with way-stops. Marco Polo was amazed at what he found in 1252. 'You must know . . .' he wrote, 'when the Great Khan's messenger sets out on these roads, he finds a posting station every twenty-five miles . . . called *yambs*; at every post the messenger finds a spacious and palatial hostelry for his lodging. . . . And at Cathay at the large river called Pulisanghin . . . the river is crossed by a magnificent stone bridge . . . fully 300 paces in length, eight in width. . . .'

There were, then, ways, roads, and tracks almost everywhere, but there is no prototype among ancient roads for the Roman road, that well-laid, metalled road resting on a sound road-bed and – when properly engineered – capable of enduring for centuries. Where, then, did the Romans get this idea of road building?

Virgil has Aeneas say that the Romans obtained their road building techniques from Carthage, and among Romans it was presumed that the Carthaginians had been the first to pave their roads with stone slabs. This is doubtful. With very rare exception, even the Romans did not pave their roads in Africa; roads were paved only in cities. A paved Carthaginian road has yet to be seen or reliably reported upon in North Africa.

The achievement of Roman engineers Much of that which became Roman was inherited from the Etruscans. Their cities, often widely distant one from the other, had communications. The Via Flaminia, for example, which connected Rome with the Adriatic, was an old Etruscan track before Rome reformed it. Many bridges are Etruscan, reconstructed with Roman arches. Pavements have been found in ancient Etruscan cities. And yet there has never been found an Etruscan road of sufficient length to determine its building techniques so that it could be compared to a Roman road.

Thus we assume that the Romans were the inventors and perfecters of the deep-laid road-bed and the cambered paved road that have survived as communication arteries for two thousand years. There is little or no engineering precedent for this in the ancient world. The road is a Roman achievement.

Where the Tiber was shallow enough to ford, foot traffic crossed it.

The Pyramid of Cestius on the Via Ostiensis. The Romans copied the Egyptian pyramidal form in the tomb of Gaius Cestius, erected about 12 BC

The Via Appia, 'the queen of roads' was constructed to join Rome and
Capua. It was subsequently extended to the port of Brindisi

The Porta San Sebastiano in Rome, formerly known as the Porta Appia, is adorned with marble blocks from ancient buildings

At this nodal point, two productive areas, Latium and Etruria, were brought into formal contact. In time came the bridge. It was first constructed of wooden piles, without iron so that it could be cut down in emergencies. The Pons Sublicius, as it was called, was put in the charge of the High Priest whose title was Pontifex, 'bridge maker'. An ancient track that became the Via Latina crossed the bridge from the northern side and connected with an old Etruscan track that went to Veii, the ancient Etruscan city. When it was paved by the Romans in 171 BC this track became the Via Cassia.

The Pons Sublicius was the bridge that Horatius Cocles defended in 508 BC; it was he who urged his followers to cut it down while he kept the Etruscans at bay. It was rebuilt as a stone bridge after the Roman victory over the Etruscans in 396 BC. Eventually three Roman roads converged on it and three radiated from it. From that bridge Rome conquered all Italy and in time the entire world.

The oldest Roman roads

The Via Appia, laid down as far as Anxur-Terracina on the Tyrrhenian Sea in 312 BC, may or may not have been Rome's oldest formal road, for it was laid on another, older road – the Via Norbana, which went to the town of Norba. Yet the Via Appia was at least considered by all Roman historians to be the oldest. One of them wrote: 'That year (312 BC) was marked by the famous censorship of Appius Claudius . . . his memory is cherished because he built . . . the Via Appia.'

The Via Latina, already mentioned, came out of the Latium country near ancient Tusculum and was paved by 240 BC. The Via Salaria, which was the principal road to the Sabine country north-east of Rome, had a proper road-bed but remained a gravel road – a *via glarea* – until the second century.

The Via Ostiensis, which moved from Rome to Ostia and which was probably the first Via Salaria, was a dirt road until it was paved in the second century BC. It ran from Rome to a fortified post – the Ostian *castrum* – set up about 338 BC to guard the salt beds.

The road that became the Via Praenestina went to Praeneste (now Palestrina), which had once been an Etruscan stronghold. This road had begun as the Via Gabina, which ran only a few miles from Rome to the quarries at Gabii. When Sulla, one of the Cornelii, became master of Rome, he built the sanctuary of Fortuna at Praeneste, paved the road which led to the sanctuary and called it Via Praenestina.

The Flaminian Way, following an earlier Etruscan route which remains anonymous, was rebuilt in 217 BC by the Consul Gaius Flaminius. It was carried to the river Nar where stood the Etruscan fortress of Narnia.

The Etruscan track which went to the cities in Etruria was paved before 200 BC as far as the XXI milestone. It was probably named Via Cassia after the Consul Cassius Longinus under whose aegis it was paved. An ancient track that went leisurely through Etruscan lands between the lakes and the sea to Vetulonia was paved in 225 BC and called the Via

The Pons Aemilius, called the 'Ponte Rotto' or 'broken bridge' by modern Romans, marks the site of the earlier Pons Sublicius, where Horatius Cocles resisted the Etruscans

Clodia. The Via Cornelia, paved as the name suggests by one of the Cornelii family, went to the old Etruscan city of Caere (now Cerveteri) twenty miles north-west of Rome. The important coastal artery, also laid over what was doubtless an Etruscan track-way, was paved for a short distance in the same century by one of the Aurelii Cottae after whom the road was named Via Aurelia. Finally one of the earliest roads, the Via Tiburtina, was built in 307 BC, very soon after the Appia itself, and led to the city of Tibur on the Anio river. A few years later it was extended by Valerius towards what is now Avezzano, this extension acquiring the name Via Valeria after its builder.

All of these *viae* as well as the less used roads of Tiberina, Nomentana, Labicana, Tusculana, Laurentina, and Ardeatina bore the name of the city to which the road led or the name of the man who instigated its construction; they were all short roads not much over twenty miles in length except those three titans – the Viae Appia, Flaminia and Aurelia which were over one hundred and fifty miles long.

This, then, was the state and position of the earliest Roman roads when in 218 BC Rome was faced with the invasion of Hannibal. The building of

The Via Appia (section). The surface of the road was covered with closely fitted polygonal blocks of stone

A Roman structure on the Via Appia, near Terracina.
The Temple of Jupiter Anxur dominated the town

This detail of a relief from the Roman Forum shows
the type of carts that traversed the Roman roads.

roads in Italy ceased, as we can tell from the dearth of inscriptions. Not
until Hannibal was defeated in Africa by Scipio Africanus did the Romans
return to road building. Three hundred years later they had paved the
entire known world.

The rules for the building and maintenance of roads, their width and
administration, were given by the Roman patricians in the Twelve Tables
as far back as 450 BC, 138 years before the Appia was laid down. Roads
were to be no broader than 4·80 metres, a measurement which allowed
the widest vehicles to pass each other. The law of road-building then
referred principally to Rome's streets. Later, writes Jérôme Carcopino,
the roads were to reach an impressive length of 60,000 *passus* (89 kilometres or $55\frac{1}{2}$ miles). But even when the Via Appia was built the width
of precisely 4·80 metres was observed.

The Roman engineer who erected public buildings, bridges or roads
was titled an *architectus*. If Vitruvius's ideal were followed he had to be
'. . . a man of letters, a skillful draftsman, mathematician, one familiar
with history, philosophy, music (so as to know how to tune catapults by
striking the tension skeins) . . . not entirely ignorant of medicine, familiar
with stars, astronomy, calculations. . . .'

*Qualifications of a
Roman engineer*

The Via Praenestina leads to Palestrina (anc. Praeneste),
the site of the monumental Temple of Fortuna

The *architectus* had attached to his staff a surveyor (*agrimensor*) and a leveller (*librator*), and each legion had its *architecti* and surveyors. However, it was the Roman soldier who carried out the actual work of building Roman roads. A spade was part of a legionary's equipment. Besides his offensive arms each soldier carried his ration of grain, cooking vessels – he lived mostly on porridge – cup, basket, saw, hatchet, sickle, pick and spade, for in the legion it was necessary that he should be woodsman and navvy as well as soldier. On the march the legions had to construct an entrenched camp every night. It was a short step from entrenchment to road building.

When the Roman peace settled on the conquered lands the Emperor Augustus, fearful that his legions would become debauched by sloth, thought that they could not be better employed than in making new highways in all parts of his empire. The legionaries occasionally thought differently, and Tiberius was forced on several occasions to put down revolts. Livy notes that when Flaminius had freed Etruria from war '. . . he built a road from Bologna to Arezzo to keep his army from being idle'.

To lay out a road, the linesman set out with surveyor's poles, a line which was called *rigor* was laid down, and the straight line was corrected by the surveyor until it was 'in line'. Right angles were obtained with a *groma*, a simple and effective device. It was a wooden cross-piece laid on a swivel arm; from each of the four ends of the cross-piece hung plumb lines so that it could be held level; with it the Romans effectively laid out right angles to make a grid. When the line of the road was determined, it was ploughed or dug out.

Much has been written on 'the straight Roman road'. The Roman engineer did not follow an obstinately straight line; of the twenty roads that entered Rome only one – the Appia – maintains a relatively straight line into the city. It is true that the Roman-built Watling Street in England does not deviate much for twenty miles at a time. Many roads in the desert, if there are no physical obstacles, are straight.

But straightness was a secondary consideration in early road building. The Romans knew that the straight line is dangerous; movement on it can be anticipated. Persia was betrayed to Alexander by its straight roads. But Romans had to deal mostly with hilly terrain; mountains and prodigious valleys in Italy, deeply recessed wadis in North Africa where there could be no 'straight road', no perfectly aligned road. Rather the Romans used 'directional straightness': generally a road was driven as straight to its goal as possible.

Once the road was aligned and the width determined (widths of roads vary widely, from three feet nine inches up to twenty-four feet), the pliant earth or subsoil was removed until the builders struck solid rock or gravel. The Greek historian Polybius witnessed the construction of a road and described how the surveyors measured and aligned it and how the soldiers dug out a ditch – the *ruderato*. Then followed the construction of the road-bed. It was filled with rubble, rough stones and flints held together with sand or coarse gravel and rammed down with human-operated rammers. Over this was a layer of smaller stones, not one of which was larger than would fill the hand. Over this another layer of gravel was laid, and finally the pavement of thick polygonal blocks.

Like Polybius, the poet laureate Publius Papinius Statius, chronicler of some events in the life of the Emperor Domitian, seems to have watched with his own eyes the building of such a road – the Via Domitiana which connected Naples to the Via Appia at Sinuessa. In his poem 'Silvae', he describes how the road builders first dug out the full width of a ditch that was to be the road, continuing until they reached rock surface. The road-bed was then filled with crushed stone to a depth of eighteen inches. Then it was filled with a lighter material, a watertight layer. Into this lighter material the truncated paving-stones were closely packed.

The Latin term for building a road was *viam munire*. It sums up the process exactly, for *munire* means 'to build a wall', and the Roman road was actually a solid wall, generally fifteen feet high and three to four feet wide, lying on its side. Unfortunately for our understanding of Roman road building techniques, the description of the correct construction of a pavement as given by Vitruvius has been erroneously applied to the construction of a road. In *De Architectura*, Vitruvius describes the Roman techniques of erecting masonry walls and pavements, the foundation and depth of which depended on the nature of the soil. Into the excavated *fossa* a rubble of stone was dumped and rammed down. Its thickness varied with the nature of the soil. Over this was placed a nine-inch layer of coarse concrete stones and lime, next a six-inch bedding of fine concrete including potsherds and lime, and then the final course of blocks of cut stone. This description of a pavement has been used by almost all who have ever mentioned Roman roads, as being the manner in which Roman roads were built. However, when the road was constructed of polygonally shaped, thick selce-lava stones, the deep-set road-bed was not always necessary.

Vitruvius' account of building techniques

Foundations for roads as well as for buildings depended on the nature of the terrain; where there was neither moisture-bearing clay nor marsh and a reasonably solid surface, the road was laid down with only a minimum of foundation, no more than what was necessary to carry the massive pavement; roads that have been examined all over Italy in widely separated areas do not reveal anything of this often quoted deep-set road-bed.

The Roman theory of road building was simple and effective. If a stone-laid road was set upon a proper foundation, firm and unyielding, or if it was solidly paved, such a road would need the minimum of maintenance. It could, and often did, last a century without repair. This is confirmed by epigraphy.

The nature of the road's construction naturally depended on the terrain; there were rural dirt roads (*via terrena*) and secondary roads (*viae rusticae*) which serviced farms and villas away from the principal consular roads.

The *viae vicinales* were those that belonged to and were administered by the community; they could be dirt, gravel or paved roads. The *viae glareae* (*sternendae*) were gravel roads – most North African roads were such – with a carefully prepared road-bed and a gravel surface instead of a stone pavement. Their construction is often confirmed in inscriptions – 'via glarea sternenda ab miliario'. Most of the early Roman roads were *viae glareae* before they were paved with the massive pavement that we have come to know them by. Over marshes, the Roman engineer first built a causeway, the most famous being the twenty miles of the Via Appia raised on a causeway that passed through the Pontine marshes. Wooden piles were sunk into the morass, the interstices between these were filled with large rocks and rock was piled and rammed until the causeway rose six feet above the flooded flatlands; on that the Roman road builder set a pavement of green-black volcanic stones. Pliny wrote that '. . . we may say it was a miraculous work in filling up that troublesome marsh (the Pontine) as if another Hercules were forcing up the road by great and spacious banks to bear the burden of immense stones of the Appian Way'.

Other coastal roads also employed raised or causewayed parts of road; the Via Severiana, built in AD 200 along the shore of the Tyrrhenian Sea to connect Terracina – where the Appia comes down to the sea – and Ostia, the port of Rome at the mouth of the Tiber, has parts of its 200 miles raised on a causeway. An even greater problem was solved by the northern coastal road, the Via Popilia on the Adriatic. This audacious construction connected Ravenna with Patavium (Padua), passing over four river estuaries and an almost continuous marsh for one hundred miles (160 kilometres). Only in recent years has this strikingly engineered Roman road been revised.

The Romans elsewhere met and circumvented marsh and moors. When a road in Rochester, near the Medway valley, was excavated, it was found to have rested on wooden oak-piles driven into the marsh-land over which was laid a road-bed of a depth exceeding four feet. In the marshy moorlands estuary of the Rhine – in Belgium, Holland and Germany – the Romans copied the *moorstrasse* of the native inhabitants and laid down log-roads which they called *pontes longi* – these crossed the moors, swamps,

Adjacent to the Forum of Trajan in Rome is the Market of Trajan, a semicircular structure where the financial and commercial exchanges were transacted.

Left, above: A detail of Roman paving near Aquileia. One can still see the ruts left by centuries of wheeled traffic

Left, below: A well-preserved stretch of the Via Flaminia, with closely set paving stones

Right: A street in Herculaneum with its original paving. Along with Pompeii, Herculaneum was buried during the eruption of Vesuvius in AD 79

rivers, rills and streams up to the gloomy pine forests of Germania. Tacitus records how Caecina, a general of Germanicus, when ordered to return to the Rhine inland from the sea coast '. . . was to take a familiar route . . . he was to proceed as quickly as possible across the *pontes longi* . . . the long log bridges. . . .' Further a moor-road bearing the name of Via Mansuerisca ran from Trier to Maastricht, in Holland; seven kilometres of it still exist and a model of it is exhibited in the Brussels Museum.

The Romans never solved their problems by evasion. The Via Flaminia is a case in point. At the pass of Furlo where the rock surface drops into the Candigliano river, the Etruscans had been content with a narrow, laboriously built retaining wall. The Romans first cut a tunnel in 220 BC, so narrow that it admitted only one wagon at a time. Later, in AD 78, Vespasian ordered a new tunnel forty metres (132 feet) long, capable of allowing two vehicles to pass abreast; this tunnel was chiselled out of the solid surface called the *petra pertusa* – the pierced rock.

Roman engineering feats

In order to push the Via Valeria to the Adriatic, the engineers had to drain the Lacus Fucinus and lay a road close to it. Pliny reckoned this operation – the digging and tunnelling of a mountain for the purpose of draining the lake – 'among the greatest and most remarkable works', employing a multitude of workmen for many years. The Via Cassia in its northern route was forced to climb the series of extinct craters about Lake Bracciano; to avoid a one in five gradient the builders of the Via Cassia cut through the rim of the lip of an extinct volcano (Baccano). The cut is more than 1,500 metres long, twenty metres (sixty-six feet) deep; the width of the road is held to six metres. Nor were Trajan's engineers perplexed by the Pisco mountains that descend to the sea at Terracina. In order to shorten the road, so that it need not climb 500 metres to Anxur above, the workers made a sheer cut of thirty-six metres of the rock face. Their pride in doing this is revealed by their inscribing at intervals of every ten Roman feet numerals to indicate the depth of the cutting.

Tunnels are not infrequent throughout the Alps; a section of the Alpine road that passed at Bons from Vienne on the Rhône to Grenoble on its way to the Little St Bernard was a one-way tunnel 246 centimetres (8 feet 11 inches) wide; the wheel ruts are standard at 144 centimetres (4 feet 9 inches).

A similar one-way passage involving remarkable rock-cutting was built by Agrippa in the time of Augustus. To keep the road above the often turbulent rivers of Val D'Aosta the engineers cut a pass eighty metres (264 feet) long into the bed-rock, a vertical cut with a road-bed four metres wide; a triumphal arch and a milestone marked XXXVI miles from Aosta. The list of such engineering feats could be extended.

Such geographical problems confronted the road makers after every conquest. An archaeologist who made one of the few stratigraphical cuts of a Roman road in France was struck by the fill of the roadbed; the type of stone he found did not occur within one hundred miles of the

Roman road and had to be brought that distance. If the Romans preferred to go over a hill rather than go around it, they were guided by the logic of engineering and military strategy. They did not like to make a cut that would disturb the original earth surface and would require retaining walls and drainage. Such a cut would tend to gather water or snow and could serve as a place for ambush.

Roads appeared in Sardegna as early as 238 BC, and the finely laid stone pavement can still be seen going along the coast at Nora near Cagliari. Roads in Sicily were begun almost at the same time as those in Sardegna; while the Punic wars raged on land and sea, the Via Valeria was being built in 210 BC. As Sicily is volcanic and as Mt Etna continued to pour its lava down towards the sea, the roads in Sicily were mostly along the coast.

Spain's network of roads was begun early, for the Romans warred against the Spanish Celts and the Phoenicians as early as 200 BC. Some of the greatest names in Rome made their mark in Spain: the Scipios; Metellus; Cato; Julius Caesar; finally Augustus, who concluded two hundred years of strife by initiating a series of roads that criss-crossed Spain. A traveller could walk the Via Augusta from Cadiz (Gades), which had one of the pillars of Hercules, along the coast of Spain into France and along the coast of Italy, where the road became the Via Aurelia, all the way to Rome without once wetting his feet. Of the 372 roads under Rome's control, thirty-two were in Spain.

The Romans built highways in Dalmatia before building them in France. From Aquileia, the port city of the Adriatic founded in 181 BC, issued a road which later became the Flavian Way. It coursed down the coast of Dalmatia as the Via Gabrina, running through rugged terrain to Dyrrhachium, present-day Durazzo. There, as the Via Egnatia, it continued into Greece, down to Thessalonica, and to the Hebrus river. It was built before 145 BC and Julius Caesar and Mark Anthony used the Via Egnatia to march into battle against Pompey in Greece.

The first Roman road in France beyond the Alps was built in 118 BC, yet Rome's advance into Gaul was still a cautious one. Pompey built the first road over the Alps in 77 BC. Eventually there were as many as sixteen routes over the Alps, but only six of these were available for wheeled traffic; one much-used road connected Turin with Arles in Provence. During the six years he spent in the Gallic campaign, Julius Caesar began the system of Roman roads which was to unify Gaul.

Julius Caesar's road system unified Gaul

Agrippa, who had built the Pantheon and turned the city of Rome from brick to marble, extended his building zeal to Gaul. There he built five Roman roads and many bridges and left his monument in the famed aqueduct, the Pont du Gard. But it was Claudius, born in Lyons, who ordered his engineers to complete a network of roads that was France's only road system until recent times. It was also Claudius who opened the road through the Brenner Pass.

Left: Funerary urns assembled in the courtyard of the museum in Aquileia
Right: Carts hauling wine and oil vessels must have been familiar
sights along the ancient roads of the Roman Empire

The international network of the Roman Empire was not landbound. Vessels plying the seas connected the ports of the Italian peninsula with overseas ports

Roman roads began to proliferate in North Africa once Augustus decided to revitalise the territory of ancient Carthage. A network of roads spread out all over what is now Algeria, Tunisia and Morocco. These roads were connected with Libya by a long coastal road, begun in AD 96 by the Emperor Nerva during his two years as ruler.

It was Trajan, born in the Spanish colony of Italica, who spread the network of roads in the area of Asia Minor and the Near East. He incorporated five roads of Egypt into his system. A road was pushed across the Sinai peninsula and linked to the cities of the Nabatean kingdom. A dual system of roads connected all the great caravan cities, Petra, Damascus and Syria. In the consolidation of the Roman Greek colonies in what is now Turkey, Trajan's engineers connected his new roads, after AD 100, with those built one hundred years before.

During the Dacian wars, Trajan extended a road along the Danube, from the Black Sea to Regensburg, that linked up with the road servicing the *limes* defences, so that when he finally completed the Roman fort at Ulpia – now in Holland on an estuary in the North Sea – he had in effect joined the Black Sea to the North Sea with one continuous road 1,500 miles (2,400 kilometres) long.

Roman highways in the Syrian desert were constructed all the way to the mouth of the twin delta of the Tigris and the Euphrates and then

The Milvian Bridge, where Constantine defeated Maxentius in AD 312 linked up with a complex series of stone fortresses, built in order to contain the Parthians.

Hadrian, the last of the great road builders, further consolidated the Roman road network. Most of his building was defensive. He improved the German *limes*, bringing strategic military roads up to the line of fortifications facing the Germanic tribes; he built the famed wall in northern England to prevent the Caledonians' incursions into Britain and then improved the road system to facilitate troop movements to the wall. In the Near East he dedicated the most remote Roman intrusion to the God Terminus. He pulled back the Roman legions from Dacia and, to prevent its use, dismantled the bridge that Trajan had built across the Danube.

The last great road builder

Roman road building continued up to and after the decline of Rome. One of the Emperor Theodosius's last official acts, in AD 395, was to issue an edict 'On the repairing of the highways and bridges'. The roads, so went the edict, 'have been honoured with the titles of great names. . . . Therefore no sort of man of any dignity must desist from the construction and the reconstruction of our highways and bridges . . . we also oblige the Divine Christian Church to participate in this work. It is our will that all men vie in their zeal in repairing the public ways. . . .'

The bridge, which one Roman quaintly called 'the little brother of the road', was another one of the monumental achievements of Rome. From the time that King Ancus erected the Pons Sublicius across the Tiber (the

same wooden bridge which Horatio defended) until one thousand years later when the central authority of Rome had ceased to function, the Romans erected over two thousand bridges, of which more than half were in Italy.

Every type of bridge except the suspension bridge was used: clapper bridges of limited span, one and two slabs, crossed rills and brooks, and wooden bridges. These last were common until replaced by arched stone-bridges. Many had stone piers sunk into the bed-rock of the river while the bridge proper was constructed of wood.

The Tiber bridges The Tiber was eventually crossed by ten stone bridges which were expected to last forever. The Pons Fabricius which crosses to the Tiber Island (with the Pons Cestius in tandem on the other side), begun in 62 BC and improved in 21 BC, was built by L. Fabricius whose name is carved on it. To make certain that the bridge was solidly built the Senate withheld payment for forty years, a rather over-cautious attitude seeing that the bridge is still in use some 2,000 years later.

It has been said that the Roman engineers, being unable to calculate stress, made their structures of unnecessary solidity. But what is wrong with solidity? The Pons Milvius, the present-day Ponte Milvio, which serviced five of the main northern routes, Tiberina, Flaminia, Cassia, Clodia, and Amerina, was built with just this solidity. It was built before 220 BC, rebuilt by Aemilius Scaurus in 109 BC, and there it still remains more than 2,000 years later, open to full vehicular traffic, scorning the scouring of its piles by Father Tiber. Many solid bridges built or repaired by order of Augustus are to be seen all along the Via Flaminia from the Tiber to the Adriatic Sea. Beginning with the massively beautiful bridge which carried the Via Flaminia over the Nar river at Narni (a tributary to the Tiber in Umbria) and which was built by Augustus in 27 BC, upward of fifteen bridges are to be seen along the way. Many were destroyed not by nature but by war; a number of them were blown up in World War II in order to impede pursuit.

All the Roman bridges have long since disappeared in Britain; although those laid on stone piers at London, Corbridge, Wroxeter, Caerleon, Caister, Castle Comb, and Rochester could perhaps yield up their stone abutments. Pons Aelius was built across the river Tyne (the name Aelius being derived from a part of Hadrian's name); it survived until 1248. Dredging the river for a modern bridge revealed stone piers and sculpted shrines to Neptune (with his dolphin) and to Oceanus (with an anchor). These deities were supposed to protect the bridge against flood and destruction. Chollerford bridge hard upon Hadrian's Wall over the north Tyne was a 184-foot Roman bridge; all of the remaining parts of the cutwaters and abutments are dressed with scrupulous workmanship, the stones being held together with iron cramps. Archaeologists found here a sculptured phallus, a good luck charm found on many Roman–British bridges.

The Ponte Fabricio, erected in 62 BC by L. Fabricius is the oldest
surviving bridge in Rome. It leads to the island in the Tiber

In Germany Roman bridges have mostly disappeared; evidence of them is wholly literary. Julius Caesar was the first to span the Rhine with a trestle bridge, minutely described in his account of the war in Gaul. The great Roman bridges that spanned the Rhine at Köln (Colonia), Koblenz (Confluentes), Deutz, and Mainz have all disappeared save for pitiful stone remains protruding from the alluvium of the Rhine. (However the iron-shod piles of the bridge at Mainz have been dredged out.)

France has managed to preserve several bridges, all in Provence. There are bridges throughout North Africa, several in Algeria and Tunisia are still in use. Jordan and Syria have a few survivors; Turkey has many. Greece has none to display, but the bridge at Skoplje in Yugoslavia, a late Roman product, survived centuries of use, and even the recent earthquake failed to shake it down.

Nothing is left of Trajan's bridge built across the Danube by Apollodorus of Damascus except some of the stone piers that appear in low water. It was built, six miles below the famous gorge known as the Iron Gates, during Trajan's campaign to subdue the Dacians (in present-day Roumania). The greatest single structure engineered by Rome, it was built on twenty stone piers, each 125 feet high and sixty feet wide, placed 170 feet apart. The upper part, the bridge proper, was of wood, designed by Apollodorus (a Hellenised Syrian) to have diagonal bracing: 'the first example', says a recent writer, 'of the truss which depends for its strength on the rigidity of the three beams fastened together to form a triangle'. Although Hadrian removed the wooden part, the design has been immortalised on coins cast at the time, as well as in the carving on Trajan's Column in the Forum. This carving should be an accurate record since the column was designed by the same Apollodorus who had built the bridge.

It is amazing that any specimens of Roman bridge-masonry could have lasted even one century, but some have lasted twenty centuries. Flood, frost, and most of all traffic vibrations above and angry waters scouring the piers below cause weakening. Yet many bridges have survived, especially in Spain, where they are all over the landscape. There is a long bridge at Salamanca which crosses the Rio Tormes, and further down on the same road, the Via Argenta, at Merida the road is carried across the Rio Guadiana for half a mile on sixty arches, many of which are the original Roman ones. However, the most famous surviving bridge is the one built by Lacer and dedicated to Trajan. It was designed to carry the Roman road across the Rio Tagus into Leviathan (Portugal). The six arches stand 158 feet above the river and support the tremendous bridge, 640 feet in length. Built by Gaius Julius Lacer, it was dedicated to Trajan, at the expense of the citizens of the surrounding cities. The inscription states:

'*Pontem Perpetui Mansurum in Saecula*' ('I have created a bridge that will last the ages').

The Bridge of Augustus which carried the Via Flaminia across the Tiber
near Narni. The railroad now passes under one arch of the bridge

Miliaria – milestones that marked the *milia passuum* that was the Roman mile – became a general feature of the roads after 124 BC. Although way-markers appeared on the ancient Via Appia before 250 BC, the organisation of the growing road system took place during Rome's social revolution.

The Gracchi brothers, Tiberius and Gaius, attempted to improve the lot of thousands of impoverished Roman citizens with new land grants and work schemes. While this programme pleased the masses it did not please the patricians. Both brothers were eventually murdered, but not before Gaius Sempronius Gracchus, in order to create labour projects, '. . . busied himself', (according to Plutarch) 'most earnestly with the construction of roads and erection of milestones . . . he had them measured off, that is every road by miles – and had stone-pillars (*miliaria*) placed in the ground to mark the distances. He caused all the roads to be divided into miles and marked with stone-pillars, that is milestones, signifying the distance from one place to another'.

So the quarrying, shaping, and carving of data on milestones became a huge public works operation. It could well have utilised the efforts of thousands. Each milestone was about eight feet in height and twenty inches in diameter and weighed about two tons. The placing of these milestones two feet under the earth, often in their own stone niches, and the carving of the inscriptions was a formidable task.

Roman milestones were placed every Roman mile (1,000 Roman paces). Such a Roman mile was 1,620 yards (1,480 metres) and thus somewhat shorter than the standard measurement. Not all roads were so marked but once there were thousands of such milestones.

Way-markers are common enough on all man-made ways and tracks. The ancient Britons marked the primitive Fosse with a cairn of stones; they also notched trees to give direction and perhaps some primitive method of distance-reckoning. In India, Alexander found roads marked with pillars. Egyptians marked their desert roads with stone-cairns and also, it is suggested, by an occasional glyph that gave direction or distance. The Egyptian god Min was the protector of roads and travellers. He is always shown with the right arm raised to the royal flail (salutary symbol of terror), while with his left he holds his erected phallus, huge and divine.

Persia had roads, way-stations and presumably way-markers which Darius I (521–485 BC) set up. In pre-Hispanic America the Incas maintained a lengthy road system with bridges, halting-stations (*tampus*), and every four miles slender monuments of laid stone (*topos*) that marked distances. When the road went over high passes the Incas made an *apacheta*, an immense cairn of stones upon which travellers would throw an absolution stone.

Greek roads were measured with piles of stones. A formal way-marker never seems to have been devised except for the *hermae* which came into use in towns during historical times. These were square stone-pillars topped with a bust of Mercury, the god of travellers.

The Romans systematised the milestone markers. In 20 BC Augustus was made commissioner of all the highways in the vicinity of Rome. 'In this capacity', says Dio Cassius, 'he set up the Golden Milestone' which Suetonius reminds us was erected 'in the shadow of the Temple of Saturn'. This was an immense pillar, but although it was called the *miliarium aurem* it was in fact only gilded bronze. On it Augustus had engraved all the principal cities of the empire with their distances from the Golden Milestone.

The Golden Milestone

Although all the roads of the Roman world were supposed to converge on that stone, actual distances seem to have been measured from the old Servian Walls. Later as it became inconvenient to reckon all roads from the Golden Milestone, the system was changed; roads were measured from the principal city. However, the metropolitan milestone still kept its aura of sanctity since Constantine the Great called it *umbilicus Romae* – the navel of Rome.

The initial function of the miliarium was to mark the Roman miles. It gave needed information to the traveller and the military commander marching his troops along the road; it also helped in the administration of the road. Locating a fallen bridge or a piece of washed-out road was made easy by the knowledge that, for example, on the eighth milestone of the Via Valeria the road was in need of repair.

The milestone also served to locate the various aqueducts of Rome.

Milestones have loomed constantly in Roman history. Christianity had its official Roman recognition at a milestone on the Via Flaminia. Nero, fleeing from Rome, learned at the fourth milestone on the Via Nomentana that he had been declared by the Senate 'an Enemy of Rome' and thereupon ended his life.

In the beginning these massive stone markers were simply inscribed. They gave the distance from the Forum, the name of the emperor or legate who had either ordered the road to be built or had financed it, or the name of the consul under whom it had been constructed. Later the emperor's titles were added and the mile-markers became wordy. The finest milestones and the most widespread were those of Trajan, who built and restored so many of Rome's roads. Born in Italica, Spain, in AD 76, reared as an honourable career soldier, and raised to the purple out of sheer merit, he was adopted by the elderly Nerva, who, with the consent of the Senate, designated Trajan his heir to office. Trajan gave more of his personal wealth and funds from the royal estates to the construction of roads throughout the world than any other ruler.

Milestones were not only guide-posts and way-markers; they were also a form of propaganda, showing the paternalism of the emperor and impressing upon the traveller who consulted them the many years that Trajan had served Rome. They were, too, an appeal to posterity for remembrance. Later, in the times of the Severi, after AD 200, the self-adulation recorded on milestones grew so flamboyant that titles and

The Roman theatre at Gubbio was built in the first century. To the ancient Umbrians, whose religious centre it was, the town was known as Iguvium. Under the Romans it was known as Eugubium

distinctions covered the entire road-marker from top to bottom, and one had to read through all this verbiage to find out what road one walked. The number of the mile, unlike that on Trajan's milestones, was found at the very bottom of the miliaria.

To the epigrapher and the archaeologist the inscriptions on milestones are a form of history and are published in the *Corpus Inscriptionum Latinarum*. They are vitally important for the history of the Roman road, as well as a useful record of the activities of emperors during their reign. A few emperors who were traduced by their contemporaries, such as Tiberius, Domitan, and Caracalla, are having their reputations slowly brought into balance since the inscriptions tell of their labour for the State.

Milestones were also erected by those who repaired (*reparavit*) a road. One archaeologist, using only the inscriptions of known miliaria found in Spain, was able to write about the repair of roads in Spain during the Roman Empire. An impressive compilation, his study records road-building activity from 32 BC until AD 383. It reveals that Caracalla, dismissed by most because of his 'tiresome and dangerous personality', ordered in AD 214 the complete rebuilding of every major road in Spain.

The well-preserved Roman theatre of Gubbio has tiers,
promenade, and an area for orchestra

From milestones in North Africa we learn that in AD 123 Hadrian
'... paved the road from Carthage to Theveste with the III Legio
Augusta....' Another road was built to go to Timgad (in Algeria) by
Trajan's order in AD 100. Some roads were built or repaired at private
expense ('*Pecunia publica ... ad Forum pecuariam viam sternundam coeraverunt ...*').

When in 1850 the French General St Arnaud marched his legions
through the Kanga pass in the Atlas mountains he reasonably believed
that he was the first man who had ever traversed so impassable a defile.
Then he found carved on a rock an inscription stating: 'The Legio III
Augusta built this road in AD 145'.

After milestones there were the *itineraria* to guide tourists, military commanders and commercial travellers over the Roman roads. The *itineraria*
were schematic maps with symbols to indicate such geographical
features as mountains, rivers, and lakes, as well as way-stops, official
mansiones (night quarters), military bases (*castra praetoriana*), and post-
houses, (*mutationes*) where horses were kept in readiness. The itineraria also
gave the distances between points on the road.

Caesar and Mark Anthony as consuls planned to map the whole known

Roman Itineraria

53

Right: A Roman milestone, near Rimini. These stone columns were erected at intervals of 5,000 Roman feet throughout the empire. Recorded on the columns was the number of miles from the town from which the measurement was made, as well as the name of the person who had built the road or raised the milestone and the name of the emperor during whose reign the road was built. Numerous examples survive, many in museums (*opposite*)

Ruins of Aeclanum, an ancient town on the Via Appia near Benevento. The town was captured by Sulla in 89 BC, and it became a colony under Hadrian

Excavations at Aeclanum have uncovered remains of walls,
an acqueduct, baths and an amphitheatre

world and employed four Greek geographers to begin the task, but the
incidents of the Ides of March ended that. It is known that Augustus kept
for his own use a golden engraved map of the Roman empire with jewels
representing the principal cities. In his reign, Agrippa, builder of the
Pantheon and monuments and roads in different parts of the empire, *Roman world maps*
mapped parts of Germany, Holland and Belgium. These were incorporated
into a larger map. In the time of Vespasian a sculptured chart of the earth
was put up near the Pantheon; there was also an *Itinerarium Maritimum*
with distances of coastal towns, measurements of sea transits, the angles of
trajectus, the ports and the islands. From this, presumably, the table of
the great *Itinerarium Romanum* was made.

As these itineraries were drawn on papyrus and rolled, they were
perishable and expendable. Only one example of these itineraria is known,
and this is a copy from a later period. This is the world map of the Roman
road system housed in the Nationalbibliothek in Vienna. Called the
Tabula Peutingeriana, it is painted in five colours on parchment. It is

composed of eleven sheets, 6·82 metres in length and thirty-four centimetres in width. It is a twelfth-century copy of what is believed to have been a third-century original Roman itinerary of the Roman road system from Britain's coast to India and from Africa to the Rhine. It is fully possible that the Roman original was copied from the gigantic world map which, sculptured in stone, was reported to have been placed in the Roman Forum as well as by the Pantheon.

This is the Ptolemaic map of the world schematic in form, with an attempt to show geographical features – rivers, mountains, forests and lakes. There is a list of place names and of distances between places. There are symbols to indicate temples, harbours, lighthouses, cisterns, coloniae, civitates, praetoria and mutationes. There are symbols for many different buildings, including the storehouse (*horreum*) and the tavern (*taberna*), where travellers could rest, eat and drink. Cisterns, where water was held, are always indicated by the word *aquae* (waters), and, to be doubly sure that the traveller knew water was there, the artist drew a large building in which there was a reservoir of water, coloured blue. Towering lighthouses are so obviously marked that no one could mistake the tall tower with flames and smoke pouring out of it.

A barrack-fortress where the imperial guard lived, the *praetorium* is clearly differentiated from other buildings, and the word *praetorium* is written above it. Temples such as the Templum Augusti are clearly marked so that the traveller would know where he might worship, and harbours are well drawn.

These itineraria for various roads, as well as for the whole empire road system, were obtainable in Rome and elsewhere from bookseller–publishers; all were copied by hand and were therefore costly. They were in the public domain, so there were no royalties to pay. Needless to say publishers grew rich.

Roads, milestones and itineraries were all part of the road system, but all this would have meant little if there had been no way-stops and halting stations.

Ancient halting stations There were various types of way-stations. The *mansio* was controlled by the central government and a traveller generally needed an official passport to use it. *Mutationes* were stations in which horses, oxen or mules were changed. Here there were grooms and veterinarians (*equarii medici*) to care for the animals. There were cartwrights and postilions, and wheelwrights were posted nearby, for the wear and tear on springless vehicles must have been considerable. The halting-places appeared every twelve to eighteen miles along the entire length of the Roman road system, which means that there were over 4,000 such buildings that had to be serviced throughout the Roman world. Yet, despite this, not one has been identified on the European continent; one has been found in Egypt and the author's expedition found a *mansio* in the interior of Tunisia, stationed between two milestones.

One might doubt that there were so many stations were it not for the evidence of the anonymous pilgrim of Bordeaux. In the year AD 333, during the reign of Constantine, a Christian from Burdigala (Bordeaux) completed a pilgrimage from his native city to Jerusalem by way of the Alps and Milan, passing through what is now Yugoslavia and Turkey. On the way this anonymous pilgrim kept a journal of the miles he covered and the number of *mutationes* and *mansiones* he passed; as the *Itinerarium Hierosolymitanum* has come down to us, he covered 3,998 Roman miles and listed the staggering number of 408 way-stops, an average of one every ten miles. And these existed and were functioning during the decline of Rome.

Tabernae were public inns and had, in general, a sordid reputation; pick-pockets abounded and the accommodation was poor and frequented by the riff-raff of the Empire, if the Rabelaisian graffiti on the walls of one of Pompeii's *tabernae* is typical. In ordinary times tavern-keepers, cooks, and bakers and other persons 'following infamous callings' were not even considered honourable enough to be run through with a pike: they were excluded from the army. Tabernae and their keepers were the butt of the satirists; Martial begins one satire with 'Recently a craft taverner imposed upon me at Ravenna. . . .' Horace, travelling to Brindisi, stopped overnight at the Foro Appii located in the centre of the Pontine marshes. He found the place '. . . jammed with boatmen and sharp inn-keepers'.

Public inns and taverns

Apparently there existed a law, enforced by supervision, that those whose houses were placed strategically by a road give succor when called upon by a traveller. On the way to Capua, at the bridge called 'Ad Ponte Campana', Horace writes in his satire 'Rome to Brindisi with Stops' that:

> 'Our next roof was a small farmhouse at the bridge
> Where you enter Campania and where
> The padrone is always *required by law*
> To furnish you with food and fuel. . . .'

Not all the taverns were disreputable. The Tabernae Caediciae, where the Via Appia at Sinuessa turns eastward to the mountains, was famous for its wine and food. 'The wine we'll drink', wrote Horace to Torquatus, 'is second Consulate Taurian / Poured off at Villa Petrinum near Sinuessa / below the salt flats of Minturnae.' The ruins of this villa and tavern are still to be seen at Sinuessa, as well as its huge *magazzini* which held hogsheads of wine, cheese and ham. The way-stop of Caudium was farther along the Via Appia, and the poet remembered that '. . . the taverns of Caudium next took us in / and into its well-stocked larder. . . .'

The *caupona* was another type of inn, usually located near a *mansio*. Not many of these have survived but the *caupona* at Pompeii appears to have been cramped, undecorated, and frequented by drovers, bullock-drivers, drunkards, and prostitutes; the walls are covered with lively and obscene graffiti.

Around these way-stops a nucleus of buildings often evolved first into a

The Italian countryside abounds with remains of the Roman past. Here is a common *cellarium*

hamlet, then into a town and eventually into a city; from taverns into settlements, from settlements into cities – such was the evolution of many cities in Germania. Salzburg and Mannheim, for example, had their rude beginnings as way-stops on the Roman roads. Two cities even retain, in mutilated form, the names of taverns. Rhinezabern in the Rhineland and Saverne in Alsace.

On the Via Appia *mansiones* appeared at an average of one every fifteen miles; further north there was one every eighteen miles. Two factors seem to have governed the distribution of *mutationes* and *mansiones*: topography and distance. They were naturally closer together in troublesome terrain, as over the Alps, and further apart where the topography of the land was less difficult.

Ox-drawn vehicles travelled eight Roman miles a day in summer, ten in winter. The imperial post, using horse relays, could cover fifty Roman miles in twenty-four hours. There were exceptions: Tiberius travelled from France to Germany to be at the side of his brother Drusus Germanicus

A former *taverna* on the Via Appia. Inns for travellers were built as early as the second century BC

Above: A fourth-century relief of a sacred procession. A magistrate rides in a
carriage drawn by two mules
Below: A funerary relief showing an Etruscan chariot similar to the Roman *carpentum*

Above: The arrival at a *mansio*. This relief shows the apostle
Philip and the eunuch of Queen Candace in a *carpentum*
Below: A two-wheeled vehicle drawn by a single horse

63

Imposing marble columns of the ancient Roman city of Aquileia,
once the greatest port on the Adriatic

who was dying of gangrene; going by relay of chariots he travelled at the rate of twenty miles an hour, five hundred miles in twenty-four hours. Pliny thought this was 'incredible celerity and a wonderful thing'.

Romans had a wide choice of conveyances: for those who could afford it there was the *raeda*, a splendidly ornate carriage in the shape of a bathtub and large enough to seat a whole family. It was pulled by oxen or mules. The *currus* was a two-wheeled chariot and required the driver to stand while using it. The *cisium*, a swift, light gig pulled by two horses, was the mail cart. The *monachus*, a two-wheeled affair, was made especially for women, who, unlike most in ancient society, drove it themselves. The *carpentum*, an ornate and heavily contrived apparatus, was a covered affair and pulled by two mules.

Then there were other vehicles for commerce and farming. Oxen pulled a *plaustrum* whose tripartite wooden wheels rimmed with iron, were the wheels that Ovid referred to when he wrote '. . . more thinned by constant use / the Appia is more worn by the coursing wheels. . . .' This was allowed to move no more than eight miles a day, as was the *carrus clabularius*, a huge, four-wheeled wagon whose wheels were set with an iron rim. While these did not allow for speed, yet there were no frontiers, no customs barriers within the Roman empire, and travel, albeit slow and uncomfortable by modern standards, was faster than any other until the general use of the railroad. Sir Robert Pell, while riding to London in 1840 to receive his appointment, did not travel any faster than a Roman *praetor* on a Roman road.

Post services were bound up with the operation of post-stations. The mails were reorganised by Augustus and were operated as the *cursus publicus*. This office saw to the training of postmen and the upkeep of post-stations. Since they were exposed to the elements, the postmen wore a headgear called *petanus*; it is the same type of leather helmet worn by Mercury but without the wings. Post messengers were used exclusively for official correspondence. There was in addition a private post service, the *tabellarii*. This service was operated by trusted slaves and used only by the well-placed; even then it was not too secure. Complaints were many. These came especially from that persistent letter writer Cicero. Of Spain Cicero wrote: 'Our messengers have regularly been captured there. It has become dangerous on account of increasing robberies. . . . They always search our messengers. Unless letters came by sea, I wouldn't know what happens there. . . .' Seneca speaks of several weeks, or even months, of delay. 'I received my letters many months after they were sent off. . . .'

The financing and building of roads were problems that Rome never solved satisfactorily. Road-labour was of the basest kind; the digging of a fosse in the wayward earth, the quarrying and breaking up of stones for the fill, the shaping and placing of the heavy, iron-hard paving-stones was exhausting work under any conditions. Details of revolts of road workers often appear in the classical literature. Slaves, criminals and war-

Reorganisation of postal services by Augustus

Left: Among the fine ruins of Ostia, the port of ancient Rome,
are the granaries and warehouses of the Horrea Epagathiana
Right: The well-preserved architecture of Ostia shows the characteristic
arrangement of elongated bricks employed by Roman masons

prisoners were used as navvies to do the exhausting work of quarrying the rock and transporting it. The Emperor Trajan himself, writing to Pliny the Younger who was in Nicomedia and had asked for guidance about the use of condemned criminals, wrote: 'Employ them in work of penal nature . . . like repairing streets and highways'.

Numerous revolts among the legions broke out because of the onerous task of road construction. Although the legionaries were engaged in road-making before and during military campaigns, it was then only considered part of their soldiery duties. In Britain, Galgacus, a chief of a clan of Caledonians, in AD 86 led a revolt, complaining to Julius Agricola, the governor, that '. . . the Romans consume our hands and bodies in making roads through woods and marshes. . . .'

The legions of Tiberius also rebelled while extending roads throughout what is now Austria and Yugoslavia. According to Tacitus, they seized their commander, loaded him down with impedimenta, made him work on the roads and asked him if 'he enjoyed all these heavy burdens'. Toward the end of the Empire soldiers forced to work on roads took direct action; they killed Gordian, one of the 'barrack emperors'. However, the legions were well organised, with their corps of *architecti*, engineers, carpenters, and masons, and road building was an integral part of the expansion of the realm. In many places throughout Africa there are inscriptions which state with obvious pride that 'the III Legio Augusta built this road'.

Slaves and war-prisoners were used as navvies to do the exhausting work of quarrying the rock and transporting it. When, however, this type of labour was not available, the legionaries fell to themselves. The quarried stone used to build Hadrian's Wall came from Fallowfield Fell, where there is a quarry face rudely inscribed '*Petra Flavi Carantini*', meaning that a legionary of that name had worked the stones (*petra*) of that area. On the Gelt near Brampton the inscription reveals that the quarry was worked by a detachment of the II Legio Augusta during the consulate of Aper and Maximus. The slaves who quarried rock, however, were anonymous. After the Hannibalic wars, slaves and war-captives were numerous in Italy. Thousands of them – Moors, Jews, Egyptians, Arabs, Cappadocians, Germans, Greeks – were turned to road making. But the soldier of the Roman legions bore the brunt of road making.

The paving of Roman roads   The actual finishing of the massive paving-stones was doubtless left to experienced masons who directed the cutting of the stones. This was precision work as each stone had to be fitted to and aligned with the others in the mosaic pattern of the pavement. A Byzantine historian who followed Belisarius to Rome in AD 536 marvelled at the preciseness of the stone paving of the Via Appia: 'The Consul Appius caused all the paving-stones to be polished and cut so as to form angles and had them jointed together without any kind of cement. They adhered so strongly that to look at them they do not seem to be jointed at all but to form one whole mosaic of stone. . . .' In addition, the massive road had to be cambered, that is, so engineered that the centre of the road was higher than the sides so that water would drain off it.

Road building was expensive, even with slave labour. In the beginning, road construction was financed by contributions from those land-owners through whose estates the road moved, and from fines and exactions levied upon those who trespassed on the public domain without official permission. A community of shepherds was fined a certain number of work-service days and had to work on the Via Appia. Private donations also contributed, and sidewalks and benches were often the gifts of humble donors.

A citizen's testament written in AD 30 states: 'I bequeath to the Commonwealth this sum, for the repairing of the Via Aurelia that runs through our colonia'. Many of the greater roads were financed by individuals. Roman legions penetrated Gaul in force for the first time in 120 BC, and the conqueror, Domitius Ahenobarbus, thought he could leave no better monument to his victory than the building and paving of a road through the Pyrenees to the Rhone Valley; he named it Via Domitiana after himself.

Censors, who had charge of public morals and public works, were expected to finance sections of road personally. Emperors, beginning with Augustus, set the pattern of largesse; he offered to finance the repaving of the entire Via Flaminia, the 250 miles of road from Rome to Ariminum (Rimini). Further, he 'suggested' that those who had grown rich through war booty should aid in financing the repaving of the Flaminian Way. The road was financed section by section and built by the Consul Calvinius Sabinus. Where the road ended in Rimini, a triumphal arch was erected to Augustus.

The highway commissioners (*curatores viarum*) were empowered to collect taxes for road repair and new road construction. Toll charges were levied at the city gates; imports and exports were taxed. Tolls seem to have been collected at many bridges and heavy dray wagons were taxed.

The cost of building an entire Roman road has as yet not come down to us, although epigraphers continue to find new inscriptions and the Corpus is constantly being enlarged by these findings. Records of costs, prices and work performance – since the Romans were precise about these financial transactions – are available, but not in a form that would enable us to determine, for example, the cost of the construction of the entire length of the Via Flaminia – costs of foundations, road-bed, retaining walls, drainage, bridges, culverts and tunnels on the whole 250-mile length from Rome to Rimini.

It is difficult to convert the Roman monetary standard into current values. Robert Graves claims that: 'The gold piece ... was the Latin aureus, a coin worth 100 sestertii or twenty-five silver denarii (silver pieces); it may be thought of as worth one pound sterling or five (pre-war) American dollars'.

In Cicero's time the cost of regravelling a twenty-mile stretch of the

A sculptured frieze with a lively scene of a chariot race in the circus. The chariot driver was called an *auriga*, and either two or four-horse teams were used, the *biga* and *quadriga*

Via Caecilia cost 15,000 sestertii; according to Graves's calculation, this would be equivalent to $750. The town of Verulae contracted to have 2,000 feet of its streets paved at a cost of 86,000 sestertii ($4,300). Hadrian, at his own expense, repaired a section of the Via Appia of 15,750 *passus* between Beneventum and Aeclanum (Eclano). This part of the Via Appia is fifteen feet wide, and the cost was twenty-two sestertii per foot. The Roman–Etruscan city of Tarquinia had had three thousand passus presumably of the Via Aurelia repaired close to its own borders at an overall cost of 200,000 sestertii; here the cost was 13·3 sestertii per foot.

The Forum Sempronii (now Fossombrone), an important city in Umbria off the Via Flaminia, was paved in AD 200 with massive volcanic stones; 1,165 feet of this precisely laid pavement of road eighteen feet wide cost 26,000 sestertii, or twenty-three sestertii per running foot. And 414 feet of road between Cereatae and Marinae were repaved in stone during the time of Trajan at a total cost of 8,590 sestertii or 20 sestertii the running foot. As slight as this information is, it does set up a pattern of costs of road reconstruction during the century of the four 'good emperors' – Trajan (98–117), Hadrian, Antoninus Pius, and Marcus Aurelius (161–80) – when the money had not yet been debased.

In AD 208 Septimius Severus completed the last great consular road of any length, the Via Severiana, which connected Terracina to Rome's port, Ostia. It was a well-made highway and a part of it can still be seen where it approaches the gates of ancient Ostia.

Although no new roads were built after that time, the old ones were under constant repair; rebuilding and repairing continued up to the time of the Emperor Theodosius.

In an edict dated AD 394 it was noted that private estates through which the roads passed would be liable to taxes for their upkeep 'according to the number of acres or the number of people sustained by the estate'. Further, repairing of the highways and bridges was one of the honours sought by consuls and men of dignity. 'Therefore, no sort of man, of any dignity, degree, or honour must desist from the making and repairing of the ways and bridges.' This edict also included the church. At first it had been exempt from contribution toward the upkeep of Roman highways but was now by this edict 'liable to the same charge and condition'.

Roman roads brought unification to all peoples. This was the theme of the poet who wrote that all the world's people were entwined under a single name – Romans. They were world citizens who shared a common law. All were Roman citizens, peers in their world. They were Roman citizens whether they lived in Africa or in Hither Asia or on the banks of the Rhine river. All looked to Rome. There was a single coinage and a single law. There were no frontiers and no major customs barriers. Travel was open and free. On the Roman roads, police guarded against highwaymen; inns, taverns, and halting stations were open to all.

A Roman bronze coin

II · AFRICA

Hannibal and road building in Africa

Hannibal's invasion of Italy and his eventual defeat in Africa left an indelible mark on Rome, giving impetus to the creation of a vast road system.

The natural expansion of Rome would have been to the north of Italy. This had been the original intention, as is shown by the construction of the Via Aurelia toward Pisa and the building of the Via Flaminia linking Rome to the Adriatic. The invasion of Hannibal delayed the northern expansion of roads and committed Rome to building in Africa.

Hannibal had left Spain with 90,000 men and thirty-two elephants and crossed the Alps to crush Rome, and he almost did so. He spent seventeen years on Italian soil, alternately fighting and plundering Roman cities. He was never defeated. Before he was recalled to Carthage in 202 BC he had a bronze plaque cast which recorded his exploits; he set it up in the Greek temple at Croton. Then he sailed to give battle to Scipio Africanus who months before had landed in Tunisia and threatened Carthage. Scipio defeated him on his own soil at Zama.

In time, however, Carthage recovered. It was then that Cato rose up at the end of every debate and uttered the words that every schoolboy knows, 'Delenda est Carthago' – 'Carthage must be destroyed'. Carthage was so obliterated that a Roman reported that its very ruins had disappeared.

In 30 BC, however, Augustus posted in North Africa the III Legio Augusta, a body of 12,000 troops with native auxiliaries. They were to control, over the next 300 years, more than one and a half million square miles of North Africa. In no other part of the Empire was the civilising aspect of the legions so well illustrated. They pacified the tribes, built roads and cities, and patrolled the vast empty spaces of the desert.

In 19 BC Augustus sent 30,000 colonists to Carthage with orders to rebuild it. Slowly they laid down coastal roads; with Roman caution they felt their way into the interior, reconstructing the old Punic dirt roads and reorganising the older Libyan and Punic settlements. Roman Africa now stretched from the Syrtes bordering Egypt, all along the Mediterranean, to the Pillars of Hercules which guarded the passage to the Atlantic. All was now under Rome.

At Bulla Regia houses were built with underground rooms to provide refuge from the African heat. The ancient city of Bulla Regia, once the residence of the Kings of Numidia, was situated on the road from Carthage to Hippo Regius

South of the Roman provinces of Africa and a part of Numidia (Algeria) lay the rugged range of mountains known as the Mons Aurasius. Here the army, under the orders of Tiberius, in AD 14 was to control the passes which came down in easy stages from the Aures Mountains to the plains of Tunis. Near the site of an ancient Libyan fortress, once occupied by Carthage, the legion built the city of Theveste. It was at this time that the legions built the first Roman road of length in Africa. It ran from Theveste down into the Tunisian plains, through the desert to the oasis of Gafsa, and ended at Gabes on the sea.

Roads in Africa were not constructed in the same way as roads in Europe; here they were gravel roads, *viae glareae*. The subsoil was a hard desert pavement. The roads were made of crushed stones put into a road-bed when necessary, and cambered but not paved. Only when the road entered a city was it paved with polished, rectangular white limestone laid in a herring-bone pattern.

In AD 42 Claudius formally annexed Mauretania, the vast area of desert and mountains with pockets of fertile land that stretched from the boundaries of Numidia to Tangiers. A Punic track was enlarged into a Roman road that was gradually rebuilt and extended until it extended to the western end of Tangiers (Tingi). The extension of the road southward to Rabat created a continuous coastal Roman road from the Atlantic to the Nile, a distance of 2,800 miles or 4,480 kilometres.

The most western of the metropoleis of North Africa was Volubilis. It was a Punic–Roman city and unlike many North African cities it was not of para-military origin. Volubilis was considerably inland although connected with the coastal road, and it continued to develop through the centuries and reached its apogee with the Severi. The Emperor Caracalla raised an arch there, dated AD 217, which still stands with its dedicatory frieze.

As Roman Africa grew in opulence, its marauders grew in number. Berbers and other inhabitants of the interior were attracted to the cities that colonists were erecting in the once unproductive sands, and so the forces of the legions had to be garrisoned there to offer protection.

The small para-military city of Theveste was built. In order to give a direct line to a supply port, Vespasian, who had commanded a victorious army in the conquest of Britain and who had since been raised to the purple, ordered his legions in AD 75 to build a road from Theveste in the Aures Mountains down to the coast. The road ended at Hippo Regius on the Mediterranean. A Punic city and seaport before the advent of the Romans (it became Bône under the French and is now called Annaba), Hippo Regius had been a military supply depot for the Carthaginians centuries before.

Later, in AD 81, the III Legio Augusta was ordered from Theveste at the eastern end of the Aures Mountains and moved to its western end in order to protect Roman cities from the incursions of nomads. The military

Marble floor from Musti. The fine materials used in this
flooring are an indication of the affluence of Roman Africa

city of Lambaesis was ordered built. This permanent military city is an
example of a formal Roman military camp and is the finest extant.

Lambaesis is actually a gigantic rectangular enclosure. Each of its four
walls included a gate. The main road leading to the centre of the city is
broad and finely paved with gleaming white limestone. In the exact centre
where it meets with the cardo, the east-west main road, there stands a
magnificent triumphal arch. An aqueduct brought down clear water from
the Ain Drinn. There was a forum for business, temples for worship, a
theatre for the more sophisticated and an amphitheatre for the more
earthy sports; Lambessa, as it is called now, was a complete city.

On a dreary, treeless, windswept plateau on the last spurs of the Aures
Mountains at 4,000 feet altitude is the site of one of the most magnificent
military camps the Romans ever constructed and a testimonial to Rome's
utter indifference to a hostile environment. This is Timgad (ancient
Thamugadi). As originally designed in AD 110 by L. Munatius Gallus,
an imperial legate of Trajan, the military city was constructed as an almost
perfect square, 370 yards on each side. It was walled, but the walls are
gone now; it had four gates but these too are gone. Timgad was founded
not just for the defence of the area but also to reward certain legionaries

75

of the Legio Ulpia Victrix who served under Trajan in his Parthian wars, for he kept his promise to settle the veterans of his legions. The work of preparing this settlement was left to the III Legio Augusta. It took ten years, between AD 100 and 110, to complete the building of the city.

It was the Roman roads in North Africa which became the catalyst of Roman civilisation. They gave the legions quick passage to any given strategic point and prevented the incursion of desert tribes. The roads also allowed the Berber farmer to get his agricultural products – mostly wheat, wine and olives – to the market place. Roads bound together the cities that sprang up because of the Roman presence, and even more important, roads led to the huge estates where large-scale agriculture was carried on.

The ancient cities, once Carthaginian, were revived. If they did not fit into the Roman concept they were torn down and the building materials reshaped. The military cities of Theveste, Lambaesis, and Timgad supplied the architects, the surveyors and the engineers. Within a century of the Roman take-over of North Africa and the arrival of the III Legio Augusta, Numidia (Algeria) and Mauretania were covered with 4,000 Roman miles of all-weather roads.

Four thousand miles of African roads

This Romanisation also had its effect on the native population; Berbers and Carthaginians alike began to think as Romans. Latin became the common language.

Roman Carthage in time reflected the immense majesty of the Roman peace. Five of the major African roads terminated at Carthage's large commercial harbour, and vast sums were lavished on its reconstruction. The most accomplished architects, masons and sculptors were sent from the distant provinces. Trajan built the roads, Hadrian built the aqueducts. Antoninus Pius rebuilt the huge cisterns that distributed the water, and later reconstructed the famed Baths of Antoninus. His adopted son, Marcus Aurelius, erected theatres, amphitheatres, and a colosseum in Carthage, as well as in many inland cities.

Septimius Severus, born in Leptis Magna in Tripoli, built libraries that provided for advanced institutes of learning. There was an Odeon concert hall in Carthage, a theatre world-famed for its luxurious setting, a Temple of Memory – and the embowered Via Coelestis, two Roman miles in length. The magnificent harbour was made even greater than it had been under Punic rule and attracted ships from all over the Roman world.

Schools of learning at Carthage were considered inferior only to those of Rome, and from this Africa which Horace had once derided came a stream of native-born writers, grammarians, lawyers, philosophers, orators, historians, and rhetoricians and, when the time was ripe for it, early Christian saints. It is said that 'Africa, not Rome, gave birth to Latin Christianity'.

It was wheat, the Tunisian wheat, which was the principal reason for North African prosperity. The importance of Tunis as a supplier of wheat to Rome is attested as early as AD 68 when the proconsul Clodius Macer

The arch, the typical element of Roman construction, was carried to Africa. The solid arch-bearing piers of a Roman aqueduct (*above*) at Musti in Tunisia and arch-roofed structures (*below*) still survive

Among the most interesting remains of Roman Africa are the splendid marble and mosaic floors *Left, below :* the Tunisian rose-quartz marble flooring is from Simitthus. The rich mosaics are from Algeria and Tunisia *Left, above :* Ammaedara (mod. Haidra, Algeria) *Right, above :* Sufetula *Below :* Thurburbo Majus

revolted against Nero and kept three thousand grain ships in the harbours; for months Rome was threatened with famine.

Roman cities proliferated. Archaeologists have identified in Tunisia (Africa) and Algeria (Numidia) a total of 357 cities, some of which had a peak population of over thirty thousand.

Almost every city was provided with paved streets, public baths and toilets, temples, luxurious houses and places of amusement. While an amphitheatre or a circus was a luxury, a theatre was almost a necessity. Every Roman city of any size had one. Twenty-seven amusement centres, theatres, stadiums, hippodromes and amphitheatres have been found in North Africa.

All this varied activity required road communications. Epigraphical evidence shows that the coastal roads in North Africa were constructed in the first century.

Tiberius ordered the building of another road, that, radiating from Carthage eastward, followed the twisting course of the Medjerda river. A three-arched bridge, built in the time of Tiberius across the Beja river, still carries vehicular traffic after 1,930 years of use. The first five large Roman settlements, each 15 miles apart, were connected by this road.

Bulla Regia was the largest Roman city on this route, 160 kilometres from Carthage. One of the most spectacular of Tunisia's cities, it lies near the Medjerda river in the centre of an immense wheat-growing plain. At the height of the summer it is furnace-hot on the surface, and the patricians in Bulla Regia met the heat by having two houses, one above ground for the winter, and a subterranean one for the summer. Six such subterranean apartments have been unearthed; archaeologists believe there are more than one hundred waiting to be dug out.

Fifteen miles east of Bulla Regia and the next stop on the road are the marble quarries at Simitthus (now Chemtou). The imperial estate owned all the mines – gold, silver, copper or lead – that were found in the land. The imperial household also owned all quarries of marble; these were called *metalla* and were administered by the emperor's intendants. Such a one was Simitthus. Here an outcrop of marble, known doubtless to the Punics, was fully exploited by the Romans; the famous red Numidian marble which Hadrian brought to ornament his villa in Tivoli came from here.

Across the Medjerda river Hadrian's engineers constructed one of the finest and largest bridges of all Africa. The bridge was forty feet above the river and had eight arches and a total span of 250 feet. It is now in complete ruin, brought down, no doubt, by the raging waters of some African tempest.

Hadrian also had built the road which is known as the 'transport highway', a special road 65 kilometres long extending from Simitthus to Thabraca, a bay port lying on the Mediterranean. All this was in order to transport the red Numidian marble to Rome.

Ruins of the Baths of Antoninus near the harbour of Carthage. The baths were built in the second century to adorn the new Roman Carthage

On the same main Roman road within sixteen kilometres (to illustrate how closely placed were these North African cities) lies Tebursuk.

The name does not even appear on the third-century Roman world chart, yet Tebursuk, if judged by its ruins, was once a large and elegant city. Discernible among the olive groves planted on top of it are the remains of a theatre, public baths, houses, a forum, and a well-preserved triumphal arch which marks the road's egress towards the east. The whole of it is buried under an extensive grove of trees so thickly planted that the ruins are almost indiscernible from the air. One enters the city over the deeply rutted Roman road, crossing a one-arch bridge in good repair. A miliarium by the side records the mileage in Punic.

These are but a few of the buildings and cities that appear on a section of Roman road only 192 kilometres long. Along those 192 kilometres there were eleven cities situated an average of 17 kilometres apart, and all within two days' travel from Carthage.

The second main road, the Via Hadriana, leading from Carthage eastward, kept to the west bank of the Medjerda river, paralleling the other road and only ten kilometres away.

The Via Hadriana, a strategic highway that led from Carthage to the three military cities of the III Legio Augusta in Numidia, was first built by Tiberius, reconstructed by Hadrian a century later, and kept up by Roman emperors until Constantine. It was eighteen feet wide. Excavations and cross-sections establish that in general there was no need for an elaborate roadbed, since the land is mostly exposed limestone. Where necessary, the roadbuilder followed the usual practice of digging out a ditch (*fossa*) in excess of the width of the planned road. The earth at the bottom of the excavation was made solid by means of heavy rammers. Then followed a nine-inch rock fill of stones. The road laid on top of this bed was surfaced with a thick course of gravel, laid and cambered to ensure the run-off of occasional rain. Rain fell usually in spring, and the onset of a shower was followed by fierce heat so that within hours even a dirt road became as hard as poured cement.

On this stretch of road there are still evident the ruins of seven large-sized cities, ten dams and bridges, seven milestones more or less in their original positions, and three triumphal arches. The largest of the cities within this short space of road is Thugga, the second largest is Musti.

Thugga (later Dougga) was a provincial capital of a large zone 100 kilometres (seventy miles) south-east of Tunis; it is the best preserved of any Roman city in Tunis, complete with villas, residences, temples, baths, and cisterns. The Roman road enters the city under an arch raised in AD 205 to honour Septimius Severus, the first African-born emperor of Rome, on the occasion of his creating Thugga a *municipium* entitled to its own laws and magistrates. The arch is massive and simple with two Corinthian columns and two niches designed to hold statues (now missing). To the left of the gateway is a three-storied, seventy-feet-high Libico–Punic

Dougga, the best preserved Tunisian Roman city

Dougga (anc. Thugga), preserves this arch erected in AD 205 to Septimius Severus, the first African-born emperor of Rome

The Via Traiana in Jerash, Jordan. Roman influences
are as evident in the Middle East as in Africa

Dougga, Capitolium. This Temple of Jupiter, Juno and Minerva
was built by Marcus Aurelius and dominated the city

Djemila, Algeria. *Left:* the multi-seated latrine. The latrines were flushed with constantly flowing water *Below:* Timgad, a two-seated latrine

mausoleum, a monument to a Numidian prince. It was raised to Ateban, son of Lepmatath, son of Palu, and was put up sometime about 200 BC in the time of Masinissa, the Numidian chieftain who helped the Romans defeat Carthage. Ornamented with Corinthian columns, it has a frieze of horses pulling war chariots. Other fragments of Libico–Punic architecture at Thugga include a megalithic wall, a sanctuary to Baal, and a temple to Saturn with strange Punic carvings. The city street leading from the Arch of Severus is of polished white limestone and laid in the usual herring-bone pattern. Drains are provided every twenty feet as catch-basins for rainwater. This street led to the Baths of the Cyclopes, a complex of ruins notable for a multi-seated latrine attached to it. It was flushed with constant running water; even the wash-basins are still intact.

The street meanders between rows of houses, leading to the forum, which was restored in the time of the Antonines, AD 166–7. The rose-red marble of the columns came from the quarries at Simitthus. The forum adjoins the *area macelli* – the birth-place of the four winds. A large compass, showing the principal directions, is carved into the marble flooring by the side of the Capitol. The theatre of Antoninus Pius, built in AD 168, is constructed in classic Roman style; the hemicycle was partially hewn out

A roughly carved Punic relief uncovered in the ruins of Carthage. The city was
finally destroyed after the Third Punic War, which ended in 146 BC

The ancient city of Musti, in the centre of the wheat-growing area
of Tunisia, preserves ruins of gleaming limestone structures

Leptis Magna, the Forum. Leptis Magna was the largest of the
African coastal cities. The ruins, including a circus, theatre
and baths, rival those of Rome in magnificence

The Gateway of the Inscriptions, an entrance to Seressi (mod. Oum-el-Abouab, Tunisia)

of the rock. The stage, orchestra, tribunal, and many of the original stone seats are intact or restored, so that performances can still be given there.

Thugga appears to have been a favourite imperial city; the principal temple was erected by funds supplied by Augustus, and it was further beautified by many other emperors.

Musti, which lies within sight of Thugga, only eight miles away, is the geographical centre of the Tunisian wheat-growing area.

It is built of gleaming limestone with splendidly carved facades and a flooring of remarkable mosaics, many of which still survive. However, the ancient Roman city has lost its form since it was made into a fortress by the Byzantines in their struggle against the Vandals.

The formal Roman road entered Musti under an arch which is now ruined, and made its egress on the eastern side under another arch. In Musti were found two milestones, one bearing the name of the city. A well, fifteen feet in diameter and seventy-five feet deep, gave the city 1,000 cubic feet of water daily. It has functioned for over 2,000 years.

Maktar (anc. Mactaris) lies on the Via Hadriana forty miles to the south of Musti. It was the provincial capital of the area and was erected in a well-watered site at an altitude of 3,000 feet. The forest of La Kesra rises above it. The modern city flows into and around the Roman ruins; Punic

Gateway of the Inscriptions, detail

tombs mingle with Roman and Christian. There are the ruins of an amphitheatre, a forum with its marble paving still intact, a triumphal arch built
by the Emperor Trajan in AD 107, and two large thermal baths in an
excellent state of preservation. The bare stone arches of an aqueduct that
once brought water to the city from the forest above it now stand in an
open field. There are ruins of a temple to Apollo, a *schola* or ancient club,
and a wide scattering of crisply carved marble bas-reliefs. The battlefield
of Zama was near enough to Maktar to make this city the headquarters of
Scipio Africanus the Younger when he led Roman troops against Hannibal's
formidable army.

Fifty miles to the south of Maktar, in a forested area, is Sufetula. It lies
within a semi-arid area which is scarred by dry water-courses, and next to
a seasonal wadi-course. In Roman times it was a considerable city, as its
ruins and roads suggest; four Roman roads joined there. In the walled
city there are three nobly proportioned temples dedicated to Jupiter, Juno
and Minerva. An aqueduct which conveyed water from the 3,000 feet high
Djebel Mrihla is revealed only by its arches, fallen and broken. A triumphal
arch, a quarter of a mile from the cultural centre of Sufetula, now Sbeitla,
suggests how extensive the site once was.

On the same main Roman road only forty-two kilometres (twenty-four

Overleaf: The grandeur of the civilisation transmitted from the hub of Rome
is nowhere more impressive than in the magnificent ruins at Leptis Magna

miles) is Cillium. It is better known as the Kasserine Pass, since one of the battles in World War II was fought there. At its entrance there is an impressive and fairly well preserved mausoleum. Its towering size and noble proportions would not be out of place on the Via Appia. The epitaph of 170 lines, the longest single inscription in North Africa, tells all who pass to stop and read that here is buried Flavius Sabinus, and reviews the 110 years of his life.

The farmlands about Cillium still yield wheat crops which people still harvest with a scythe; camels still pull the ploughs as do oxen. Only the cultivation of wheat can explain the former affluence of Cillium. For it has a theatre, hewn in classical style out of the rock. An impressive monumental arch with an inscription *'Colonia Cillitana'* leads to the city, now almost wholly destroyed.

Thelepte, which is thirty-one kilometres (nineteen miles) further along the same Roman road, is now in an area of titanic desolation. It seems the most unlikely place for the Romans to have created a city. Along formal streets, many of which are stone-paved, there is a veritable forest of columns; all about there are ruins. While there is no triumphal arch at Thelepte, there are remains of a thermal bath; the ruined arches rise as high as 100 feet. It once was a massive structure, one of the largest Roman baths outside of Carthage. These baths were designed to accommodate five hundred or perhaps a thousand people at a single time, and where are the populations which would have sustained it? Bedouins now use the once luxurious baths as night stalls for their camels.

The only geographical explanation for the existence of Thelepte is that it lay in a strategic position. From it, one road, seventy-five kilometres long, went north-east to Tebessa, the earliest Roman garrison city; the other road of equal length led across the fierce desert to Gafsa.

Gafsa (the Roman Capsa) is an oasis. At an opening in the arid hills, along what once was the old Roman road, there is a harmonious line of dark date palms and white houses. Minarets dominate the horizon. 'Archaeologists', wrote Norman Douglas, who was there in 1911, 'have discovered in the district of Gafsa alone over a hundred Roman wells and reservoirs of every shape and size'.

Gafsa was founded, so say Arab historians, by Nimrod's armour-bearers; others say that it was Melkarth, the Libyan Hercules, who was the hero of its colonisation. The Egyptians ruled it at one time, and later the Carthaginians regained it, calling it Kafaz. After the destruction of Carthage it was the retreat and treasure house of the Numidian kings.

In 106 BC the Roman legions came to Gafsa to put down the revolt of Jugurtha, the Numidian. They found the surrounding country barren and desolate. The heat-laden winds 'rise in the desert like a veritable tempest at sea,' wrote the Roman historian Sallust. 'The plain being unbroken and without vegetation, the wind, which nothing impedes, raises the sand in violent clouds . . . fill the face and eyes.' The Roman military commanders

Sufetula (mod. Sbeitla). The splendid remains of this Roman city, fifty miles south of Maktar, include temples to Jupiter, Juno and Minerva

Sabratha, lying on one of the great African caravan routes, preserves
monumental ruins, including the Baths of Oceanus and the Temple of Isis

in Numidia, facing such a hostile land, taught their legions to be flexible
in their tactics. They made forced marches through the desert at night.
So trained, they filled bullock skins with water, crossed eighty-one kilometres of desert, and surprised Gafsa. The hostile desert was no longer a
protection to anyone.

Little of ancient Gafsa remains, but the wonderful Roman reservoir can
still be seen. It is twenty-five feet deep, fifty feet wide and seventy feet long.
Spring water entering below is so clear that small iridescent fish can be
seen in it, flowing through a large opening. Well-laid steps come down to
the pool and the water flows out into another deep reservoir; it is crowded
throughout the day by Arab children.

The strategic Roman road between Gafsa and the port of Gabes, built
originally by Tiberius in 14 BC, had the principal purpose of allowing the
III Legio Augusta relatively easy movement across the vast area so as to
prevent the desert tribes – the Gaetuli in mountainous Numidia (Algeria)

and the desert-based Garamantes in Libya – from attacking Roman cities and villas. The distance from the military garrison city of Tebessa, the first headquarters of the III Legio Augusta, to coastal Gabes was 185 Roman miles.

Between Gafsa and Gabes there were five Roman way-stops. The Romans must have found the last ninety miles from Gafsa to the coast a little journey in hell, for the area is all desert. In the first ten miles out of Gafsa the Romans had to pass the first salt marsh, the Chott el Guettar. Here the depressions (the *chotts*) are dried-up arms of the sea. In ancient times, says the legend, the fleets of Atlantis rode here at anchor. The rains that fall are held in these shallow chott-lakes. The water evaporates in the heat and leaves a residue of salt; the glare from it is so intense that it can cause purblindness.

Gabes (ancient Tacape) lies in a large gulf, Syrtis Minor, and is a protected port. For the interior-based III Legio Augusta the shortest route to the coast led to Gabes. Five principal roads entered Gabes. The north road went to the large Roman centre of Thysdrus, famed then for its vast groves of olive trees and its enormous amphitheatre. This immense structure now looms up in isolation from a featureless land, but when it was built by Gordian in AD 238 the area was thickly enough populated to fill twice weekly the circus which could hold 30,000 spectators at one sitting. Of all the colosseums built it was inferior in size only to that of Rome. The city was extensive as were its villas. Water was so abundant at that time that a magistrate in an inscription congratulated himself for his feat of having adorned the whole city with fountains.

The coastal road, which was extended during the short reign of Nerva in AD 98, was the great artery that bound all of the Mediterranean African provinces together, from Alexandria in Egypt to the Pillars of Hercules. Nerva, who died within two years of taking office, merely began the road in Africa Proconsularis; it was to his adopted son Trajan that fell the task of financing its extension into Libya.

The great coastal road of the Mediterranean provinces

The Roman road that connected Carthage with the 'three cities' of Tripoli was laid over classic ground; Egyptians, Greeks, Phoenicians, Cretans and Syrians lived and died there centuries before the word 'Roman' was ever heard over the land.

The deserts of Libya (ancient Libu) went out from the Nile; 'a great belt of sand', wrote Herodotus, 'stretching from Thebes in Egypt to the Pillars of Hercules (Tangiers)'. Yet these deserts were never empty. Sections of them have been continuously inhabited for 20,000 years. Herodotus preserved a list of the tribes that dominated Libya. In Cyrenaica, where the Greeks later settled and built a splendid concourse of coastal cities, lived a tribe who used 'four-horse chariots'. Then, 'proceeding in a westerly direction one comes next to the Nasamones . . . who in the summer leave their cattle on the coast and go into the desert to a place called Augila for the date harvest'. This oasis of Augila or Awjilah

Overleaf: Timgad, Algeria, the main street ending at the Arch of Trajan. Called Thamugas by the Romans, the city was begun in AD 100 at Trajan's orders

(Jalo) is still there, 222 kilometres inland from the coast, and so are the date palms.

A tribe once adjoined the Nasamones, called the Psylli, but they became extinct. Since their lands were on the edge of the great sand sea of Calanscio, 'the south wind dried up all the water in their storage tanks'. Upon this they decided to declare war on the south wind. They marched out to the desert where the wind blew to attack it, but it buried them in sand. Next in order came the Gindances whose women were famed for their libidinousness. Then the Lotophagi who lived off the fruit of the lotus ('as big as a mastic-berry and as sweet as a date'), and this was where one found cattle 'which walk backwards as they graze'. Next – and this 'next' is a huge geographical straddle of a thousand miles into Tunisia – were the Machlyes who lived about the 'great lagoon of Tritonis', which is the Chott Djerid, a salt flat fringed with marsh-verdure and ringed with oases, doubtless once an inland waterway that stretched from Gabes on the coast to the oasis of Tozeur. The Argo, said the myths, was lost in this maze and Jason was bewildered in trying to find his way out of it until 'Triton appeared and told Jason to give him the tripod in return for which he would show him the channel. . . .'

Herodotus, in view of the fact that he never travelled beyond Egypt, used very well 'the stories which the Libyans tell'. For he related that 'further inland to the southward, in the part of Libya where the wild beasts are found, live the Garamantes'. It is these Garamantes who later enter Roman history. They were a powerful tribe, holding lordship of oases and of caravan routes that moved from Central Africa, bringing gold, ivory, ostrich plumes, slaves, skins, and carbuncle stones to the trading stations on the Libyan coast.

The Libyan gebel   The dominant geographical feature of Libya is the *gebel*, a rock plateau that rises to a height of 2,100 feet immediately behind the coast. The climate here tends to be Mediterranean; there is seasonal rain. Olives, grapevine and date palms have been cultivated since earliest antiquity. It is along this coast that the Phoenicians, mentioned in Homer and the Bible, set up, as early as 1000 BC, trading stations called the *emporia*. By the fifth century the three cities of Sabratha, Oea (Tripoli) and Leptis Magna had been settled by the Phoenicians as trading stations for the ivory, gold, and carbuncle stones that came on the long caravan route from Central Africa. It must be assumed that the water table of the inner Sahara was then higher than it is now, for desert wells lay within a day's trek all along the way, and there were intermittent grazing lands. Goods were carried by oxen and horses.

Oea (Tripoli) had a natural port; Sabratha had none and lay on the open sea; Leptis Magna had the small natural river port formed by the Wadi Lebda. Carthage developed these cities on a small scale, meanwhile holding the Greeks at a distance and placing the limitation of their westward expansion at the Gulf of Syrtes.

Dougga, theatre. The theatre of Dougga was built in AD 166–9

The fall of Carthage in 146 BC brought these cities of the emporia into the Roman empire. Sallust writes that Leptis, one of the three cities, was founded by the Tyrians and 'is situated between the two Syrtes'.

Of the sea, on which trading ships sailed, he found that 'near the coast the water is very deep; farther out, it is a matter of chance; parts are deep, other parts, under certain weather conditions, are full of shoals. For when the sea runs high, and the winds lash it into fury. . . .'

These conditions did not prevent trade. In 106 BC, with a Roman garrison in attendance, the first Roman businessman came to the emporia. He left us his name – Herennius.

Sabratha, the most westerly of the three cities, was reached by the coastal Roman road, the Way of Nerva. It extended through the sand dunes into Libya.

Sabratha was the goal of one of the great caravan routes of Central Africa. The route went through the oases that lay at the foot of the precipitous *gebel* back of Sabratha, passed over the edge of the high rocklands of Al Hammadah al Hamra to Ghadames. This oasis was located at the point where three countries, Tunisia, Algeria and Libya, now conjoin. Ghadames (Roman Cydamae) was to be one of the key fortresses of the African *limes*, but millennia before this Ghadames was one of the *entrepôts* to the four great trade routes, the one that led to and through the Sahara to Lake Chad, and from there to the Niger and into Central Africa, a distance of 2,000 miles.

Into Sabratha poured the riches of Central Africa – gold dust, ivory, ostrich feathers, dye-stuffs, hides, and above all live animals to supply the Roman circuses all over the world.

Cities of the tripolis   After the fall of Carthage, Sabratha gradually became Roman. It was extended until it bordered on the sea. The Roman coastal road enters the city as its *decumanus* running east and west along the coast. Forums, temples, and basilicas were tightly clustered on the sea-side. Further along were the baths of Oceanus and the Temple of Isis. The pride of Sabratha was its theatre, which had the Mediterranean as its background. The stage floor is laid in mosaic; its front, the podium, is decorated with reliefs representing gods and allegorical figures. The theatre proper is Augustan; the stage, however, was erected in the time of the Antonines.

Tripoli was the largest of the three cities that formed the tripolis. It is sixty-five kilometres (forty miles) from Sabratha. It had a large natural harbour, ample fresh water, a very fertile hinterland, and seemingly endless groves of olive trees. Nothing Roman is to be seen in Tripoli today except the once splendid triumphal arch erected to Marcus Aurelius and Lucius Verus in AD 163 under which the coastal road, the Via Nerva, passed.

Leptis Magna, the third city of the tripolis, is by any measure the greatest city on the entire Mediterranean coast between Carthage and Alexandria. Its fame is historical, architectural and gastronomic.

'The town of Leptis', wrote Sallust, 'was founded by the Tyrians who are stated to have sailed there (in the eighth century BC) on account of civil disturbances (in Lebanon)'.

Leptis is situated between the two Syrtes, two enormous bays lying almost at the extreme east of North Africa. In a small natural port, where the Wadi Lebda debouches into the sea, the Phoenicians created their first trading settlement. Olive oil, ivory, and slaves were the standard merchandise; soon was added another – the silphium herb. Known elsewhere as 'devil's dung' or asafoetida, it was widely used in Roman cookery. Pliny the Elder devoted a whole chapter in his *Natural History* to the silphium.

Leptis Magna became part of the new Roman province of Africa founded in 23 BC. Within a few years a certain Calpurnius Piso had begun to restore the old parts of Leptis and build the new. In the year AD 1 the theatre, almost as luxurious as the one in Sabratha, was erected. New forums were erected over old ones; luxurious baths, private and public, were raised as fast as new water sources were found to animate them.

Five years later, in AD 17, Leptis Magna built its first interior Roman road. Italian archaeologists working in the area have uncovered a milestone 1·85 metres high and forty-four centimetres in diameter, bearing an inscription that tells us that in the reign of the Emperor Tiberius, one Aelius Lamia (in AD 15) opened up forty-four Roman miles of road into the arid interior. This Via Lamia as it was called was later marked with milestones put up in the time of Caracalla. The road opened up the land and good communications allowed the farmers to plant groves of olive trees further inland.

It did not take the desert tribes long to react to this new Roman encroachment. Deprived of their coastal grazing lands, the Garamantes began to raid the new settlements.

The III Legio Augusta, however, led by Cornelius Balbus, took positive action against them, pursuing the Garamantes through Ghadames, where they overran a Garamantian outpost, across the high and inhospitable plateau Al Hammadah to the oasis of Brak and beyond to the caravanserai of Sebha.

In AD 69 the desert tribes under the Garamantes again besieged Leptis Magna. The siege was broken only by the arrival of cohorts of the III Legio Augusta under Valerius Festus. The Garamantes, loaded down with booty, must have taken their traditional route back into the desert. Festus found a shorter route, 'four days shorter than the other road', known to the Romans thereafter as the *Praeter Caput Saxi*. He waylaid the Garamantes, slaughtering them and returning with the loot.

Later, during the time of Trajan's rule, the Romans seemed to have come to terms with the Garamantes. In AD 100 two commanders, Septimius Flaccus and Julius Maternus, marched for thirty days through the Libyan Sahara past Sudan and into Ethiopian country. Aided by the Garamantes, they captured the Ethiopians, running them down with the Garamantes's four-horse chariots.

The Roman incursions into the desert had one purpose: the protection of Roman cities. When the Romans found they could not control the enormous waste-land, they drew back and set up a defence in depth, a *limes* beginning in Libya and stretching from Thubactis (modern Misurata) across the desert of Libya to the marsh-chotts of Tunisia, and beyond this to the aridities of the Atlas Mountains and the deserts of Numidia, near the pillars of Hercules. The *limes*, starting at the Mediterranean, extended 1,200 miles.

Three main fortresses were erected: Nu Ngem, which guarded the Leptis–Fezzan road; El-Gheria El Garbia, which protected the Oea–Tripoli route to Germa, and the Ghadames (Cydamus) fort, which con-

The Roman desert limes

trolled the gateway for the caravan routes into the central Sahara. The defence in depth was achieved by establishing a series of fortified farms. These, perched on the highest points of the gebels overlooking the desert wadis, are some of the most striking archaeological remains to be seen in the aridities of Libya. These forts are so numerous that, although a study has been made of the *limes*, the number of forts and fortified farms has never been exactly determined.

Leptis Magna, along with other coastal cities of the emporia, developed rapidly once it had acquired an effective defence. The immediate Roman roads in the Libyan hinterland were made 'formal', that is, they were marked with milestones. Libyan roads were at best cleared *pistes* or trackways. There has yet to be discovered in all this area, outside of Roman cities, a single stretch of ancient paved road. Italian archaeologists, and later British archaeologists, have found milestones, but they are surprisingly few. Most are dated during the time of Septimius Severus and his son Caracalla.

In the time of Vespasian (he had once been proconsul in Africa) the Temple of Magna Mater in Leptis Magna was built. Upon the advent of Trajan, and the completion of the coastal road, the Via Nerva which extended eastward from Carthage, the city was given the title and rights of a *colonia*. A four-portalled triumphal arch to Trajan was raised in its market in AD 109 by public subscription. Forums, markets, baths, temples, a circus, a palestra for gymnastic exercises, theatres and villas proliferated. So many marble columns adorned the city that even after a thousand years the sands had failed to cover them. Over 600 marble pillars were removed from Leptis to ornament the palace of Louis XIV at Versailles.

Septimius Severus of Leptis Magna
Septimius Severus's residence in Leptis, his birthplace, during the years AD 203–4 brought the city to its height of power and beauty. He added to Leptis by beginning the *centro Severiano*, a single structure which included a colonnaded street, a forum, a basilica, and a nymphaeum.

It was the engineering projects, however, that earned Severus his great renown and caused a triumphal arch to be raised to him. The Wadi Lebda was canalised. A few miles east of Leptis an artificial lake was made on the littoral to receive the waters of the Wadi Caam (the ancient Cinyps river), conducted to Leptis by means of a subterranean aqueduct. This was the ancient Cinyps river. Dams, barrages, sluices, and waterfalls were all parts of the Severian harbour project. The natural basin, the mouth of Wadi Lebda, was artificially enlarged into an irregular polygonal shape, 400 metres in width and length. The sea walls were protected by huge stone ashlars weighing as much as a ton each. The promontory that protects the mouth of the Wadi on the north side was extended 300 feet into the sea and built up from the sea bottom with a solid facing by huge ashlars held together by bronze clamps. At the end of this was a huge octagonal lighthouse. The south mole, protected from the open sea by an artificial sea wall and sand and earth works, had the main wharves. There is a temple, a forum, and along the wharves a series of storehouses. Much of this is still in an excellent state of preservation.

After AD 300, the stones of Leptis Magna cease to speak. The city was in crisis as was most of Africa. Within there was a struggle between the Catholics and the schismatic sect the Donatists, and from without the desert nomads had, with a camel corps, outflanked the *limes* and threatened the city.

In AD 363, the city was under siege. The garrison refused to defend it unless they were given their salary arrears. The demand was not met, and Leptis was sacked.

The coast road continued east of Leptis Magna. It passed through regularly spaced halting-places, often cities of considerable size. It passed under the arch of the Philaeni, known to modern troops in the Desert War as the Marble Arch, which marked the boundary between Carthage and Greek-occupied Cyrenaica. Here the Roman road entered a constellation of cities which had been developed by the Greeks since the sixth century. It passed through Benghazi, Tocra and Ptolemais; at Apollonia, the seaport of Cyrene west of the modern Derna, was the *entrepôt* to Cyrene (which lies further inland). Roman roads were formalised into streets once they entered the former Greek colony. By the time the coastal road passed through the cities the whole of the colony was Romanised, although the architecture and language remained Greek.

The road acted as a catalyst; by linking all these cities, it helped to unify Africa's vast spaces. When the road reached the Greek–Roman village of Antipyrgos (mod. Tobruk) it entered Egypt.

Inscriptions from the Baths of Antoninus, Carthage, referring to the Numidians and to Carthage

III · EGYPT AND THE MIDDLE EAST

The great Roman coastal road from Tangiers to Alexandria (in Egypt) was, if one measured a straight line, 2,100 miles long. Its last course lay along the menacing sands close to the sea, and the way was marked only by cairns of stones although there were regular way-stops which sheltered water sources. The goal of this coastal road was, of course, Alexandria.

There were five principal roads in Egypt. The first was the coastal road, which Strabo called 'the way of the sea'. It crossed seven of the streams of the Nile and followed the coast to Palestine, Sidon, Tyre and Lebanon. Under Trajan after AD 100 the road was rebuilt along the Mediterranean and extended from Alexandria to Antioch and along the serrated outer edge of Anatolia to the Bosporus.

Before Egypt came under Roman management, however, Egyptian roads were merely rudimentary. The Nile was of course Egypt's first highway, its river road, which ran uninterrupted up to the first cataract. The roads leading to the gold mines were mere desert tracks marked by cairns of stones; wadis, dry water courses, were used as roads. At the well-known quarries about Assuan, short lengths of road were made in order to get the quarried stone to the Nile. Some of the roads, varying from five to eight metres in width, that ran into the higher lands of Nubia were walled with sun-baked brick.

But there were no roads with prepared surfaces as the Romans knew them; at best the ground was cleared to a width of five metres, the way was marked with cairns of stones, and at the end of each day's march there was a well. There were several short lengths of paved processional roads within the precincts of towns or sacred areas. When the chariot was introduced into Egypt after 1500 BC, and the roads were levelled, but even then there were complaints about the 'tiresome narrowness of the pharaonic roads'. These did not fully satisfy the Romans when they arrived.

Rome's involvement with Egypt stemmed from the Caesarian wars.

Roman hegemony after Actium

With the victory at Actium came the emergence of Octavian as Augustus and Egypt became the fief of his principate. It was ruled by a proconsul answerable only to Augustus. Under Roman management Egypt became one of the granaries of Rome; it produced annually 1,625,000 bushels of

This road in Amman, Jordan, laid out by the ancient Romans leads past the restored Roman theatre

The Great Sphinx of Giza, 189 feet long, represents a civilisation
that had existed for centuries before the arrival of the Romans

wheat. Alexandria was the emporium of commerce and manufacture: glass, linen, weaving, papyrus, agriculture. There was trade with India, Arabia and Ethiopia. Most trade goods passed through Alexandria.

Land communications in Roman Egypt developed slowly during the following century. Two roads, although not continuous, went along the east and west banks of the Nile. They remained unpaved. No milestones were erected; the Romans merely adopted the Egyptian system of marking the way with cairns of stones. Nor did the Romans make a more general architectural impression on Egypt; there are surprisingly few remains. Trajan opened the roads more for strategic reasons than for economic ones; thus Egypt remains one of the few areas of the Roman world where there is a dearth of inscriptions.

The destruction of Alexandria, during the Jewish–Greek civil wars in AD 115, gave Hadrian and his *architectus*, Decrianus, an opportunity to rebuilt it. One hundred and seventy miles up the Nile, Hadrian also rebuilt the market place of Hermopolis Magna (now El Ashmunein) and improved the two roads along the Nile.

Later, on the other side of the Nile, Hadrian built Antinoöpolis in memory of his young friend Antinous, and laid down the Via Hadriana, the only formal Roman road in all Egypt. An inscription found at Antinoopolis states that by an order of Hadrian a road was built from that city on the Nile across the desert to the Red Sea and along it southward to the port-city of Berenice at 36 degrees south latitude. Berenice was the *entrepôt* for shipping from India and the Arabias. There are today, however, few traces of the hydreumata, stations and garrisons mentioned in the inscriptions. No milestones have been found to confirm the road. A few sections of cleared track or way have been seen, but nowhere is the surface paved. The conclusion recorded in the *Tabula Imperii Romani* is that the formal Via Hadriana has vanished. Yet there is evidence of its use in early Christian and Nabatean graffiti carved on rocks at Berenice, and in the remains of a Roman temple.

The Via Hadriana in Egypt

The fourth road of Egypt was in reality five roads. All of these coursed across the high eastern desert escarpment, ranging from 800 to 2,500 metres in altitude, and terminated at seaports on the Red Sea. Where the Nile makes a fish-hook bend, the Egyptians built Tentyra (Dendera). This city, thirty-seven miles south of Luxor, was erected in magnificent solitude. It had been the capital of the sixth *nome* of Upper Egypt. Across from it on the east side of the Nile was Caenepolis (present-day Qena), from which place stemmed two roads. One, which we shall refer to as the Via Myos Hormos (although the road carried no such designation) extended north-east to the seaport of Myos Hormos (Abu Sha'ar). There it connected with the Via Hadriana. Seven Roman forts at ten mile intervals guarded the road, which traversed the mining district known as the Mons Porphyrites, where there were extensive granite and porphyry quarries. The second road, the Via Mons Claudianus, breaks off from the Via

Myos Hormos at the first station, Aras. Its direction is for the most part easterly; its terminus is the same Myos Hormos on the Red Sea. Roman forts and wells dot the entire length of the road. At Mons Claudius the Romans built a temple in addition to numerous stone dwellings to house the miners.

Coptos, ten miles south of the river-port of Qena, was the starting point of two other roads. One of these, the Via Coptiana, is the only Roman road mentioned in many sources from Roman times. The two roads bifurcated at the first station. This way-stop was called Phoenicon. Here the road which we shall refer to as the Via Leucos Limen, sixty miles long, takes the shortest route almost directly eastward to the Red Sea and the port Leucos Limen (now Quseir). It has seven forts, spaced at regular intervals, and a long series of signal stations. At Hammamat, the third station of the Via Leucos Limen, there are several inscriptions to Pan – the Roman patron of desert travellers – carved on the walls of caves. There are other inscriptions in demotic which suggest that the road was Egyptian before it became Roman. The road terminates at the sea and connects with the coastal Via Hadriana.

The principal route, the Via Coptiana, began at Phoenicon. Camels were used for the journey, and there are watering stations placed at intervals. Many of these stations are still to be seen: Didyme, where there are graffiti and invocations to Pan and Min; Afrodito; Compasi, where amethysts were mined; Jovis; Aristonis; Falacro, where another road from the Nile joined; Apollonos; Cabalsi; Novum Hydreuma, and Vetus Hydreuma, where the coastal Via Hadriana turns inland and joins this road.

Together the roads proceeded to the large seaport of Berenice which lay protected in 'Foul Bay'. Berenice, we learn from Pliny and others, received sea cargoes from other ports to the south and was linked in turn with organised caravan routes to the Nile, and therefore to Egyptian markets. Strabo, the Hellenised geographer from Cappadocia, stated that the Temple at Berenice was founded and built by Ptolemy Philadelphus. In the early nineteenth century it was discovered by the archaeologist Belzoni, who found many inscriptions with Roman and Ptolemaic dates. More is yet to be discovered, for Berenice still lies under the sands.

There was a final road, it seems, that led from Idfu (Apollinopolis) to the gold mining regions of the eastern desert. It had four way-stations and forts, placed at regular ten mile intervals, until it connected with the larger Coptos–Berenice road at the Falacro station.

The fifth road of Egypt was the Sinai–Aqaba road. The track was very ancient, older than the memories of the authors of Exodus. The road went along the side of the Bitter Lakes below Suez, turned due east and coursed across the Sinai Peninsula for 120 miles – a four days' journey – to Aqaba, the Red Sea port of the Middle East.

It was the Emperor Trajan who opened up the Middle East. His

Two Roman milestones, more than seven feet high, overlook the
Wadi Mojib (anc. Arnon River) from the Via Traiana

decision to make war on Parthia and push the Roman frontiers beyond the Euphrates in order to secure Rome's interior trade lines brought Roman legions into Petra. In AD 106 Petra was annexed and made a Roman province. After that Trajan's engineers began to build the road to Aqaba.

The port of Aqaba

This city, at the head of the Gulf of Aqaba (the north-east arm of the Red Sea), is now the meeting place of four nations – Jordan, Egypt, Saudi Arabia and Israel; then it was all Roman. Nothing is known of pre-Roman Aqaba. Even its ancient name is in dispute; the Peutinger Tablum lists Addianam, other sources refer to Aqaba, or to Aila, an even older Nabatean name. There are no ruins, there are no remains of docks or warehouses, there is nothing Roman or pre-Roman, and yet we know from the records that it had been the *entrepôt* of trading ships for centuries.

Trade ships arriving at the Gulf of Aqaba on the Red Sea brought produce from Arabia Deserta, Arabia Felix, Ceylon, India and beyond, and for centuries caravans were funnelled through it to Petra. Cinnamon came from Ceylon, as did cloves; nutmeg and mace came from Malaya. Ginger root came from the wild parts of India. Pepper was a Roman passion, and the filling of the pepper-bins by the Tiber was so important that there was a curator of pepper. So famous was this depository that when the Goths appeared before the walls of Rome in AD 408, they demanded three thousand pounds of pepper merely as the basis for negotiations. All these spices fulfilled the trade ideal: they were easily transportable, cheap at the source, dear at the market.

Pearls came from the coast of India; the best were from Ceylon. 'I swear before the gods', said a returning Roman trader, 'that the bottom of the sea seems to be covered with them'.

Coral – also highly valued by Roman jewellers – covered the bottom of the Red Sea, giving the sea its colour and its name.

Diamonds were found in the gravel of Indian rivers and were a trade item; the Romans called them 'adamantes', the invincible stones, since there were no tools that would cut them. India also traded in sapphires. And there were jade, crystals, rose-quartz, carnelian, jasper, agate, onyx and beryls.

Then, too, there were the slave trade and the ivory trade. The Romans had a passion for ivory; seats for judges were made of ivory and Caracalla's horses fed out of ivory mangers.

All this luxury trade was carried by ships to the port of Aqaba. And it was from this port that the engineers of the Legio ix Hispana began to build the great arterial road that was to run from Aqaba through Amman, Philadelphia, then on to Bostra, Damascus, and finally to Palmyra in the Syrian desert. The road was laid down along the Wadi-el-Butm. Although there is no longer evidence of the road itself (it has been swept away by periodic floods, the most recent having taken place in 1964), five miliaria still mark its course.

One hundred miles northward, the road having passed through desert

Petra, the 'rose-red' city of the Nabateans of Jordan, preserves
gorgeous rock carved chambers with delicately modeled façades

a lateral road – still marked with milestones – led to the city of Petra.

Petra was built by the Nabateans, a Semitic-speaking Arab people Originally nomads, they turned from piracy to trade and extended their kingdom into Jordan, parts of Syria, and Arabia Deserta. The first historical reference to them is on the 'List of Enemies' of the Assyrians the text is dated 647 BC. They were known rather early to the Romans According to Strabo, the Romans knew that the capital of Petra was 'in a hollow somewhat less than two miles in circumference, surrounded by inaccessible mountains with a stream running through it. . . .'

A good description of it, for out of the void of desert drabness suddenly bursts this wadi formed out of layers of sandstone in vivid colours and swirling patterns. As the rock surface is soft, the Nabateans carved and hewed the city out of the rock.

No precise date exists for Petra's origin. The most famed of the hundred of tombs dotting the wadi is the first building to be seen in the city when one emerges from the darkened, mile-long Sîk canyon. It is known as 'the treasury'. The facade of El Khazne is sculptured from the rosiest-red of all the rocks of Petra. The style of the architecture is Greek, the period i first century, the effect is awesome. The temple is cut like a cameo, a miniature *tholos*, a structure of extreme elegance.

While still under Nabatean rule, Petra controlled the caravan routes from the south, since the original trade route went through a waterless desert west of Petra. In order to gain the northern route, all caravans had to take the narrow exit through the Sîk. So, in AD 106 Trajan annexed Petra; later, Hadrian renamed it 'Hadriana'. After that began its full Romanisation.

The Sîk road that led into Petra was paved; in the city itself a fine Roman road of gleamingly white limestone was laid down. A wall was erected to give dignity to the forum; a Temple to Zeus and a triumphal arch to Hadrian were built, and an amphitheatre was hollowed out of the side of a sandstone cliff, gigantic enough to seat 10,000 spectators.

Engineering achievement of the Via Traiana

Petra's influence, however, disappeared with the *pax Romana* since the main Roman road – the Via Traiana or Way of Trajan – by-passed the city. The engineers of Legio IX Hispana who built the road with native labour used the materials at hand. Above Shobak, north of Petra, the builders used large flat slabs of basalt, there being a volcanic outcrop there. Further on, where the road crosses a hill 4,500 feet above sea level they used heavy, round field-stones for paving. Cyclindrical columns seven feet tall and weighing over two tons, were placed as markers at every Roman mile; an aerial survey made of this road in 1946 found forty such milestones in succession.

Fifty miles south of Amman the earth opens in an immense rift, the Wadi-el-Mujib. It is deep, wide, and precipitous; when water-filled, it river flows into the Dead Sea. The Roman road negotiated this canyon descending five hundred metres on one side and climbing up on the other

The magnificent façades of these carved structures were cut from the
top downward out of the predominantly pink limestone

Left: The Roman road leading to Petra, which was first
inhabited by Edomites in the ninth and tenth centuries BC
Right: Jerash (anc. Gerasa), one of the three great
caravan cities, with Petra and Palmyra, preserves splendid
temples of Artemis and Zeus

Fifty miles further north, the road comes down to Amman lying under and between its seven *gebels*. This city was once called Philadelphia. Its large amphitheatre is still extant.

Less than thirty-five kilometres further north is Jerash (Gerasa). Milestones still mark parts of the Via Traiana as it goes towards Gerasa. Of Greek origin, Gerasa was one of the cities of the commercial league known as the Decapolis. It was one of the three famed caravan cities (the others were Petra and Palmyra). It is the finest and most completely preserved Roman provincial city in the Middle East. A nymphaeum still stands on the main street. There are two theatres, both with Greek inscriptions, one at each end of the city. Temples, baths and a wide scattering of house sites complete the caravan city. It seems incredible that this site should have slipped from memory until the German traveller Seetzen came across it in 1806.

Jerash, the best preserved provincial Roman city

Entering Gerasa, the Via Traiana passes through a triumphal arch, runs beside the ruins of a hippodrome, and leads into an immesnse stone forum laid in a unique, irregular elliptical shape. The Via Traiana becomes the principal street of Gerasa, colonnaded from one end to the other. The original paving-stones of polished white limestone still lie in their original positions.

At the north gate the Via Traiana leaves the city under an inscription: 'Built in AD 115 by Claudius Severus, legate of Trajan'. Beyond it, the landscape is uninviting. Black basalt strips criss-cross the sparse tilled land; plants springing up from the lava fissures are twisted and thorned; dark basalt hillocks and mountains rise out of the plain.

Yet this Druze plain is littered with things Roman. There are remains of olive presses and cisterns; grape motifs dominate the sculptured remains, reminding us that once, under Roman domination, vines grew here and the land was very fertile.

Busra, as its ancient name – Nova Traiana Bostra – implies, was re-founded by Trajan; it was a way-stop on his great paved caravan route. Busra is on the road to Damascus.

Damascus, which had been in existence for over two thousand years before Trajan brought his road to it, owed its existence to the Barada river which came out of the snow-covered Mt Hermon thirty kilometres directly east. That river, beginning as a slender thread, made Damascus an oasis and an emporium.

The Middle East had been attracting Roman traders for two centuries before the region fell under Roman domination in 63 BC. From that date, Rome, having become aware of the wonderful natural resources that had fallen to her, set out to organise the area. First came communications. By 47 BC roads were sufficiently passable to allow Julius Caesar to advance by forced marches from the Aegean coast at Tarsus across the high, rugged land, rent by rivers and valleys, to Pontus. Within days he was ready for battle with King Pharnaces, who had taken advantage of the

The sandstone of Petra is famous for its rich patterns of colour

Civil Wars to attempt to dislodge Rome from Asia. The Pontic Wars were for the legions only a small exercise in tactics and 'Caesar', he himself says, 'laughed contemptuously at the empty bravado of Pharnaces'. Within a hour both battle and war were over; Caesar's elation at the speed of it is summed up in the words '*Veni, vidi, vici*', which were inscribed on a tablet carried before him in his triumph. His legions were left behind to garrison Pontus and to construct the main road over an ancient trade route that led to Ancyra (Ankara). Then Caesar set out to view the rest of the way to Galatia and Bithynia, settling disputes, assigning prerogatives to kings and states and setting up a road board to superintend the building of new ways.

The strategic roads that led to the *Limes Syriae*, and the number of fortresses, fortified farms and military outposts dwarf anything that Rome ever attempted on the Rhine, in North Africa, or in Britain. The *Limes Syriae* stretched out like a spider's web for 625 miles; forts with tall, stone fighting towers were linked with military stations placed every twelve miles. For centuries scholars looked with incredulity upon the mass of Roman roads in Syria that were drawn on the *Tabula Peutingeriana*, the

Palmyra, halfway between Damascus and the Euphrates River,
boasts some of the most imposing remains of antiquity

Above: The walls of Palmyra were built by Justinian late in the history of the city, which is mentioned as early as 1100 BC in Mesopotamian inscriptions
Right: The limestone pavement and some of the columns of Hadrian's Forum in Jerash date from the first century. Jerash conducted trade with Persia and India

Palmyra's so-called 'Street of Columns'. The first modern travellers visited the site in 1678

third-century Roman world map. Yet the existence of these roads was confirmed by aerial surveys made by French archaeologists during the years 1934–42.

Palmyra lay in the geographical centre of this defence complex. Since it was an oasis, offering a perennial supply of good water, it was the key to the caravan traffic route. It was reached by Trajan's road from Emessa (Homs), 200 kilometres distant, and it was later linked by the *Vallum Diocletianum* directly to Damascus through 225 kilometres of desert.

The Roman road to Palmyra still retains in places its original pavement; there are occasional fallen milestones with eroded inscriptions. The road approaches Palmyra by the Way of the Tombs. The Palmyrene tombs are stately towers; a few are still intact and wonderfully preserved within, with their elaborate blue or gold decorations painted on stucco.

After the Way of the Tombs, the Roman road enters Palmyra through the gateway of the wall that Justinian built in the sixth century of our era, and then turns into the long colonnaded street of paved limestone. A water conduit pipe once ran beside the road, and it can still be seen branching off into buildings that formed the residential centre. A well-

Emperor Augustus fostered Palmyra as the meeting place between Rome and Parthia

preserved theatre stands directly beside the road. Surrounding it are shops, residences, fountains, temples and caravanserais, which give an impression of the wealth of this city that governed the great caravan trade with the East.

Palmyra acquired its pre-eminence in Trajan's time; it became a desert emporium. To this centre came cotton, golden trinkets from Parthia, jewels from Babylon and cloth dyed with Tyrian purple. There was myrrh from Arabia, rare woods and spices from Persia, richly woven textiles and live birds, especially peacocks, which were much desired by Roman gourmets.

Eminence of Palmyra under Trajan

In the time of Marcus Aurelius there was also trade in Chinese silk. A group of Roman traders in AD 170 passed through Palmyra on their way to the Shiraz plain, there to meet a Chinese trade mission. 'The Ta-Ts'in [the Chinese name for the Romans] traffic with Persia and India', says the Chinese record. 'They are honest in trade. They have no double prices. Their kings wish to send embassies to China to trade in silk.' A pound of silk cost one pound of gold, but later, when communications with China worsened, the price as posted on Diocletian's list was three pounds

of gold for one pound of silk dyed with Tyrian purple. Trade made Palmyrene citizens rich. The portraits of women found on tombs show them ostentatiously dressed, their ears spangled with ornate earrings, their fingers encased with rings.

A parallel communication to Trajan's interior road in the Middle East was the coastal 'Way of the Sea'. As a primitive pre-Roman track it went back to dimmest antiquity; 'the overland journeys', wrote Strabo of this road, 'are made on camels through deserts and sandy places'. The track began at Alexandria in Egypt, followed the long sweep of the Mediterranean shore into Palestine and Lebanon and went on to Antioch and along the Anatolian shore to the Hellespont.

The Egyptians, as early as 1950 BC, used it when they traded with Tyre and Sidon for wood and purple dye. It was designed for pedestrian and mule traffic. When the wheel was perfected, domesticated onagers – wild asses – were used to pull huge, solid-wheeled carts. Still later, after 700 BC, after camels had been introduced from Mongolia, they were used by caravans.

This ancient track connecting Egypt with Tyre was an important trade route. Ancient Tyre, which was on a fertile coast watered by the rivers from the heights of Anti-Lebanon, was well known for its trade. The prophets of the Old Testament were livid with resentment over Tyre's wealth; their enumeration of the splendours to be found in the purple land gives an idea of Tyre's opulence. Tyrian imports are listed as silver, iron, tin from Cornwall, lead from Spain; ivory and ebony from Edom; horses and horsemen from Armenia; brass from Cilicia; linen and wheat from Syria; cassia from Damascus, not to mention camels, wine, and sheep. Tyre had two export items: cedars from Lebanon and the purple dye. The mollusc – source of that dye that gave Tyre its fame and wealth – is now possibly extinct; there are only high mounds of murex shells as a tangible memorial to that once-great dye industry.

This coastal road had already been paved before the time of Trajan. The same way passed through Sidon, which is listed in the Roman itineraria as both a seaport and a way-stop on the road. From there the road went to Beirut.

As 'Berytus', this city had a certain fame; its climate and fertile soil made it a favourite with the Romans. Augustus had given the city the name of his daughter, calling it Julia Augusta Felix; it was filled with temples and courts, none of which remain today. It was also a seat of learning; Septimius Severus founded an Academy of Law there in the third century.

After Beirut the coastal road crossed the Nahr-el-Kelb (the 'Dog River'), which rises out of Mt Sannine, drops into deep canyons, then disappears into caverns to re-emerge near the sea. (Because the water went underground, the river was believed to be related to Anubis, the Egyptian god of the underworld; hence the name 'Dog River'.) Here the mountains

A tomb portrait of a Palmyrene lady, a contemporary of the rebel
Queen Zenobia, whom Aurelian led captive back to Rome

come down to the sea, and, long before the Romans, a passage had been cut out of the solid rock. Everyone who used this road had to pass this defile and on the limestone cliffs by the bridge that spanned the river armies of every age seem to have cut inscriptions. Here Esarhaddon, the Assyrian, records his return from his victories in Upper Egypt; another account tells of Nebuchadnezzar's feats against the forces of Phoenicia; and although there are no remains of the Roman road or its bridge, there is a Roman inscription: the Legio III Gallica, Caracalla's troops from France, was stationed there and repaired the road.

Before the Way of the Sea reaches Byblos there is a lateral road which turns off to go to Afka and the sanctuary of Adonis. The modern road, which has been laid over the old Roman one, climbs up the limestone outcrop into the terraced hills.

At 3,000 feet altitude there are the remains of a temple built for the worship of Adonis. Now called Shir el Meidan, this temple is in ruins but stands nobly among the mimosa and poppies. It was ordered destroyed by Constantine the Great after he was told that pagans still practised sacred prostitution and ritual copulation there.

Far below the winding road is the Adonis river. It moves down to the sea, creating numerous spectacular gorges. In the spring during the heavy rains the river flows over exposed iron-ore deposits, and when it debouches into the Mediterranean it is a bitter red, colouring the waters for a considerable distance. This red stream was regarded as a symbol of the flowing blood of Adonis who, according to the Greek myth, was fatally wounded in the thigh by a wild boar.

Beyond Byblos the 'Way of the Sea' went through Tripolis and Antaradus (where it connected with a lateral road to Emessa and Palmyra); it then followed the coast to Laodicea (now Latakia), famous for its tobacco as well as for its earlier stigmatisation by St John for its 'lukewarmness'.

Beyond Laodicea, the Roman road turned inland to Antioch. It entered Antioch through the Daphne Gate, passed the wall of Theodosius II and the earlier walls of Tiberius, finally leading to the great colonnaded street of Agrippa. Founded by Alexander the Great, Antioch was for centuries the capital of the kings of Seleucidae. It is indicated on the Itineraria Romana with a symbol of a throned emperor which shows it to have been of equal importance with Rome and Constantinople as an imperial residence. It was one of the largest cities of the Roman Empire and one of the great commercial centres of the ancient world. And yet today there is not a trace of its former greatness.

Fortunately, in the late eighteenth century a young French artist, Louis François Cassas, engraved his 'Views of Antioch'. He drew the four-arched Roman bridge that crossed the river Orontes (it was still there in 1787), Justinian's walls, the Roman road, as well as the wall of Tiberius and the gateway of the road that led to Beroea-Aleppo. Apart from these memories, nothing remains of Antioch.

Antioch, an imperial residence

The Adonis River, whose waters are reddened by iron-ore deposits, was considered by the ancients as a symbol of the flowing blood of Venus' lover

The fabled land of Anatolia was penetrated from the south by four strategic Roman roads. These military ways were laid over much earlier trade routes, the age of which is unknown. From the high lands, snow-bound in the winter months, flowed the Tigris and the Euphrates, which helped to create the fertile crescent. Myriads of other rivers and rills cascaded down from the heights of Anatolia to the narrow coastline that rimmed this land-bridge between Asia and Europe.

The Hittites had occupied the central highlands as early as 2000 BC only to disappear during the violent struggles to control the fertile plains of Syria. They were succeeded by the Phrygians who kept up a century-long attack on the Assyrians until their Cadmean victories cost them their national sustenance. With the rise of the Lydians we enter the period of written history. Herodatus tells us of Croesus, 'by birth a Lydian, monarch of all the nations west of the river Halys, which flows from the south between Syria and Paphlagonia and issues northward into the sea we call Euxine. . . .'

Sardis on the Hermus river – which flowed into the Aegean – was the Lydian capital. 'It was opulent', said Herodatus, because the Lydians were 'the first nation to introduce the use of gold and silver coins and the first who sold goods in retail'. When it was conquered by the Persians, Sardis became the terminus of the first trans-continental highway, the Susa-Sardis route, the 1,600-mile-long royal road of the Persians.

Croesus had built the first formal ways in this land. He must also have bridged the river Halys with one of the earliest bridges known, when to carry the war to Cyrus he set out to lead his army to wage battle 800 miles south-east of his own kingdom.

Croesus was defeated by Cyrus, who attacked his cavalry with mounted camels: when the Kingdom of Lydia fell, the Persians consolidated their newly won empire and built the long Sardis-Susa road, which later served as a basis for the Roman road system in Turkey.

The road began at Susa in the Tigris-Euphrates delta, moved west to Babylon on the banks of the Euphrates, then north to the city-state of Nineveh, west to Nisibis across the upper tributaries of the Euphrates in Syria, to the Greek coastal city of Tarsus, northward once again through the pass of Cilicia – known as the Cilician Gates – through which all land communications had to pass, into Laodicea and on to Sardis; later the road was extended to coastal Ephesus. Thus the Persians linked the Persian Gulf to the Mediterranean. It would take a man 'walking 150 furlongs (eighteen miles) a day', says Herodotus, 'precisely ninety days to cover the distance between Susa and Sardis'. There was a total of 111 post-houses on the royal road. A messenger service was set up, the first such organised system known; mounted couriers could cover 150 kilometres a day.

The first organised courier system

These were the lands that Alexander the Great entered during the years 334–2 BC, using the Sardis-Susa road as a means of speeding his troops. It was the place of Troy-Ilium, and here on the road between Ankara and Sardis Alexander the Great cut the knot tied by King Gordius of Phrygia. Two of the seven wonders of the world were there: the Temple of Diana at Ephesus and the tomb of King Mausolus (from which is derived the word *mausoleum*). Diogenes was born at Sinope on the Black Sea, Herodotus at Halicarnassus on the Aegean, and Strabo at Amasia.

Anatolia gained the attention of the Romans when they found that Hannibal, their old enemy, was acting as military adviser to Antiochus III, king of Syria, one of the Seleucid kings who had established his fief out of the ruins of Alexander's empire. P. Cornelius Scipio Africanus Minor, the same Africanus the younger who had destroyed Carthage, appeared here in 183 BC to oppose the attack that Antiochus – with Hannibal's advice – had meant to launch. Hannibal's death and Antiochus's defeat by the Romans loosened the control of the last king of Pergamum, who reigned over a concentrated galaxy of cities. Fearful of chaos, he willed his entire kingdom to Rome.

This event brought the Roman businessman to the Middle East. On the upper river Mysia (which flowed into the Aegean) there were timber and gold; zinc and gold came from the Troad region. The area about Lydia, formerly the kingdom of Croesus, yielded pinewood in the upper reaches and gold on the Tmolus. The wines and water of Anatolia were famous throughout the Mediterranean. The isle of Chios off the coast at Smyrna had a famous marble quarry, and nearby Lesbos had deposits of marble, iron and lead. Miletus, south of Ephesus, was famous for its wool which was gathered from sheep and goats pastured in the high hinterland plateaux and woven into cloth and dyed with purple. The hinterland plateaux provided horses, cattle, wild animals, ostriches – sought after for their feathers and skin – and elephants.

Roman trade in the Middle East

Samos and Chios wove tapestries; Sardis was a source of carpets, gold and jewellery. Pergamum was famous for its parchment. Magnesia came from the city of Magnesia on the Smyrna-Sardis road. Used as a laxative in Roman and Greek medicine, magnesia served Roman engineers as an insulating substance in fire-brick manufacture.

When the Romans took over Asia (their expansion limited then by the power of Pergamum), they sent to it one Manius Aquilius as proconsul. He was there for three years. Inscriptions on milestones (six have been found) show that he was building roads there as early as 130 BC.

On 13 September, 88 BC, the Romans throughout Anatolia were butchered. There were, at the lowest contemporary census, eighty thousand Romans – men, women and children – living throughout Anatolia. Romans were pulled from sanctuaries, counting-houses and homes and massacred by order of Mithridates VI, king of Pontus, with the active aid of the Greeks. The event profoundly shocked Rome. It is part of Roman road history since this event brought Roman wrath down on that land. The legions were led by the finest generals, Sulla, Pompey and Lucullus.

Overleaf: Palmyra, Valley of the Tombs *Left:* The Roman road crosses this bleak landscape on its way to the caravan city
Right: The monumental size of the tomb of a Palmyrene merchant testifies to the city's wealth

Pompey scoured the coasts to liquidate piracy; Sulla and Lucullus dealt with the interior enemies. By 64 BC, contrary to Rome's original intentions, almost the whole of Anatolia was annexed; later it became a series of Roman provinces. And with that the building of roads began.

In 47 BC, the legions of Julius Caesar marched over the still uncompleted main route from the Cilician Gates to Sebastea (Sivas) on the upper Halys river, and then to the city of Zela. Caesar had left his mistress, Cleopatra, and their child Caesarion in Alexandria and had sailed to Syria to gather his legions and to give battle to Pharnaces, the son of the king of Pontus who had massacred the Romans in Anatolia. Pharnaces had taken advantage of Caesar's involvement elsewhere to overrun the country. His chariots, armed with scythes, attacked the Roman legions but were rendered harmless. Then the legions enveloped them in a pincer movement and the whole battle was over in an hour. 'Caesar', writes an anonymous historian of the Pontic Wars, 'was transported with incredible delight'.

With that Caesar set off to the Aegean coast, settling disputes, assigning prerogatives to client-kings and ordering the building of the roads.

Augustus, in full undisputed control of the empire, in 6 BC turned his attention to the road problem in the interior. In the lake district his engineers began two roads out of Antioch in Pisidia. One moved southeast, crossed the rolling country, passed the snow-capped peaks of Sultan Dag, and went through a narrow defile to Iconium (present-day Konya). Milestones reveal its length and the date of its construction: the eighteenth year of Augustus's tribunate (6 BC). Later the road was extended to the important although isolated Greek colony of Lystra. It was here, not many years after the road's construction, that Paul of Tarsus, while trying to win the colony over to Christianity, was stoned and left for dead.

The other road began at Antioch and went through mountainous terrain to the colony of Comana. The distance as given by the milestones was 122 Roman miles. Both roads were named Via Sebaste after Augustus, the Greek *Sebastos* being equivalent to the Latin *Augustus*.

The Aegean coastal road was the first to be put into order along its entire length. It was widened to a standard 6·8 metres (22 feet 3¾ inches) gauge; levelled, graded, paved where necessary; many bridges were built along it, since the Aegean coast is fragmented by ten large rivers and numerous streams.

Although the coastal road carries no name, the inscriptions reveal that it was repaired and repaved over and over again during a period of three hundred years. It was in effect the same 'Way of the Sea', as Strabo called it, that began in Alexandria and continued along the entire crescent-shaped Mediterranean shoreline.

The Anatolian coastline – that of present-day Turkey – is for the most part narrowly confined. The mountains rise abruptly from the sea-coast, with peaks as high as two miles above sea-level. Northward and westward where the galaxy of Greek-Ionian cities is located, the coastline is serrated

The Temple of Bacchus at Baalbek dates from the first and second centuries. The scaffolding used in the reconstruction of the temple recalls the building methods of Roman engineers

and fragmented; it posed geographical barriers for land communication until the Romans arrived with their developed techniques.

At Adana is the first large city north of Syrian Antioch. It is located in wide, fertile valley created by the Sarus river. The river bifurcated at it mouth so the Romans were forced to bridge both branches; after two thousand years the 310-metres-long bridge still retains fourteen of it original twenty-four arches.

Tarsus next appears as a way-stop on the official Roman itinerary; nea here a lateral road mounted the foothills and passed through the fame Cilician Gates, a natural pass that offered the only easy way to the mountainous interior. It had been for centuries in the hands of brigands unti Rome cleared them out. Thus, Aristides, in the time of the Antonines wrote that 'the Cilician Gates no longer hold any terror. . . .'

Further along the coast another Roman bridge had to be put across th Mersin river so that the road could reach Pompeiopolis, a city famed i the classical period for its long, ornamentally colonnaded street.

The road led to Seleucia by way of Selinous (now Selente), which lie opposite the isle of Cyprus. Selinous was notable in history. Trajan died an was cremated there, and his will was dictated naming his nephew Hadria his heir.

From Selinous westward the road followed the coast, connecting a galaxy of cities. First was Aspendus (now Belkis), built beside the rive Köprü. It still retains its Roman theatre, financed by Antoninus Pius an built by the architect Zenome. A milestone found *in situ* on the road informed the traveller, then as now, that it was repaired by the sam emperor who had ordered the building of the theatre.

The cities of the region of Pamphylia received the personal attention o Hadrian. A gateway over the Roman road raised in 130 BC was dedicate to him. The climate was mild since the high valleys intercepted the col winds from the hills, thus the region attracted, as the opulence of the ruin show, a large contingent of Romans.

From Side, famed for its slave market, the road went inland so as t avoid the serrated coastline; its goal was Cnidus. Here travellers on th Roman road could make a short detour to see the tomb of King Mausolus - one of the seven wonders of the world. The Roman foundation of Cnidu dates back to 129 BC, making it one of the earliest of the Republic's citie in Asia. Nearby are Alinda; Caunus with its large theatre; Xanthu (modern Kinik) with its evidences of Roman road, gateways, walls an monuments; Heraclea; Milas of the famous Axe-Door of Euromas, an Halicarnassus, the birth-place of Herodotus.

Next on the continuing coastal road are the famous triad cities (thre cities all within one hundred miles of each other), Ephesus, Smyrna an Pergamum.

Ephesus, Hadrian's favourite city Ephesus was Hadrian's favourite city; he had his engineers bridge th Meander river and rebuild the road (many of the surviving milestone

Beehive houses near Aleppo. Built of sun-dried bricks, the walls continue upwards in diminishing rings to form a domed roof

record this reconstruction) up to the gates of the city. He completed the theatre begun by Claudius in AD 50 and gave Ephesus the right to mint its own coinage. One of the cities given to the people of Rome by the king of Pergamum, Ephesus was famous for its Biblioteca Celsiana, built by C. Julius Aquilla in AD 135 in honour of his father C. Julius Celsus, governor of the province of Asia. It contained a vast number of books and scrolls. The donation included a sum for the acquisition of further books.

Smyrna (Turkish Izmir) was the second of the triad. Founded in 3000 BC, it has been famed as a port since earliest times. Homer is said to have lived there. It was administered by Rome from 27 BC; after the earthquake of AD 178 Marcus Aurelius ordered it entirely rebuilt at his own expense.

At this point the Roman road into the interior turned northward and went along the Gediz (Hermus) river towards Sardis which lay up the river.

Archaeologists have confirmed this site as 'Golden Sardis', the capital of the Lydians, for numerous examples have been found of the coinage of Sardis, stamped with their royal device, a lion and a bull in combat. It was, as Herodotus avers, the first place to use gold and silver coinage, or more precisely the electrum alloy of these metals. The Pactolus river, he wrote, is the river which brings the gold dust down from Tmolus; it flows through the market place at Sardis.

The Roman road then followed the trail of the Royal roadway inland from valley to valley up to Cotyaeum (Kutahya) into the heartland of forest and mountains. Wild horses came from here, cattle and heavily woolled sheep, as did fruits – apples, pears, walnuts and quince – much of them new to Rome for fruit culture came late to the Roman farmer. Water was an Anatolian delight; there were so many kinds that the natives served different waters during a dinner as the Romans served wines.

The road then went through a mountainous region, with snow-crowned peaks, cascading rivers, and lakes. Lions and leopards still inhabited it. There were ostriches, hyenas, and onagers; elephants, bears, wild boar and panthers were numerous. While Cicero was governor there he was beseeched by Caelius, writing from Rome: 'Now about the panthers: please send to Cibyra for them and have them despatched to me. . . .' Caelius was again writing to him from Rome (September 2, 51 BC) '. . . in nearly all of my letters I have mentioned the panthers [he needed them for a show that he would be expected to give as *aedile*]. It will be a disgrace to you if, while Patiscus has sent Curio ten panthers, you do not send a great deal more. . . .' In October he was still writing about panthers, '. . . please take pains, as I'm always asking you, to let us have something in the way of beasts from where you are', and finally in February, '. . . it will be a disgrace to you if you don't get me my panthers from Cibyra.'

From Cotyaeum the road went to the Porsuk valley on to Dorylaeum which lay on the Porsuk river; thence it passed through Justinianopolis and to the historical site of Gordium. It was here that Alexander the Great

ut the Gordian knot. A section of the Roman road marches across high
rid hills. Sixteen feet wide and still in good condition it was bound by
igh curb-stones, the sub-surface laid between them and then gravelled.
he road led to Ancyra (modern Ankara).

Early in its history, Ankara had been the capital of the Phrygians, but
he Romans seem to have been established there as early as 170 BC.
he *Tabula Peutingeriana* – the Roman itinerary of the third century –
ives Ankara the six-walled symbol of a large state, indicating that it was
he largest and most important city-state in the entire Middle East outside
f Antioch.

Ankara was a favoured Roman colony. It had a citadel with twenty
owers and enormous baths, as well as a temple to Augustus, the Monu-
nentum Ancyranum, on which was carved the 'Res Gestae', the apologia
f Augustus for his life and deeds.

Ankara, the citadel with twenty towers

The lands south of Ankara – a rugged and fiercely mountainous area –
lso included the coastal area of the Black Sea. This region was honey-
ombed with roads; the legendary 'straight Roman road' is here nowhere
isible. The very nature of the terrain made such straight roads impossible.
he central plateau is a continuous mountain massif with a bewildering
uccession of snow-covered peaks; an immeasurable quantity of water
escended through twisting ravines and valleys. Moreover, the roads
subjected to diurnal heat and nocturnal cold, alternately freezing and
hawing, were given to structural fatigue. Whereas the Roman engineers
alculated that a road laid over a good sub-surface foundation and paved
vith huge volcanic pavement could last between seventy-five years and a
entury without major repairs, in Anatolia the expectancy was fifteen
ears. An important road that ran like an inverted 'V' from the marshes
bout Caesarea to Sebastea and to Melitene (one of the three fortresses
uarding the border) was reconstructed fourteen times over a period of
26 years. Archaeologists have found milestones from the time of Trajan
AD 97) through a succession of emperors to the time of Constantine
AD 322), each stating how the road was reconstructed.

Although commerce was never long forgotten in the Roman world, the
oads in Pontus were, in the main, strategic; they were built and maintained
or the relatively rapid passage of troops to carry offensive war against the
erpetual threat of the Parthians. Vespasian, in AD 72, organised these
efences as well as the roads. He was followed by his son Domitian. Under
he Flavians a strategic road was begun or improved from Trapezus (on
ne Black Sea) inland to Satala, the first large fortification below the
Pontic Highway', the main trunk road that went east-west between the
osporus and Armenia. The strategic north-south road continued to
Melitene, the middle fortress, and then fifty miles south to the final great
ortress of Samosata on the upper Euphrates river. Roads, with fortresses,
ere constructed across the narrow waist of Anatolia, 280 miles from the
lack Sea to the Mediterranean Sea.

Trajan had set up an elaborate frontier system – forts, posts, roads – to prevent an incursion of Parthians into the areas which Rome had marked as her own. During the time of the Republic fierce wars had been fought, always ending in defeat or in dubious victory. In 53 BC at Carrhae, Crassus the millionaire suffered the worst defeat suffered by the Romans since Cannae; 20,000 men were killed, 10,000 made captives, and Crassus himself was flayed and his skin stuffed with straw. From then on Parthia was a Roman preoccupation. Augustus had no intention of a passage of arms with them; at most he tried to retrieve Roman honour by negotiation.

Many examples of Roman roads are still to be seen in Anatolia. Caesarea (translated into Turkish as Kayseri) was situated at a road-junction in the geographical centre of Anatolia, that is at the same distance from sea to sea and border to border. It still retains its roads. A group of young road-explorers recently found a section of road, '. . . a perfectly preserved Roman road which led from Caesarea-Mazaca to the Cilician Gates'. They found the pavement of the road 'remarkably durable'; it had been widened in the course of the centuries until it had a width unusual for formal Roman roads, $21\frac{1}{2}$ to 28 feet (6·60–8·60 metres).

Roman roads in Anatolia

The road survived by dint of constant maintenance; a gravel road (a *via glarea*) with stones laid between curbs and rammed down with an overlay of gravel it had need of continued maintenance. When paved, the stones were set down with direct contact on the earth without elaborate sub-surface preparations. The aridity of Anatolian highlands made them unnecessary. This ancient route left Caesarea-Mazaca eastward across a high and treacherous terrain. It had to pass towering Bey Dag (10,000 feet altitude) and cross another high range to reach Cucusus (Göksun) and Samosata, the fortress city that guarded the pass-highway on the Upper Euphrates. On the Samosata-Zeugma road (*zeugma* is Greek for bridge) there are remains of Roman bridges; one has a span of 250 feet.

The Pontic Highway, which coursed the east-west axis of Anatolia, was connected with the Black Sea coast by numerous lateral roads; every valley stream seemed to have a road beside it, each one connected with a coastal road. Unlike its Aegean counterpart however, it was not a continuous route. Its greater length began at Themiscyra in direct line with Sebastea and proceeded with numerous hiatuses toward the Bosporus. On its way it passed the port-city of Sinope, one of the great cities of the Black Sea, built, according to legend, by the Argonauts. Arrian of Bithynia, the Greek geographer employed by Hadrian to make a survey of the Black Sea, said in his report, 'At Sinope . . . I looked down on that same sea from the hilltops whence our Xenophon first beheld it of old'.

The road from Sinope followed a tortuous terrain some miles back from the Black Sea. It then connected with the main Pontic Highway which led to the Bosporus. The Bosporus, that narrow water passage which led to Europe, was reached by a tortuous road, but on the other side of Anatolia the road was broad, well known and well travelled.

Massive hewn blocks of stone form the Trajanic road between Antioch and Aleppo

Pergamum, the first Roman capital of Asia (willed to the Romans by King Attalus), lay close to the sea. It was famed for its hot spring; its Greek hospital, the Telespheros with its sacred underground passage for the sick; its theatre built by the Antonines; its basilica, the largest in Asia; and finally for its library containing 200,000 scrolls. It had been begun by King Eumenes in 200 BC and, as it was a rival of the Alexandrian Library in Egypt, the Egyptians refused them papyrus. Because of this the founders of the library perfected *pergamena*, or parchment which was made by scraping the skins of goats or lambs until soft and flexible. Books were henceforth paged instead of rolled.

From Pergamum, the Roman coastal road went through Troy and to the edge of the Hellespont.

There were inns along this road if one is to judge from the remaining itineraries, and a continuous line of way-stops: *mansiones* for the well-placed travellers, *tabernae* for the others. Still there is very little literary evidence about inns in Asia Minor. One historian finds it significant that Aelius Aristides never dared stop at an inn on his way from his home at Cyzicus to his classes at the furthest western tip of Anatolia, but preferred to journey through the night rather than stop. There was a famous inn at Carura because of the hot springs there, frequented by affluent Romans.

If inns were not safe – all innkeepers were considered cut-purses if not cut-throats – conditions were often worse on the road. Brigandage was endemic in Asia Minor. There was a determined Roman effort to stamp it out, but it was never fully suppressed and broke out again in the third century when Rome had lost its hold on Asia Minor. There are various inscriptions to those who fought the highwaymen; one guard met his death at the hands of brigands.

The Roman coastal road then went along the edge of the Hellespont, past Abydos where Xerxes bridged the Hellespont in 480 BC so as to attack Greece. It continued through the city of Priapus and following the shore of the great inland sea of Marmara it went on to Prusa, lying under the shadow of Mount Olympus.

Prusa, founded by Prusias, king of Bithynia, in 300 BC, was Romanised by 73 BC. It is well known in history. Pliny the younger and Trajan exchanged letters over it. Pliny was sent to Bithynia by Trajan on a special commission to look into the affairs of this troublesome province.

Near Prusa along the main road was Nicaea. Situated on the edge of a large lake, it was an important way-stop on the highway that led to the straits of the Bosporus. Strabo said that 'Nicaea is quadrangular in shape . . . has four gates and its streets are cut at right angles . . . the gates can be seen from one stone that is set up in the middle of the gymnasium'. Many famous people were born there including Dio Cassius, who wrote a history of Rome in Greek.

The main Roman road now turned westward to move again toward the Bosporus. At the end of the bight of the sea of Marmara stood Nicomedia.

It owed its name and origin to the Bithynian king Nicomedes, who rebuilt it in 262 BC. When the Romans took over the city, they extended its shipyards, making it an important port. In AD 117 Nicomedia flourished under the Roman peace.

The final way-stop before the highway reached the Bosporus was Libyssa. Here the road passes close to a broken monument which held the ashes of Hannibal, the 'enemy of Rome'. Hannibal had been sheltered by the king of Bithynia but, when he was found by the Romans in 182 BC, rather than disguise himself and attempt to escape, he is reputed to have drunk hemlock, saying, 'It is now time for me to end the great anxiety of the Romans who have grown weary waiting for the death of a hated old man'.

From Libyssa, the Roman road proceeded directly to Chrysopolis. Here, as the Roman itinerary shows, there was an immense lighthouse.

Chrysopolis communicated with the other side of the strait of the Bosporus by means of an efficient ferry service. The two-mile channel was too deep for a bridge, too wide and swift for pontoons.

For the centuries of Roman supremacy, the Bosporus was the gateway to the Balkans.

This Phoenician–Roman sarcophagus relief of a sailing ship is evidence of the continuing importance of Phoenician merchants in the Roman Empire

IV · THE BALKANS

All the glories that had been Greece fell under Roman rule by 148 BC
Although there was an attempt to maintain a semblance of autonomy i
some of the Greek city-states, in practice the whole of Greece became
Roman province.

Roman roads in
Greece

With the Romans came their roads. Assuredly, the Greeks had ha
roads previously, but except for the processional roads leading to temple:
these were at best cleared tracks. To the Greeks, a road was a series o
ogmoi, that is, parallel ruts which had been chiselled out of or worn int
the bedrock. These ruts were the width of wagon wheels (eight inches wide
and six inches deep. At places the wheel-ruts had switchpoints and siding
like railways; such a wheel-rut junction may be what Sophocles meant b
the place 'where the three great roads meet'.

Roads such as the Romans constructed were unknown. Pausanius i
his *Description of Greece* wrote, '. . . the roads here were easier for mules tha
men'. Mountains had *klimakes* (ladder-roads), steps cut into the rock t
facilitate climbing; they were passable for loaded mules and loaded mer

This paucity of land communications was caused by the nature of th
terrain. Greece is a mountainous country; its ubiquitous hills divide
Greece into small, self-contained political units, nearly all of which touche
the sea. These city-states, each built about an acropolis and a market place
were chronically at war with each other. Thus, it was felt that the mor
inaccessible a city-state was, the more protected it was from attack. Plat
expresses this view in his *Laws*: '. . . the land-steward must make movemer
as difficult as possible for enemies, but for friends . . . as easy as possible, b
attending to the roads, that they may all become as level as possible. . .

To the Greeks, 'mountains protect but separate (people), the se
frightens but unites (the people)'. The sea enveloped Greece; even th
most remote district had access to the sea. Thus, although the Greeks ha
little in the way of land communications, they used the sea as a highwa

The Aegean was a sea road by means of which a sailor could move fror
island to island without ever losing sight of the continent. The sea roa
required no upkeep. The Greeks used it to escape from land poverty, fc
their country was one third rock, and very little of the land was fertil

The seat of the priest of Antinous in the Theatre of Dionysus,
Athens. All of Greece was subject to Rome after 148 BC

Athens, the Theatre of Dionysus. Dionysus figured
in the Roman pantheon in the guise of Bacchus

The Greeks took to the sea-road because of famine pressure – men
increased faster than food.

The Romans, on the other hand, were a land people. They were never
at home on the sea. Julius Caesar, hurrying with his legions to Spain, was
pleased with himself at having chosen a land route 1,000 miles long rather
than a shorter sea route. The Romans generally hated the sea and called
it 'a pasture of fools'. The Romans thought in terms of land. Rome had a
land army and land armies must have roads.

Via Egnatia   The one great Roman road into Greece – the Via Egnatia – was built
soon after Macedonia capitulated to the Romans in 148 BC ending the
long series of wars that had dragged on for almost a century.

History was to be made on the Via Egnatia for six hundred years.
Caesar was to march back and forth across it until he defeated Pompey;
Augustus was to bring his legions over it to defeat Brutus and Cassius; it
was to have its part in the battle of Actium involving Cleopatra and
Anthony. The Emperor Aurelian, who built the walls of Rome and defeated
Queen Zenobia, was to be murdered on the Via Egnatia by a secretary
who bore the name of 'Eros', and when Rome was divided between East
and West, the Via Egnatia was to continue to play an important part in
the final struggles of the empire. One of the last milestones in Roman road
history was to be erected on the Via Egnatia.

All the classicists agree on the importance of the Via Egnatia, but few can agree on the origin of its name. In direct line with Dyrrhachium, the terminus of the Via Egnatia, is the port-city of Egnatia, lying a few miles north of Brindisi on the Via Traiana. Egnatia was once famed. Horace remembered it and left a few lines about the port on his trip to Brindisi: '. . . Egnatia, a town clearly built when the fresh-water nymphs / were at odds with the natives. . . .' Egnatia is the only clue to the name of the road; of all the inscriptions found, none suggests an explanation.

The route of the Via Egnatia, which in effect joined the Adriatic to the Bosporus and the Black Sea, went inland from Dyrrhachium into what is now the territory of Albania to Scampa. There a bridge crossed the Genusus river; on the other side was Tres Tabernas, an official halting-place. The road then skirted several large lakes and moved to Heraclea, where the Emperor Aurelian was murdered in AD 275. The road then entered Pella, the capital of the Macedonian kings and the birth-place of Alexander the Great. After 225 Roman miles the road entered Thessalonica (modern Salonika), the Macedonian port on the Aegean Sea; then moving north-east and avoiding a jutting peninsula, the road went to Apollonia, where Lucullus died. The Via Egnatia continued through Philippi, where the battle against Brutus and Cassius was fought; then to Neapolis, which had been the base of Augustus before and during that battle; thence along the coast to Porsalia, Maximianopolis and Traiano-polis. The road then followed the left bank of the Hebrus river inland and north to Hadrianopolis (modern Edirne), an important junction for routes going northward to what is now Bulgaria, Yugoslavia and Austria. Here the Via Egnatia turned south-east and moved down to Bergule and Perinthus – where there was an official way-stop – ending at Byzantium at the southern end of the Bosphorus. On the other side lay the provinces of Anatolia, reached by a ferry service. There is no evidence that the Romans bridged the straits, although the Persians, in the time of Darius, had put a pontoon bridge across it.

Such was the Via Egnatia, 540 miles long, which connected the Adriatic Sea to the Black Sea. It was on this road that, in 48 BC, a Roman knight, Vibullius Rufus, travelled '. . . night and day, changing horses at every town to gain speed', to warn Pompey of Caesar's approach. Pompey, who had once ruled with Caesar, had left Rome, fought a delaying action until he reached Brindisi, and escaped to Dyrrachium even while Caesar's legions were battering down the street barricades. Caesar pursued Pompey to Macedonia and when Vibullius caught up with the Pompeian army Pompey was leisurely marching along the Via Egnatia somewhere east of Elbassan (Scampa) to take up winter quarters. Caesar tried to find 'a suitable place' to give Pompey battle, and on 9 August 48 BC, at Pharsalus Caesar fought his greatest battle. The Pompeians were decimated and Caesar went back to Italy, by way of the Via Egnatia, for his triumph.

Within two years the Via Egnatia was again enlivened by marching armies. Mark Anthony and the twenty-two-year-old Octavian – adopted by his late great uncle as his heir – set out to reform the state and avenge Caesar's death. The march began in Macedonia and down the Via Egnatia to seek out the Republican legions. Brutus and Cassius had spent two years gathering wealth and armies in the East. In the ranks of the legions were some of the most noble names of Rome and they sought to delay a confrontation with Octavian and Anthony in order to use the winter months to build up reserves; they had vain hopes that the desolate uplands of Macedonia would hamper the movements of the enemy. They forgot the Via Egnatia. Even though it was in bad repair, along it came the legions to avenge Caesar. There was a grim battle. In no other battle of the Civil Wars was the conflict so disastrous to the aristocracy. Cassius and Brutus committed suicide. For many weeks thereafter the remains of those to be entombed in the name of the Republic were transported back along the Via Egnatia.

Ten years later, in 33 BC, the Via Egnatia, repaired and bridged, was a strategic factor for the battle of Actium. In 33 BC headquarters were established at Patrae, at the mouth of the Gulf of Corinth. The army was at the roadstead of the Via Egnatia. Agrippa, who had built the four main roads in France and its famed aqueduct Pont du Gard, was then Admiral of the Fleet. He first destroyed the land communications and the Egyptian fleet's contact with the Via Egnatia, and then turned on the fleet itself. On September 2 Anthony and Cleopatra with their admiral Sosius sailed out to do battle. All that is known is that they escaped to Egypt and to their fate with forty ships.

Octavian, now Augustus, the first Princeps of Rome, being faced with discomfort of peace, arranged to settle some of the retired veterans in Macedonia. The Via Egnatia then took on new life.

Milestones reveal that the road was under constant repair. Hadrian repaired it when he was in Greece (AD 124) and Antoninus Pius, who succeeded Hadrian, restored the Via Egnatia in AD 158. In AD 165 Marcus Aurelius issued orders for a general repaving of the route around Edessa. Galerius personally supervised the rebuilding of the road in AD 305. Constantine had it repaired in AD 308. Finally Valens put up a recorded milestone; it is dated AD 375.

Life in Roman Greece

The Via Egnatia was primarily a *via militaris*. Whole tracts of Greece lay desolate, said Dio Chrysostom, the peasants having departed elsewhere to more fertile soil. In a period when all other provinces revelled in prosperity Greece was impoverished. Greek technicians – masons, sculptors, doctors, teachers – found employment elsewhere than in Greece. Wheat and other cereals had to be imported. The peasant lived on pancakes made of barley and rye, cheese, goat's milk, fish and garlic. Meat – be it game, pork or lamb – like wine was taken only on feast days. The olive oil produced was enough only for local needs. The Greeks cooked with olive oil, lit their lamps with it, used it as soap, as ointment, and as butter on their dry bread. Wines – those wines that Homer called the 'mirror of truth' – were locally produced and locally consumed; none reached the lucrative Roman market. What else? The sheep that grazed the 'burnt ground' were enough only to supply local needs. There was enough flax to keep a small industry at Patrae in operation; there were fighting cocks, purpura from the sea, and nuts.

Imperial Rome granted Greece more favours than any other province (for Romans were always sentimentalists where Greece was concerned), a circumstance which may have been one of the causes of its stagnation. The Romans were attracted to Greek culture. Amanuenses copied Greek manuscripts for the Roman booksellers and for the private libraries of such as Cicero and Pliny; sculptors were kept busy making copies of ancient Greek pieces and reproducing in quantity those that were ordered from Rome.

Nero was a Hellenophile; his Greek tour resulted in the building of roads and the start of the Corinth Canal. It is impossible now to apply any corrective to balance the reputation of Nero. The first five years of Nero's administration were good. Beset by his mother, Agrippina, alternately having good and bad council, he attempted to govern an empire for which – unlike previous emperors – he had had no training; it is amazing that he was able to complete anything.

Of all the Julio-Claudian emperors Nero had the most creative engineer-ing ideas. In rebuilding Rome after the famous fire, Nero employed the architects Severus and Celer. The streets were widened and laid out in an orderly grid. Later Nero was won over to the plan to dig a canal along the entire 160-mile coast between Ostia and Lake Avernus which would drain the Pontine Marshes and develop an inland waterway. The project, which had hardly been begun, was discontinued on Nero's death. Far from having been an expression of Nero's megalomania, it was a sound engineering idea; heavily laden grain ships could have moved along the canal to Rome rather than using the cramped docks of Ostia, the port of Rome.

Nero and Greece

While in Greece in AD 64 to inaugurate a road, Nero directed that it should go from Corinth the length of the Peloponneses and into the interior to Arcadia. Pausanias, in his *Description of Greece*, later made a tour of it. 'There are roads leading from Mantinea into the rest of Arcadia . . . on the road from Mantinea to Tegea there is a place full of oak trees under which the highway runs.' Pausanias thought that the way 'from Tegea to Argos is in fact a first-rate highway, suited for carriages'.

On this same tour of Greece in AD 64 Nero revived the idea of the Corinth Canal, to cut the isthmus that separated the Mediterranean and Ionian Seas. Nero actually began it, mobilising the usual workers – slaves, prisoners and hired labourers – and a technical staff taken from the legions. He swung the first mattock and carried off the first basketful of earth. The project was well under way when it was discontinued after Nero's death. A French company in 1881 discovered Nero's route by far the best of the surveys; a Greek organisation finished it in 1893. It took twelve years with modern machinery to complete it.

Hadrian was a Hellenophile and a road-builder. Because of his passion for all things Greek, he created cities, extended roads, and everywhere left his impression.

One of the most baffling and complex of the emperors, Hadrian was generous and at the same time vulpine and vindictive. He was artful and mendacious, but versatile and inventive. As an architect, he rebuilt the Pantheon and designed his own villa. He painted, he sang (to friends) and he wrote well. He was a skilled and well-trained soldier and at the same time a good civil administrator. He reorganised the civil service; he gave Rome a good fiscal policy and examined the public accounts as if they were those of his own family. The vast sums due the Treasury, 900,000,000 sesterces, were cancelled; he burned the debentures in a huge bonfire in front of Trajan's Forum in AD 118. Roman laws were codified under his direction. He strengthened the power of the Senate, yet the Senators never liked him; the populus despite his largesse actively disliked him.

Like Trajan, to whom he was related, Hadrian was born in Spain. He was brought to Rome at the age of fifteen and educated there. He was initiated into Greek literature and culture which influenced him all his life. When of age he entered official Roman service and was in almost constant attendance on his cousin, the emperor Trajan, whom he succeeded in AD 117.

Hadrian's military policy was opposed to Trajan's. He wished to place limits on Roman expansion; he wished to bind the acquired provinces more closely to Rome as a sort of commonwealth of nations. The inner restlessness of Hadrian made him 'wish to see with his own eyes everything which he had read about'.

He arrived in Greece in AD 124. Athens cast its spell upon him. His passion for building found ample score; he completed the Temple of Zeus Olympios which had been planned centuries before by Peisistratus. He visited Sparta, built a temple at Mantinea, an aqueduct at Corinth and the town of Hadrianopolis (now Edirne on the border of Turkey–Bulgaria) which became a hub of roads. The main trunk line ran from Hadrianopolis eastward to the Bosporus; the other moved to Philippopolis in modern Bulgaria and into what is now Yugoslavia. Hadrian repaired the Corinth–Megara–Athens road. It had been an ancient Greek way, called Scironian after Sciron who brought his Megarian troops over it. Pausanius, who made his tour in the time of the Antonines, wrote, 'But the Emperor Hadrian widened it and made it suitable for chariots to pass each other in opposite directions. . . .'

Hadrian also repaired the Via Egnatia. A milestone records that during his VIII year of tribunician power and his III consulship he repaired the Via Egnatia. The fragment of a letter written by Hadrian or by his amanuensis in AD 124 gives some idea of the manner in which Macedonian cities were expected to defray expenses for the repairing of the Via Egnatia. It was found at Heraclea, one of the important way-stops on the Via Egnatia; the letter is a reply from Hadrian to an unknown governor. 'Outsiders who have acquired land areas are to be subjected to the contributions incumbent upon their estates. The manner in which the roads are to be paved I have explained. . . .' There was a general edict on the repairing of the Via Egnatia and connecting roads; contribution was to be monetary and not by corvée; that is, each tax-contributor was to give money instead of work-service. One third of the contribution was to be made by outsiders, one third by the community, and presumably the final third by the imperial treasury. 'I ordain that also the Antanoi (the outsiders) are to share in the expense with you and are to contribute one third.'

Hadrian's personal reactions to Greece and Greeks did not reflect those of Rome. Greeks, especially such minor officials as road overseers, were distrusted. The building and maintenance of roads in Italy was considered an honourable public service; officials vied with each other for the position of curator of roads. In Greece, however, road-makers belonged to the lower orders, and Greek officials were usually surprised that the Romans sent out to supervise the engineering of roads actually used the money for that purpose. 'Among the Greeks', said another Greek, 'if members of the government are trusted with more than a talent of silver . . . they cannot keep their faith. Whereas Romans who are officials dealing with large sums of money always maintain a correct conduct in regard to it'. Greek contractors never complied with the Roman specifications for roads and bridges, which may account for the numerous times that the Via Egnatia had to be repaired. The Romans mistrusted those whom they called 'Greeklings'. What Cicero thought of them was more or less general: 'This I can say of the whole race of Greeks . . . I grant them literature. I grant them knowledge of many arts. I do not deny the charm of their speech . . . but truth and honour that nation has never cherished'.

Initially the Romans had little interest in the Balkans. The Adriatic Sea was cold; the weather was capricious and immediately subject to any meteorological pressure that came out of the African desert. The myriad islands, large and small, along the Dalmatian coast offered splendid havens for sea pirates, who were held in check only by constant vigilance. If any Roman proconsul suggested a Balkan venture he was reminded that even the Greeks, these land-hungry people who established and maintained colonies in many inhospitable lands, made few attempts on Dalmatia's unfriendly shores.

Roman entry of the Balkans

The Romans had been in Macedonia for almost two centuries, yet they had made few attempts to enter the Balkans from the southern route. The Via Egnatia was designed only for getting across Greece. Yet it is surprising that once Rome decided to enter the interior lands between the Adriatic Sea and the Danube the route that went from Aquileia, the northern end of the Adriatic, through Emona down the valley of the Savus to Siscia, to Singidunum (modern Belgrade) and hence southward and downward toward the Bosporus was the route which became in time the very backbone of the Empire. Up until thirty years ago the route that the Romans had laid down was the only one in all Yugoslavia that according to one traveller could be traversed from end to end with some measure of rapidity and comfort.

The development of the Roman road system in the Balkans with its accompanying wars and its civilising processes began at Aquileia, which lies in the extreme north of the Adriatic, protected from the open sea. Aquileia was founded in 181 BC. Its name sprang from an omen. While a surveyor plowed the first street-plan of the colony (a Roman custom in the founding of cities), an eagle (*aquila*) appeared above the furrowed ground. Built on a navigable river, Aquileia was the chief port of the Adriatic and became in time one of the largest emporiums in the Roman world.

Five roads to Aquileia Five important roads led out of it or into Aquileia. The Via Postumia, which cut across the upper part of Italy, connecting Genoa with many of the major cities in Cisalpine Gaul (Piacenza, Cremona, Padua, Verona), came into Aquileia. Near to it, beginning at the city of Altinum, is the Via Claudia Augusta. The Via Annia led through the marshlands along the edge of the Adriatic shore, connecting all the *coloniae*, hamlets and villas along the route. Northward straight out of Aquileia marched the Via Julia Augusta. It went through the terrifyingly high Alps. Another road branched off at Julium Carnicum, presently Zuglio, to go to the metal-rich area in the Carinthian Alps. Still another, the Via Gemina named after the Legio XIII Gemina, the troops who began building it in 14 BC, went through the Julian Alps eastward, and was laid over the ancient Amber Route. Finally the southern route, the Via Flavia, built – as its name suggests – by the Flavian emperors, made the circuit of the peninsula of Istria and then under various names and at different periods of construction coursed down the Dalmatian coast to coalesce, 425 miles later, with the Via Egnatia.

Aquileia has always been known, but major excavations were not begun there until 1925. The excavators found the port on the river Natissa, with its docks of massive limestone held together by bronze clamps. These were the remains of villas, temples, a Roman bridge, and a forum, destroyed by Attila and his Huns in AD 452. There was an entire Roman cemetery. A section of the Via Julia Augusta, complete with original curbing, was found buried under ten feet of detritus. There were found tombstones to jewellers, iron workers, wheelwrights and sculptors. Pocket sundials were an Aquileian speciality; so was the carving of amber. The museum abounds in amber – rings, earrings and brooches – affirming the Roman passion for it.

Aquileia was the western terminus of the fabulous Amber Road, one of the most ancient trade routes. The Greeks had an inordinate taste for

Hadrian's Library, Athens. The city was particularly dear
to Hadrian, who had many structures erected there

amber; they went some 2,000 miles for it. Amber, when rubbed, gives off sparks, so it was *elektra*. Their taste for it passed on to the Romans.

After the northern Italian cities were raided by the tribes coming out of what is now Austria and Yugoslavia, Roman strategists could see well enough that only a narrow waist of land was held by Rome between the Adriatic and the Danube. The Romans had their first test of strength with the Celto-Illyrians in 178 BC. By 168 BC they had won what is now Trieste. In 34 BC Aquileia was made the headquarters of Augustus. The disorganisation which followed the Caesarian wars allowed the Dalmatian pirates to move about with impunity. One of the generals, Fufius Geminus, made raids far into Illyrian territory from the Dalmatian coast; he was overwhelmed. Then Augustus brought in the admiral-soldier-architect-engineer, the famed Agrippa. He was called on, at an advanced age, to direct a guerilla operation against the Celto-Illyrians, but he died within a year. In the next year, 11 BC, Tiberius moved in and took over operations. His legions fell upon these fierce and intractable tribes and defeated them in several sharp battles, but failed to subdue them completely. The result of this imperfect conquest was a revolt a few years later which Tiberius in a grim soldier's campaign finally crushed. He secured Siscia and Sirmium, important communications centres on the Savus (Sava) river.

The fluvial geography of what is now Yugoslavia (then Pannonia, Dalmatia and Illyricum) can be rapidly summed up in the two large rivers, the Drava and the Sava. They originate in the Carinthian Alps and flow in parallel lines to the Danube. Since geography dominates tactics, roads had to follow these two great valleys. Augustus and Tiberius pushed their legions along these paths, at the same time following and enlarging the ancient Amber Route out of Aquileia.

Strabo, the Greek geographer, must have been there about this time. He states that Aquileia was founded by the Romans '. . . as a fortress against the barbarians who were situated above it [that is, in the Julian Alps]. . . .' It was an emporium for the Illyrians, where they 'load on wagons and carry inland the products of the sea, wine stored in wooden casks and olive oil'. In exchange they traded slaves, cattle and hides. From this port-city the Legio XIII Gemina began to build the Via Gemina, the road that bears its name. It moved north-east through the lands of the Illyrian tribe of the Taurisci, then through an alpine pass, *In Alpe Julia*, the divide after which all rivers drained into the Sava. Next appeared the way-stop Nauportus; its name suggests what it was: a river port. It was here that the legions of Tiberius revolted. They had been assigned, says Tacitus, to '. . . various tasks as road-making and bridge-building . . . at one point they seized one of their commanders, loaded him down with impedimenta and made him work on the roads'. When that revolt was put down Tiberius made the legions push the road on to Emona (present-day Ljubljana). As evidence of their presence there are numerous tombstones of the legionaries. The road then crossed 120 kilometres of rugged

The Roman heritage survived long after the fall of the Empire, as these Bogomil
tombs in Yugoslavia testify by their imitation of antique models

landscape until it dropped down into the Drava valley. At Poetovio was
established a river-port, and the Legio III Gemina set up its headquarters
here. From what is now Ptuj one road ran south-east alongside the Drava
river, and another went directly north climbing the Alps to the colony of
Flavia Solva into the mining centres of Noricum. The main road then
continued 110 kilometres north-east, following the Amber Route, until it
came to Savaria (Szombathely). This was a Colonia Claudia and a road-
hub. The roads went off in four directions; the main route went to
Scarbantia, and at a large lake the road bifurcated and went north to
Carnuntum. The other route proceeded to a colony on the Danube called,
in view of its watery foundation, Aquincum (now Budapest).

Roads followed and sometimes even preceded the complete conquest of

the tribes. The principal route, which bears no dedication, at least not in the milestones, went to what is now Zagreb, then on to Siscia, which was the head of the river-navigation on the Sava and which was conquered after a desperate struggle by the general Fufius Geminus. From Siscia, the soldiers of the Legio IV Scythica and the V Macedonica pushed the road by slow stages to the Danube; and where the Drava had its confluence with the Danube, Tiberius erected over an old Celto-Illyrian site the *colonia* of Singidunum.

This vast region did not submit easily to the *pax romana*. Pacification meant the continuous building of fortifications and roads. While Claudius continued to erect cities and to extend roads in Pannonia, he also began operations at the Black Sea, making Thrace a Roman province in AD 46. The Thracian shore had been long settled by the Greeks. It had mixed population of which the exiled poet Ovid has given a vivid account. 'I stood . . . on this coast of ill-omened Pontus [the Black Sea]' or in 'the cruel mountains of Scythia and Sarmatia . . . surrounded by hordes coming

Left: Athens, the Roman Agora, a market and place of assembly. The philosophical schools of Athens were frequented by many famous Romans, including Cicero and Horace

Right: The Tower of the Winds was erected in the first century BC

from the Parrhasian virgin's icy pole – the Ciziges, the Colchi, the hordes of Teretei and the Getae . . .' unchecked across the Danube basin.

Tomi (Constanta), where Ovid lived, was the anchor-city of Trajan's monumental 1,800-mile road to the Atlantic.

During the years AD 69–96, the Flavians – Vespasian and his two sons – managed to bring together the two ends of the Balkans: the provinces of Thrace, Moesia, Illyricum and Pannonia. Vespasian, one of the conquerors of Britain, had no difficulty in meeting the enemy on the rugged and inhospitable earth of Illyria. He fought, settled his veterans in newly-won cities, arranged new settlements and built roads. There are many milestones bearing his name.

His son and successor Titus was involved in triumphs and disasters; he opened the great Colosseum which his father had begun, but between the fire in Rome and the disappearance of Pompeii and Herculaneum in AD 79, his two years as emperor gave him no time in the Balkans.

But Domitian, the next emperor, made three personal visits to the Moesia border of the lower Danube to set up his campaigns. Domitian was eager to reorganise the empire; archaeological evidence shows that he succeeded. No one since Augustus had put so much energy into rebuilding Rome; statues of Domitian were so numerous that they were the jest of Rome. One daring man, according to Suetonius, wrote on one such statue the Greek for 'enough'. Domitian was a fervent roadbuilder: he repaired the Via Latina, and between AD 80 and 82 he built a road that bears his name, the Via Domitiana which connected Cumae, near Naples, to Sinuessa on the Via Appia. When he turned to the Balkans, he consolidated the vast lands lying between the extremes of the Black Sea and the Noricum Alps. In order to prevent further revolts, Domitian moved whole populations into a settled zone; in turn he placed peoples known to be loyal in areas of continued defection.

Of all the tribes that roamed the lands east of the Danube, the most troublesome to the Romans were the Dacians. They occupied a land north and east of the Danube between the Carpathians. They crossed the Danube, raided Moesia, killed the Roman governor and impeded the building of a road that Domitian was planning to hew out of a rock precipice overhanging the Danube.

The Praetorian prefect, Cornelius Fuscus, was then the operative general, and he was highly esteemed. Fuscus drove the Dacians across the Wallachian plain, and in order to pursue them he built at Orlea the first bridge across the Danube, a hastily made bridge of wooden piers. However, the Dacians used the bridge to pursue Fuscus and his legions, whom they massacred at the village of Adamklissi.

Trajan's first act, when he arrived with his forces to carry the war into Dacia, was to direct that a monument be built to commemorate Fuscus and his legionaries. Then, upon a first victory, his architect raised the Trophaeum Traiani. Near the monument was erected a city, Novae

Remains of the Roman wall in Ljubljana, Yugoslavia. As Roman Emona the city was the capital of the province of Pannonia Superior

Ruins of an arched Roman structure in Yugoslavia

Traiani, which housed Trajan's legions. Then he set the whole army to
work building the strategic roads needed for the conquest of Dacia.

The route along the Kazanpass on the Danube had to be hewn out of
the sheer rock cliffs that rose beside the river. Trajan's engineers essayed
one of the most spectacular sections of Roman road anywhere. They
quarried the rock wide enough to allow the passage of one wagon and
high enough for goods-trains, using the usual methods of prying out the
segments of rock by labouring natural rock faults. When faults did not
appear they used the time-proven method of heating the rock and then
pouring vinegar over it. This caused the rock to split; the finishing operations were worked by the masons. The road stood ten feet above the raging
Danube. Later it was extended so that it actually stood over the water.
This was done by boring deep holes directly below the rock-hewn road and
inserting huge wooden planks into them. Over these a wooden planking
was laid, which extended the road an additional eighty centimetres. The
wooden section has long ago disappeared, but the stone road is there. On
the rock-wall the builders carved the *Tabula Traiana* which recorded with
understandable pride this daring overhanging river-road.

In AD 101 at the beginning of the Dacian war, Trajan built two pontoon bridges with elaborate wooden superstructures laid on heavy-bottomed boats. Over these passed a double flow of warriors. The larger bridge was used to move the heavy siege weapons. A Roman army in movement was impressive and awe-inspiring. Catapults – massive instruments for hurling huge stones in a siege – were pulled by oxen or, when there were none, by the legionaries; the immense *onagers* hurled fire-bombs; battering rams, weighing four tons, were used to batter-in stone walls.

The territory of Dacia was marsh-filled near the Danubian plain and the foothills of the Carpathians beyond were cut by numerous rivers which often overflowed their banks. The pioneers had to prepare makeshift roads and temporary bridges to move the army. They fought the elements as well as the Dacians. They pressed on to Aquae on the river Szamos and there king Decebalus ceded part of Dacia to the Romans.

The *pax romana* lasted until AD 105. Then Decebalus was on the loose again. This brought back Trajan. The Dacians took flight and king Decebalus gave himself the coup de grace. Dacia was taken over by the Legio XIII Gemina, famed as the road-building legionaries in Pannonia. A *limes* was built, with fortresses lining the route. It was extended from the Danube to the mountains – a distance of 350 kilometres – and serviced by a road. Around the bridge-head at Drobeta the area was settled, and building went on for another century. In AD 230 Alexander Severus rebuilt the city. The ruins are still called Turnu Severin.

Dacia was completely Romanised. Its language developed out of Latin, which continued to be spoken even after the Romans left the country. So impressive were Trajan's victories that after 2,000 years they are remembered in folk memory. The main Roman road in Dacia began at the Danube near the watch tower Turris and moved westward along the higher bank of the Alutus (Olt) river. Romula was the principal city. The road continued almost in a northern direction following the river; it ended at the last Roman stronghold – a fort at Caput Stenarum at the foothills of the Carpathians. Another road followed the Danube in an easterly direction toward the great bridge built by Trajan; there at Drobeta (Turnu Severin) it moved into the interior to service the *vici*, villas and forts in the lower Albocenses district.

The restless energy of Trajan was well known. 'He expended,' wrote Dio Cassius, 'vast sums on wars and vast sums on works of peace and while making urgently needed repairs to roads and harbours and public buildings he drained no one's blood for any of these undertakings. . . .' One of his greatest engineering triumphs was the bridge he built six miles below the Iron Gates, where the Danube is narrow (quarter mile) but also very swift. Dio Cassius saw parts of the bridge long after its superstructure had been torn down. 'Brilliant as were Trajan's other achievements this stone bridge surpasses them all. Although the bridge is of no use today [he was writing in AD 190, a century after the bridge had been built] for merely

Trajan's Bridge

the piers are standing . . . they seem to have been erected for the sol purpose of demonstrating that there is nothing which human ingenuit cannot accomplish.' Dio said that there were twenty piers of squared ston 150 feet tall and 60 feet wide, standing at a distance of 170 feet from one another and connected by arches. The superstructure was of wood.

Fortunately the architect-engineer who built the bridge also designec and built Trajan's column, which is a pictorial history of the Dacian war and was raised to commemorate them. The illustrations show the bridg with only seven massive stone piers, but this may have been an artist' device since often one tree in this carved Dacian history represents a whol forest. They show a massive circular stone bridge-head on each end o the bridge.

But the great bridge was destroyed by Hadrian. Fearful, said Dic Cassius, 'that it might also make it easy for the barbarians, once the overpowered the guard at the bridge-head, to cross into Moesia . . [Hadrian] removed the superstructure'.

Consolidation of Balkan roads

It was Trajan who consolidated the Balkan roads. Beginning at Tom (now Constanta) on the Black Sea, the road followed the general directior of the Danube to Histropoli, passed through Troesmis and Durostorum where a lateral road connected it with the Belgrade–Byzantium road. I continued to Ad Novas, where a bridge had to be flung across the wide Tunok river. Then it followed the twisting Danube to the place below the Iron Gates where stood the great bridge mentioned above. Beyond thi point the road was cut into the rock above the Danube; it continuec through the Kazanpass and on to Belgrade.

At this point the Sava joins the Danube. The river is extremely wide but apparently it was bridged by a wooden trestle bridge a half mile ir length. It is recorded that the Emperor Gratian was killed at such a bridge Says Zozimus the historian, 'they . . . overtook Gratian as he was about tc cross (in AD 383) the bridge of Singidunum [Belgrade]. . . . They killed him. . . .'

So went the Danube road, upward to Budapest, beyond to the fortress-city of Carnuntum and then on to Vienna. It turned northward at Regens-burg on the Danube and eventually connected with the Roman Rhine-land road, which continued to Köln, beyond into Batavia and finally to the North Sea where Trajan built Ludodinum Traiana. Thus, Trajan effectively extended a road from Constanta to Holland. He united the Black Sea with the North Sea by means of a road 1,800 miles long.

Rome's coastal communications on the Dalmatian coast escaped the devastating wars since the whole 500-mile coast was in effect sealed off (except for a few lateral roads) from the interior. The peninsula of Istria, which like an arrow-head thrusts itself into the Adriatic off the mainland, had a road built by Augustus and connecting with Pula, the largest of the port-cities at the very tip of the peninsula.

Pula was founded after 27 BC as Colonia Pietas. Istria had natural

The Arch of Sergius at Pula, Yugoslavia

waterways and ports and was settled by veterans from the great wars. It was developed by a form of land distribution called centuriation. Land was broken up by the surveyors into rectangles measuring 776 × 710 metres: this became everywhere the standard measurement for free land granted to discharged veterans. On this section of land the retired veteran was expected to produce wheat, wine and oil In 2 BC Pula raised a temple to Augustus, which still stands, amazingly, almost in its original form. Its dedication reads: '*Romae et Avgvsto C. Divi F. Patri P.*' ('To Rome and Augustus, son of divine Caesar, Father of his country'). Pula also has the remains of a theatre, cyclopean olive-oil presses and parts of its original

wall. La Porta Gemina, raised to the memory of the Legio XIII Gemin:
who bore the brunt of conquest, stands near the arch of Sergi. Thi
triumphal arch also has withstood centuries of conflict; it remains in ar
almost perfect state. It is Augustan and dates from 27 BC. It was erected
by one Sergius, about whom nothing else is known. The inscription on top
of the arch merely reads: 'Salvia Postuma de Sua Pecunia'. The most im
pressive monument in Pula is the amphitheatre, which is almost a
imposing as its counterpart in Rome. It was begun under Augustus
enlarged by Claudius and rebuilt by the Flavian emperors. It is the sixth
largest of the great Roman arenas.

Vespasian and his sons, in the years between AD 61 and 86, rebuilt the
road from Aquileia through Trieste along the entire peninsula to Pula
This Via Flavia, as it was called, went past the amphitheatre and then to
the sea, continuing around Istria to Tarsatica (Rijeka). From this poin
the road followed the wayward coast. Since the mountains reach the sea
there is no other place for a road; thus all later roads have been laid ove;
the Roman one. Fifty miles southward is Senia, protected by a large island
Senia lay in Dalmatia, which derived its name from the Dalmati, an
Illyrian tribe.

This road has been studied in considerable detail. Archaeologists have
discovered ruins and gravestones in Arupium (Vital), where there was a
mansio; further on at Epidotium (Lesce) Austrian archaeologists found in
the last century a piece of the stone-laid road intact; at Ancus (Vebrae)

The amphitheatre of Pula is the only Roman amphitheatre of which the
outer walls have been preserved intact.
This important harbour city was captured by the Romans in 178 BC

there was another *mansio*. Although the road itself has almost entirely disappeared, milestones – some of which still lean drunkenly *in situ* – mark the way.

At the small Jador river the Roman road again reached the sea; it arrived at Salonae. Salonae began as a Greek port. It was known to Julius Caesar, who was once proconsul of Illyricum. Salona (Solin) became under the Romans one of the most important of the coastal Dalmatian coloniae; its importance is demonstrated by the remains found there: of theatres, baths, aqueducts, roads, bridges and an immense cemetery which survived virtually intact.

Of great interest is the immense palace of Diocletian, which lies at the adjacent port of Split through which the coastal road ran. In his twenty years in office, Diocletian overhauled the fiscal policies, rebuilt roads in Spain and throughout Illyria. He revolutionised the Empire by dividing it into four administrative units. Believing that religion should unite rather than disunite the Empire, he fell on the Christians, imprisoned the clergy, ordered the demolition of the churches and deprived all Christians of citizenship. They called him 'that monster of wickedness'. But the monster kept on trying to arrange the tangled affairs of the Empire. He made an edict on prices to keep down inflation. Every professional work-man had a ceiling placed on his earnings. Food, clothing, wagons, road-repairs were all given controlled prices. Then to the surprise of all he resigned office and went into retirement in his palace at Split.

Diocletian in Yugoslavia

As an old soldier, Diocletian was going to retire like one – in a fortress. It was a rectangular fort with huge towers, a curtain wall, a sentry walk, and fed by a protected aqueduct which brought in the water from the Jandor stream in which Diocletian had splashed his feet as a goat-boy. One side rested against the sea, and its main portal was in fact its port. Within, it was an almost complete city. Despite the passage of centuries during which it has been used as a medieval fortress, a church, a factory, much of the palace still remains.

The Roman road was directed through its north-south gates and so proceeded along the coast. A section of the road along this part of the coast was known as the Via Gabrina; the name appears in one inscription but does not seem to appear again. The road moved inland about fifteen kilometres from the coastal Dalmatian road to a valley. South of Dubrovnik the coastal road turned south-east as much as fifty miles inland to avoid the coast, deeply indented with bays and inland waterways. Then it follows the river valley of the Zeta, goes through what is now Titograd, skirts around the lake of Skarskoj, and enters Skadar in Albania. The road, parts of which can still be seen, is paved in places and maintains a width of nine feet. There are numerous milestones, remains of stone bridges and traces of way-stops. After Skadar the road follows the Drun valley avoiding the marsh-lands, then turns sharply westward and within ten miles enters Drao (Durres, Durazzo, etc.). There it joins the Via Egnatia.

V · NORICUM AND GERMANIA

Noricum and
security

Rome extended her power into the area called Noricum for precisely the same reason that she had entered the Balkans: security. The northern cities of the Empire in Cisalpine Gaul attracted the invading Celts; villas stood unprotected on vast estates and were easily assailed. To protect them, the Romans found it necessary to expand.

The conquest of Noricum, then, was not merely a matter of expanding into a new living-space but of setting up a buffer zone to protect Northern Italy.

The port-city of Aquileia became the headquarters of Tiberius's army for the conquest of Noricum, as it had been for the Pannonian and Illyrian campaigns. Noricum, occupying roughly the area of modern Austria, was divided into two parts and there were two ways to enter it. North from Aquileia the Via Julia Augusta climbed through Loncium at the Plöckenpass and was the most direct route to Salzburg (Juvavum). The Via Julia Augusta was built by the engineers of Tiberius's legions during 12 BC and AD 8 and named after Julia, the daughter of Augustus, who was married at fourteen to Marcellus and after his death to Agrippa and after that to Tiberius. The second route, and the longer, was over the Via Gemina which arrived in the mountain areas about Graz. The easier route – and the one that Tiberius's legions first took – broke off from the Via Julia Augusta at Julium Carnicum and entered the Alpes Carnicae to go to Santicum by the way of Pontebba. Here were the warm baths of Santicum (Villach.)

The Roman road comes into Roman Santicum above the baths. It is less than four feet in width (3 feet 9 inches) with wheel-ruts 2 feet 7 inches in width, far less than the standard width. The legions, in order to keep the road level, cut through the calcareous white marl stone; steps were cut into it later.

The main Roman road – which bears no formal name – went around the lake and stopped at Karnburg. Here was a *mansio*, indicated in the Itinerarium Romanum. Then the road went on to Virunum.

About Virunum was a constellation of *vici* and forts. The area was full of mines. A Roman site now called Magdalensberg is located on one of the

The Roman walls of Cologne, the ancient Oppidum Ubiorum,
were rebuilt and repaired in the Middle Ages

hills in the central range between the rivers Glan and Gurk. At first it was an Italic trading centre; orders were placed here for iron tools, knives, pincers, swords and the famous throwing spear, the *pilum*, as well as silver drinking cups, serving plates, and iron locks and keys. There are remains of a forum, a temple, baths, and a building which seems to have been used for the archives. There are remains of dwellings and forges and even of a tavern. The life-size bronze statue of a young athlete – the Germans call it *der Jüngling von Magdalensberg* – is perhaps one of the finest single works of art left behind in Roman Noricum.

At Flavia Solva (now Leibnitz) on the lateral road that connected the Via Gemina with the road leading to Linz (Lentia) on the Danube, the Hof of Seggau is filled with Roman sculpture; mostly these are tombstone portraits, but there are also the figures of soldiers in combat, the gravestone of a carpenter holding pliers and hammers, the representation of a centaur pursued by a maenad.

On the other Roman road that goes through the heartland of Noricum down to Salzburg, there are numerous churches containing excellent sculptures. The cathedral of Maria Saal is a famed repository for Roman sculpture; a superb piece showing a chariot pulling Hector is cemented in the cathedral wall next to the sixteenth-century epitaph of one Hans Valkenaurer. Below a Renaissance plaque with an ostentatious *wappen* is a simple Roman head-piece showing man and wife in the clothing of the third century. Above an imposing cross applied to a genre background in fresco is a Roman statue of a nude figure. Inside the church a votive stone has an inspiring nude Venus holding a shell which is used as a depository for Christian alms. The tombstone of Ulbius Gaianus, postmaster of the province, shows Ulbius driving a post-wagon with a brace of horses. This is one of the most detailed sculptures that we possess of a Roman transport wagon.

A few miles further north, the walls of the small village church of St Donat are covered with Roman tombstone portraits alongside Christian gravestones.

The northbound road – the name of which has been forgotten – has been long since incorporated into modern roads so that there are no surviving sections of the original road. Generally, however, such roads were not paved; the road-bed was of crushed stone, raised into what the Romans called an *agger*, this one is a modest ridge a few feet above the terrain. There was no standard width in the roads of this area, they varied from between fifteen and eighteen feet wide. In the Noricum Alps, the road was steeply cambered – that is, sloping from the crown to the edges – so as to provide drainage.

Within fifty kilometres or thirty-five miles after St Donat, the road crossed the river Mur, where – according to the Tabula Peutingeriana – there was a bridge. At the point now called Pichelhofen the road bifurcated. The arterial road went north, climbing the Sengsenggeberge, crossed the

Inns river by a famous wooden trestle bridge, and reached Wels, one of the four large Roman cities in Noricum Austria.

These roads were laid down by the Legio xv Apollinaris, during the years 12 BC–AD 8, at great cost in lives, Tiberius and his legionaries struggled with nature as well as with the native population.

In AD 16 the Legio xv Apollinaris made Carnuntum its headquarters; this was to be the largest Roman effort in Noricum-Austria and was to endure for 400 years.

The Emperor Claudius, continuing the work in Noricum, completed the named Via Claudia Augusta which goes through the Brenner Pass into Austria. This great arterial road, one of the principal roads into Germany and Austria, began at Altinum (modern Altino), a port-city on the immense salt-water lagoon of Venice. From the landward side it was serviced by the Via Annia, built in 128 BC, which was the coastal arterial road that connected Aquileia with Padua and Verona. Altinum began as a colony under the aegis of the famous Drusus, brother of Tiberius and father of Claudius. It was famed as a resort for Romans. A small part of the ancient city has been excavated and the excavations have revealed interesting sections of the road. This is the only road on which repairs suggest the method used to replace paving stones. The stones were apparently cut and shaped at the quarry, and the edges were marked with numerals and letters so that each stone could find its way correctly into the mosaic of the road. The gravel road, albeit buried under 2,000 years of alluvium, still keeps its alignment and may still be seen going through vineyards and cornfields. On the side of a peasant house is a sign: Via Claudia Augusta.

The Via Claudia Augusta is well documented. Forty Roman miles after following the Piave Valley it passed through Feltria (Feltre) and the Valsugana and reached Trento. Tridentium, as the Romans knew it, had been settled for centuries, but in AD 53 it took on new importance as the connecting link between the Via Claudia Augusta and the roads coming from Verona and the river Po.

Two rivers of equal size had their confluence at Bolzano; to gain entrance to the other side of the Alps, there were two possible routes to reach the river Inn. The Isarco (Eisack in German) had a precipitous valley; its pass was the Brenner, and its advantage was that its altitude was only 1,370 metres, making it one of the lowest of the Alpine passes. At Bolzano, Drusus, in 8 BC, built a bridge which bore his name, the Pons Drusi. The other river, Adige, led north-east to Merano. Drusus, it is said, chose his longer and higher route as he was fearful of maintaining the Brenner road because of the gorges in the Isarco valley and the marsh and forest about the pass itself. At Merano, however, the road continued toward the Vorarlberg of Austria. It went up the valley of the Adige or Etsch, keeping to the right side of the series of interconnected lakes. After it arrived at the Reschen-Scheideck Pass (altitude 1,510 metres), the road went zig-zagging

Via Claudia Augusta and the Brenner Pass

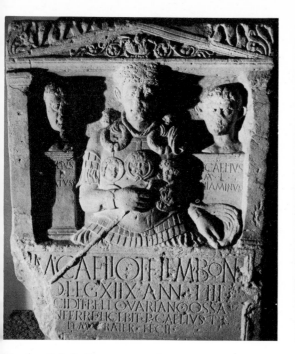

Tomb relief of a Roman centurion

Roman relief of a horse with elaborate saddle

Left: Sculptured relief of a horse-drawn Roman post-wagon, from
the tombstone of Ulpius Gaianus
Above: Cast of a relief of the column at Igel (see p. 188)

down the Alps to Landeck, passed through St Anton and Stuben, then moved through Bludenz into Raetia.

The Roman road then made its way through Feldkirch to Bregenz on Lake Constance and moved on along the lake toward Kempten in Germany. The road is still marked '*Römerstrasse*'.

Route of the Via Claudia

The main route of the Via Claudia on its way to Raetia-Noricum mounted the Brenner valley toward the summit. Claudius had one commemorative plaque set up at Feltre, in the Dolomites, and another on the road that passed the Reschen-Scheideck Pass at Rabland.

On this plaque, Claudius recorded the fact that in the eleventh year of his principate (AD 53), he had finished what his father Drusus had begun, a road that united the Po to the Danube.

The Via Claudia went to Donauwörth, but before the road reached the Pass the gorge was pierced by the Puster Valley. Here the engineers constructed a lateral road which was to lead to the warm baths of Santicum and connect with the road to Salzburg. It passed through Bruneck and Gosten (where a milestone has been found, placed there in AD 197 by Septimius Severus).

By the time the road reached Littamum (Innichen), it had passed into the eastern catchment area of the Drava (Drau); beyond this point the rivers flow into the Danube. The road, the Alpenstrasse, continued to the centre of Carinthia where it connected with a road at Teurnia. It was turned in a westerly direction by the engineers of Septimius Severus. All the milestones date from his period, circa AD 200. Severus had reason to look on Noricum kindly, for it was at Carnuntum that the legions proposed him for emperor; from there he marched to Rome.

The Via Claudia Augusta then went directly north over the area called *in alpe*, past the highest point at Radstadt-Tauern which had, as the name implies, a tavern. And so on to Salzburg.

The Via Claudia Augusta, begun by Drusus, completed by Claudius, was repaired every fifty years throughout the life of the empire and then one thousand years later by the agents of *Thurn und Taxis* who carried the European mails. It was repaved by Maria Theresa of Austria and by Napoleon. The road is still basically the same Roman road.

The Brenner Pass is 1,370 metres high. It is one of the few Alpine passes which is open most of the year. At the pass was a *mansio* which served travellers bearing the Emperor's seal and taverns and *cauponae* for the rest. The Roman way of the Romans followed the valley; then, after Matreium (Matrei), it began the precipitous descent. The Roman engineers had to erect retaining walls – some are still to be seen – for the winding and twisting road that came down to the Aenus river. Across the Inn (Aenus) the engineers placed a pontoon bridge – the *Pons Aeni*. The bridge seems to have been there in 1517 (albeit constantly repaired), when Albrecht Dürer made a water-colour sketch of it.

From Innsbruck (Veldidena) the Via Claudia went on to Mittenwald

Scarbia), Partenkirchen (Partmanum), and Augusta Vindelicum. Through the marsh areas between Partenkirchen and Augsburg the engineers used a *pontes longi* – long road of logs. German archaeologists recently found a long section of it under five feet of soil. The Via Claudia Augusta finally ended at Donauwörth on the Danube.

However, when Claudius's pacification program was expanded into Noricum-Austria, he had his legions extend the road along the Inn river route. At Innsbruck the road kept to the right (south) bank of the Inn and passed Ambras, where milestones have been found, crossed the river at Kupstein, went on to Rosenheim – famous in Roman times for its bridge, the Pons Aeni – and so toward the Danube.

The tribes across the Danube were many; the Marcomanni north-east of Regensburg were well known to the Romans. Opposite Carnuntum were the numerous and dangerous Quadi, who controlled the passage of the Amber Route. These tribes across the Danube were attracted by the towns, villages and villas built by the Romans. As protection against these tribes, Vespasian rebuilt the Carnuntum defences and barracks and constructed other defences at Vindobona (Vienna).

Carnuntum was initially a military garrison built upon an estuary of the river. It was served by the Danube road that ran through its centre as well as by the southern road coming from Aquileia. The civil part of Carnuntum on the road to Vienna has remains of dwellings and temples; the baths are extensive, and the city had its own ampitheatre.

The Legio XIV Martia Victrix kept Carnuntum on an alert war-footing while other legions came and went. From this strategic point they could be sent to repel attacks on the lower Danube or be rushed to reinforce the German *limes*; mostly they stood to arms against the Quadi, who were

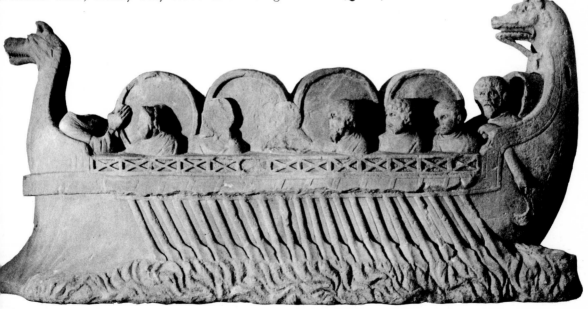

A late relief of a Moselle riverboat with grotesque heads at both ends, from the tomb of a wine merchant

perennially poised on the other bank of the Danube. Gravestones of these soldiers are many; some were buried on the Street of Tombs, and their inscriptions illuminate its history. A centurion of the Legio xv Apollinaris, Calidius Severus, had his helmet, coat of mail, and horse carved on his tomb. Another reveals a soldier and his wife; another, the tomb of a certain Gaius Attius, shows him driving an oxen-propelled four-wheeled wagon.

Long before Septimius Severus was raised by his legions in Carnuntum to the imperial purple (for which he named the city Colonia Septimia Aurelia Antoniniana Carnunti), the city had been famed for the residence of another emperor. Marcus Aurelius had his headquarters at Carnuntum, lived there, fought there and died there. It was at Carnuntum that he wrote his *Meditations*.

Marcus Aurelius was born in Rome in AD 121. Reared by Fronto, the African-born rhetorician, he was adopted by Antoninus Pius. As soon as Marcus Aurelius assumed power in AD 161, the Parthian wars broke out anew. When the frontiers were re-established and the legions returned home, they brought the plague – either bubonic or smallpox – and death was widespread. Marcus Aurelius was forced to cancel taxes as well as debts to the state. The imperial treasures, gems, crystals, amber, purple dyed silk and gold, were sold so as to obtain funds for the war, to offset the plague – and to finance the Roman peace.

Wars on the Danube

Five years later the Quadi were invading the Danube province, and Marcus marched to Carnuntum. His legions pushed back the invaders and he made his headquarters on the Danube; henceforth, he was to spend much of his reign there, joined by his wife Faustina. During one of his campaigns in Asia Minor, in the village of Halala near the Taurus range in Turkey, Faustina died. The Emperor's grief was great, and he asked the Senate to give her divine honours; her ashes were placed in Hadrian's tomb next to those of her father Antoninus Pius. In her memory he created a school for orphan girls.

The roads were put into repair, new legions were moved over them into position and Marcus Aurelius returned to the Danube for war. Population pressures from the East were forcing the tribes across the Danube into Roman territory; hordes of Marcomanni and Langobardi crossed the river and asked to settle in Roman provinces but were driven back. Marcus Aurelius decided on a war of extermination.

It was the longest and grimmest war since the time of Hannibal. Yet during it Marcus Aurelius found time to put down his thoughts in a note book. The *Meditations* were not written for publication; they were never meant to be seen. 'Time is a river,' he wrote (he faced the flowing Danube for years), 'the resistless flow of all created things. One thing no sooner comes in sight than it is hurried past and another is borne along . . .'

Early in March in the year AD 180, Marcus Aurelius was brought moribund into the Praetorium of Vienna, where he died. When the news

The Porta Nigra at Trier, the most notable Roman remain of ancient Augusta Treverorum

The Roman bridge on the Moselle at Trier, which was fortified by
the Romans about 14 BC and made a colony about AD 50

reached Rome it was regarded as a catastrophe. 'Every man', remembered
a historian, 'was weighed down by grief, not a soul in the Empire who did
not receive the news with tears . . .'.

He made the long journey home. His ashes conveyed in an elaborate
catafalque were carried along the roads that he had built and repaired.

The Rhine emerges from myriads of rills out of the Rhinewaldhorn Alps
and rapidly becomes a massive stream; as a large river it flows into Lake
Constance near Bregenz and as it emerges at the little Swiss town of
Laufenburg it is a roaring cascade of thunderous water; 320,000 litres of
water passing every second.

The bridge on the
Rhine

It was at Confluentes (Koblenz) that Julius Caesar built his famous
bridge across the Rhine during his conquest of Gaul. He wrote that his
motive in building this bridge was to deter the Germanic tribes from
crossing the river and attacking his legions; he hoped to show them that
Roman armies could also advance across the Rhine.

The making of the bridge presented great difficulties on account of the
breadth of the river [400 metres], its depth [1·75 metres] and its swiftness
[6·8 kilometres per hour]. Caesar's method of construction employed
parallel sets of piles. One pair was fixed obliquely, inclined in the direction

176

of the current. Forty feet lower down the river, another pair of piles was planted, similarly fixed together, and inclined in the opposite direction to the current. The upper pair was kept at the right distance from the lower pair by means of iron braces. The whole structure was so rigid that the greater the force of the current, the more tightly were the piles held in position. A series of these piles and transverse beams were carried right across the stream and connected by lengths of timber running in the direction of the bridge. 'On these my engineers laid planks and bundles of brushwood,' wrote Caesar.

The bridge was completed in ten days. So that neither wagons nor the cavalry would be mired down, log roads (*pontes longi*) were built up to the bridge and continued on the other side. Tacitus said that Caesar then moved '. . . into the territory of the Sugambri, remained for a few days in their territory, burning all villages and farm buildings and cutting down the crops . . ., then recrossed the bridge and destroyed it behind him.'

Although Caesar was a road-builder – he constructed roads in Spain, improved the road that crosses the Great St Bernard and built other roads and bridges – still no road bears his name. The bridging of the Rhine was his German monument.

Having stirred up the Rhine dragons, he unaccountably left the rivers and the German tribes to their own devices. The Romans thought it a bleak and fearful land covered with vast, gloomy forests. 'The country we know under the name of Germany', wrote Tacitus, 'is separated from Gaul, on the one hand, and from Raetia and Pannonia, on the other, by the rivers Rhine and Danube . . . and by the barrier of mutual fear or mountain ranges. Its northern coasts, with their broad promontories and vast islands beyond, are lapped by Ocean. . . . To say nothing of the perils of a wild and unknown sea – who would want to leave Asia, Africa or Italy to visit Germany, with its unlovely scenery, its bitter climate, its general dreariness to sense and eye?'

During the wars that followed Caesar's death, the German incursions into Gaul had grown bothersome. As a result, Augustus decided to make a conquest of all Germania. In 38 BC he dispatched Agrippa, his son-in-law, to the Rhineland; there he settled the Ubii tribe on the left bank where Cologne is now. Within fifty years Cologne had become the largest city on the Rhine and was raised to the dignity of a colony – Colonia Claudia Ara Agrippinensium, named after Agrippa's granddaughter who was born here.

Three years after the Ubii had been resettled, the Sugambri crossed the Rhine, sacked and burned the settlement, attacking the legions and its legate. This defiance brought Augustus personally to the Rhineland. In his three years there, he drafted the plan to push the frontier to the Elbe; the tribes between the Rhine and the Elbe were to be wiped out. Agrippa was to build a network of roads on both sides of the Rhine to facilitate troop movements.

The conquest of Germania

Since the lower Rhine is marsh and moor scarred with countless streams and rivers, Agrippa adopted the policy of constructing log roads. This method has an ancient history – log roads in Belgium, Holland and Lower Germany go back as far as 2500 BC – and many are still buried and preserved under metres of peat. The Romans found the indigenous log road (*Bohlweg* in German, *veenbrug* in Dutch) a quick means of communication because it was easy to build. Log planks, fashioned out of oak ten feet long – the standard log road width – were laid over fasces – bundles of brushwood – and these were secured to the ground by long wooden pegs inserted through holes at the ends of the logs which skewered the planking into fascine bundles and earth. The Romans improved the primitive log roads by digging a drain on each side and inserting brushwood which acted as a check to flooding; it also acted as a guide to the road over land often flat and featureless. At times the roads were surfaced with coarse sand and gravel. As these roads were, in reality, causeways, the Romans called them *pontes*, and since they were carried long distances over bog and moor they became known as *pontes longi*.

Log roads

Within a few years log roads were common on both sides of the Rhine; the Elbe was reached by such a road. Drusus made use of them during his conquests. The stepson of Augustus, he was commander of the legions on the Rhine, and his plan to reach the river Elbe was to advance from river to river using the log roads for communications. In 12 BC he was at the river Lippe. His legions dug the Fossa Drusi, linking it with the Rhine and tha lakes of the Zuider Zee; this gave the fleet access to the North Sea. Three years later Drusus reached the Elbe (Albis) and erected a trophy on its banks. This feat earned him, writes Suetonius, 'an ovation with triumphal regalia.'

On resuming the war, however, Drusus injured his leg. Gangrene set in and he died at Mainz, where an immense cenotaph was raised to him; the core with pieces of traventine in it is still there. 'Then his body', says Suetonius, 'was carried to Rome [along the road he had built through the Reschen-Scheideck Pass into Italy] in a coffin borne by relays of leading citizens from the various free towns and veterans' colonies which lay along the route.'

The death of Drusus did not affect the war; the push to the Elbe continued. Operational headquarters were located on Furstenberg Hill overlooking the Lower Rhine in the recently erected military encampment of Vetera. This was among the first of the forts. Quintilius Varus was posted to command the three legions. On his staff was Herman, chief of the Cherusci. His name had been latinised to Arminius; he had been enrolled among the knights, lived in Rome, spoke Latin and was a friend of Varus. Thus he was above suspicion.

Across the Rhine was the immense forest area known to the Romans as *Teutoburgiensis Saltus*. In AD 9 the tribes around the Teutoburgerwald had revolted and killed a Roman tax-collector. On secret instructions from

The reconstruction of a Roman castrum, a military encampment at Saalburg

Arminius the surrounding villages who were considered to be friendly to Rome were to ask for protection. Varus, to effect punitive measures, moved out in full force with his three legions. Through the forest the pioneers laid down a provisional log road. As progress was slow, Arminius was able to leave the column and set off the prearranged smoke signal notifying the Cherusci to ambush the Roman column. The battle raged for four days. So as not to fall into the hands of the Cherusci alive, Varus and his surviving officers committed suicide. Cassius Chaerea (later to distinguish himself as the executor of the Emperor Caligula), however, did not. He organised a detachment of soldiers and they broke out of the encirclement. All the rest were slaughtered; there were no prisoners.

This was the biggest single Roman defeat since Carrshe. The legions XVII, XVIII and XIX, mostly drawn from Italy, were decimated and never again appeared in the army lists. There was panic in Rome as if the German tribes were at the very gates. Tiberius was sent for, a new army

raised and they marched over the newly made roads through the Alps to hold the Rhine bridgeheads. Augustus was in constant gloom and at times on the verge of suicide. At night he could be heard to wake and cry out:

'*Quintili Vare, Legiones Redde . . .*' ('Varus, give back my legions.')

Germanicus, the son of Drusus, was designated to avenge the dead legions and to recover and bury their remains. 'No pity', says Tacitus, 'was to be allowed the Germans for either age or sex.' His legate Caecina was sent ahead, says Tacitus, 'to build bridges and causeways over the sodden ground' to the place where the remains of Varus and the legions lay unburied. When they reached the battlesite they found 'whitening bones . . . scattered spears, horses' limbs, human heads fastened to tree trunks . . .'.

The defeat of Varus changed Roman policy and German history; the Rhine would henceforth be the frontier; its entire length was to be fortified from its mouth near Leyden to Basel in Switzerland. The Empire was to be kept within these limits. All forts and villages on the other side of the Rhine were abandoned or destroyed, and a wide strip was made uninhabitable. The Lower Rhine was fortified from the North Sea to Lake Constance, a distance of 825 kilometres and the fortifications were connected by roads. A fortress was erected on the sea in Katwijk aan Zee, not far from Leyden. Like the others, the fortress at Noviomagus (Nymwegen in Holland) was a self-contained barracks. It consisted of a wooden palisade, sally-ports for counter-attacks, with the commander's quarters placed in the centre of the fortress on the Via Principalis. There were officers' quarters, a hospital, workshops and storerooms in the centre, and at the end the legion's barracks.

The defeat of Varus

Thus were forts and roads built along the Rhine. Within twenty-five kilometres east of it was Castra Vetera (now Xanten), the base for the Legio xxx Ulpia. This had been the base of Varus and his three legions. Trajan made it into a stone city with a Forum and a large amphitheatre. It became the Colonia Ulpia Traiana. After it was abandoned, however, the Rhine shifted its course and the city disappeared under tons of silt, although parts of the road built by Agrippa between Xanten and Cologne can still be seen.

Colonia Claudia (Cologne) was the first Rhine colony and the centre of river traffic. In addition, five roads issued from it. Cologne was a cultural centre as well as a commercial centre; it was set directly upon the Rhine banks and its walls did not enclose more than 96·8 hectares; yet it was considered to be a large city. All the comforts of Rome soon appeared. Fresh water was brought into Cologne and conveyed through a wonderfully wrought aqueduct fifty miles long and, for the most part, underground. The tunnels were provided at regular intervals with man-holes so that they could be serviced.

Julius Caesar was the first Roman to build a bridge across the Rhine;

The excavated remains of a Roman encampment at Saalburg
Many cities grew from such sites

Constantine the Great, who was in residence there between the years AD 308 and 310, built another. It was constructed like the one that Trajan put across the Danube, heavy stone piers supporting a wooden superstructure. The bridge-head was secured on the other side by an enormous fortress called Kastells (Deutz).

The principal street, still called the Hohenstrasse (High Street), runs along the line of the main Roman road toward Bonn, passing the church of St Severin, which was built over what once was a Roman graveyard and basilica.

Bonn (Bonna) is twenty-five miles away; it was a legionary headquarters and the site of a Roman bridge over the Rhine. Three milestones were found on the road, which extended southward from Bonn toward Remagen (Rigomagus). This city also had its Roman garrison; a ferry-service was maintained here until the late nineteenth century when a bridge was erected. It was over this bridge that the Allies crossed the Rhine during the last days of World War II.

The next military post on the Rhine road was Antunnacum, now Andernach. It is one of the oldest sites on the Rhine. Just opposite Confluentes, where it is believed that Julius Caesar built his bridge. Where the Moselle joins the Rhine the road passed over the usual structure of stone piers – parts of which are extant – with a wooden superstructure. The road has long since disappeared under successive layers of other roads, but Claudian milestones have been found.

Up and up went the road, past Bondobriga (Boppard) where one can see how a farmer has utilised a Roman tower for his house; up to Bingium, (Bingem), whence a well-used lateral road went to Trier. Then the road crossed the river Nahe by the Pons Drusi and continued to Mainz.

Originally named Moguntiacum by its founders after the Celtic gods Mogon and Mogentia, Mainz housed two Roman legions and dominated the Rhine at the point where it joins the river Main. The Roman fortress was built on the high ground that rises back of the river; numerous villas grew up around the fortress. That the roads were well made and in good condition is shown by the journey of the Emperor Caligula. In the autumn of AD 39 his retinue, which included his sisters, a German bodyguard and an escort of the Praetorian Guard, went from Rome to Mainz in forty days; the distance was 966 Roman miles.

The Legio XXII Primigenia Pia Fidelis was maintained in Mainz until the late Empire; evidence of its presence can be found in the tombstones and the stamped pottery. There are remains of an aqueduct and a theatre and the cement core of an immense cenotaph to Drusus. An arch raised by a wealthy merchant, Dativius Victor, circa AD 200 adorned the city; the stones from its destruction were used in the old Mainz city hall and were later rescued by archaeologists who reassembled the arch. The Column of Jupiter near the harbour has been perfectly preserved; it was dedicated to Nero by two Gallic traders. Mainz also had a stone bridge begun by

Left: The column of Jupiter near the harbour of Mainz
Opposite: Detail of the top of the column. Mainz was
the capital of Germania Superior

Domitian and completed by Trajan; the bridge-head on the other side became Kassel.

Argentorate, the next stop of importance, was a city – *civitas* – and headquarters of the Legio VIII Augusta. Actually it lay on an island between the Argens (hence the origin of its name). The barracks were built over a Celtic market place, and post-Roman buildings were in turn erected on the ruins of the praetorium; as a result it sank with scarcely an archaeological trace. After the decline of Rome Argentorate changed its name to Stradiburc (now Strasbourg) – 'the stronghold on the paved cross-road'.

The road continued its Rhineland journey through Stabulis (which lies near Mühlhausen); passing through a short tunnel at Pierre Pertuis near Basel, the road then went on to Augusta Rauricorum (modern Kaiseraugst).

Terminus of Rhine navigation   In Roman times Augusta Rauricorum was the terminus of Rhine navigation. It was also the oldest settlement on the Rhine, having been founded by L. Munatius Plancus. It was, as its remains show, an important colony. The city was composed of two sections, civil and military. The camp which housed the Legio VIII Augusta was set directly by the river (foundations of the south wall, towers and the baths are still there). At Tower Three on a Roman street that served the fortress, workmen found in 1961 a hoard of fourth-century silver plate and coins. It included a silver service (officers always travelled with their silver plate, which was one of the principal items of booty in victory), candelabra and bowls, silver fish-trays, drinking cups, silver spoons and spatulas, and even a silver statuette of Venus. In the civil section of the city, the basilica and the Temple of Jupiter lay within a rectangular forum surrounded by porticoes. The substantial remains of the forum and of the amphitheatre have enabled those two sites to be completely reconstructed. In 1955 Swiss archaeologists excavated a building whose foundations faced one of the principal stone streets; from the excavation emerged a typical Roman house. It has been restored in full detail.

The road left Augusta Rauricorum by the north gate and continued toward Rheinfelden, where it moved away from the Rhine and crossed the river Aar; on the other side of the river the legions built Vindonissa, a sizeable city with a large amphitheatre. Out of Vindonissa led four roads. One of these roads crossed the Upper Rhine by a bridge at Zurzach and then pushed on to Lorch and the *limes* fortifications. The second, the Regensburg route, went through what is now Winterthurn and finally came to an end at the edge of the Bodensee. There the cohort Herculea Panoniorum built Arbor Felix (Arbon). This fortress marked the end of the 680-mile network of forts and roads along the Rhine.

Limes Germanicus   These Rhineland forts were the traditional Roman defence until in AD 73 Vespasian decided to extend the frontier wall and began the Limes Germanicus.

Vespasian had observed that, within seventy miles after its emergence from the Bodensee, the Rhine turned sharply northward. With the Danube it set off a heavily forested wedge of land which the Romans called *Agri Decumates* (the Tithe Land). This region was thinly populated; no tribe seemed to lay claim to it. Vespasian began the annexation of it and his son, Domitian, personally directed the operation. The purpose of this annexation was to push back the German-Raetian frontier until geographical features were found on which to base a static line of defence from Regensburg on the Danube through the forest to the Middle Rhine. Frontinus was one of the generals in that campaign and in his book *Strategemata*' he explains how the legions pushed back the tribes until the defence perimeter reached from the Danube near Regensburg to Lorch on the Rems river, a straight line to the river Main, and this became the *limes* with its line of forts. The new frontier then made a fish-hook turn, moved toward the Rhine and joined it below Koblenz. The total length of the limes being 330 miles.

In this manner Roman civilisation was re-established on the right bank of the Rhine. The *limes* was not a single line; it was defended in depth by an additional line of forts along the rivers between it and the Rhine. Roads were built to service the forts; villages grew up about the forts; the *mutationes* and *mansiones* that were built to serve travellers grew into cities such as Rottweil, Stuttgart, Ulm, Wurzburg, and Heidelberg. In order to move troops along the *limes* to areas under attack, military roads were constructed. If the land was moor or bog, the Romans made log roads; if not, they built roads – literally highways – two feet above the ground and steeply cambered to allow water to drain off into carefully prepared road ditches. More often than not the roads were lined with stone curbings. The bridges crossing brooks, rills or rivers were wooden. The result was a whole network of roads constructed between the Danube and the *limes* and another network between the *limes* and the Rhine.

While commander of the Rhine army, Trajan improved the system of defences. Later Hadrian, in the years between AD 119 and 122, ordered the building of a continuous wooden palisade connecting the fortresses. The Antonines, who followed, began the conversion of the Roman forts from wood into stone structures. Finally the Severi improved the fortresses and gave them their final form.

One of these hundreds of forts was Saalburg. Its Roman name curiously enough is lost even though more is known of it than of any other similar fortification. It was built north of Frankfurt, where the *limes* shapes itself like an arrow-head pointing toward the Chatti tribe. It was a secondary fortress and lay 220 metres back from the palisades. The second Raetian cohort occupied it from AD 260 until the whole defence system was abandoned. The fort was then sacked and dismantled, and in the Middle Ages the peasants used it as a quarry.

For 1,600 years Saalburg lay as a skeleton with only its stone-lined wells and its foundations partially visible, until Kaiser Wilhelm II of Germany, a passionate dilettante in archaeology, assumed the full cost of its restoration. In this well-restored fortress, one can see how a cohort (one-tenth of a legion, or 600 men) lived while on duty. The original barracks, ramparts, gates, walls, even the locks are exactly reproduced. There is also a full catalogue of everyday objects, for the abandoned wells became the depositories of such things. When a stone-lined well ran dry the legionaries swept their refuse into it; thus were preserved the broken potsherds, hob-nailed boots, bits of armour, weapons, carpenter's tools, nails, locks, all the details of material culture which usually disappear.

The Roman road (even its stone curbings are well preserved) issued from the main gate of the fortress and led in the general direction of the Rhine towards the arterial roads over which came the trade goods.

Prosperous Trier   Within this macrocosm between *limes* and Rhine, Rhine and Gaul, serviced by a road network astonishing in its complexity Rome impressed its civilisation upon the land. Prosperous cities grew up, the largest of which was Trier. It was connected by its six roads with every important city on the Lower Rhine, and by virtue of its position on the Moselle it controlled the river traffic. When Augustus founded it in 16 BC (hence its name Augusta Trevirorum) he immediately ordered that the ancient tracks leading to it be rebuilt in the Roman manner. These ways were extended, and in some rare instances paved with flagstones. The two principal Moselle arterial roads went to Koblenz and to Cologne. As a road centre, Trier became the principal supply centre of war material for the Rhine legions, as well as a centre for wholesale merchants and transport firms. From Trier were sent out foodstuffs, cloth, wine – for the Moselle wines soon became famous – leather goods, utensils of bronze and iron, glassware and earthenware.

The prosperity of Trier was reflected in its buildings; still standing is the famed Porta Nigra, once one of many portals. The ruins of the large amphitheatre which was connected with the wall, the basilica, the fragmented remains of the two *thermae* and a large grain warehouse (*horreum*) only suggest what Trier must have been like in its heyday.

The base of the bridge that crosses the Moselle at Trier is Roman. The *architectus* planned the bridge so that it would connect with the principal street within the walled city. It was built in the fourth century to replace an older bridge built before AD 70. The fourth-century bridge presumably had a wooden superstructure resting on seven stone piers which were sunk into the river bottom; the base has a huge core of sandstone covered with lava stones held in place with iron and copper clamps. Both the bridge and the town are pictured on a medallion, a gold *solidus* of Constantine.

The road from Trier to Cologne passed over this bridge. The route has been exceptionally well studied. It was built by Agrippa, repaired by Trajan and restored by the Severi, all of whom marked it at various times with *miliaria*. This route passed the large villas and farms which were the

This remarkable column at Igel near Trier, dating from the second century, was the monument of the Secundinii family

Detail of the column at Igel showing two men driving a cart

ride of the land. Such estates had stables for livestock, workshops, bakeries and sumptuous manor houses. The interesting and obviously costly mosaics found in Nenning, Cologne and elsewhere reveal something of the manner of life along the Rhineland during the economic boom after AD 100. The fine mosaic of Bosceaz (Vaud in Switzerland) showing a country cart piled high with produce, being pulled along the Roman road by a pair of oxen gives pictorial evidence of that prosperity.

Most villas and public buildings and baths had indirect heating, the type that had been invented (or rediscovered) in 80 BC by Gaius Sergius Orata of Naples. Floors were raised and built over a *hypocaustum*, the walls were made of hollow tile, and heat was obtained by burning wood or coal in the *hypocausis* (furnace). The heat warmed the floor and issued from the heatducts in the walls.

Life in the Rhineland

Although the written record is scant, the genre-sculpture has preserved much detail. One relief depicts a mowing-machine; other sculptures show granaries that supported the livestock. The hooded cloak, a form of *loden* used by the peasants living in the damp climate, is depicted in a small bronze figure found in Trier.

Elaborate tombstones give a vivid record of the life of the cities that grew up about the Roman roads. The tomb of a wholesale wine merchant at Neumagen on the Moselle shows a Roman riverboat with the high prow and high stern carved into mythical monsters; in it are barrels of wine. Other tombs depict property-owners receiving money from tenant-farmers. There is the scene of pupils reading from a rolled papyrus, another of a woman sitting in a wickerwork chair having her hair dressed.

The Igel column still stands beside the road where it was erected by the Secundinii in the second century. Built of sandstone and an impressive seventy-four feet high, its central theme is the brothers Secundinii – Securus and Aventinus – scions of a rich cloth merchant. In one scene they are shown examining cloth, in another they are collecting rent from tenants. In another, a load of cloth is being hauled away on a cart. A kitchen scene shows cooks making bread, grinding, kneading and baking. A tavern scene shows men reclining on low couches and women (who were not permitted to recline) sitting in wickerwork chairs.

The Roman road is also recorded. One scene shows a loaded mule going over a steep, paved road; the paving stones are laid polygonally as in Italy, and at either end of the road there are stone buildings which are presumably toll-houses. The most revealing scene shows two men sitting on a mule-pulled, two-wheeled wagon; they are passing a milestone, the inscription of which reads: 'L IIII,' the precise distance from Igel to Trier in leagues. All measurements elsewhere were marked at intervals of 1,000 Roman paces, which is 1,620 yards or 1,480 metres. Only in Gaul – and therefore in this part of Germania – was there a different measurement. It was called the Gaulish League and was 2,430 yards or 2,220 metres.

An unusual feature of these roads was the directional itinerary. The ndard milestone is cylindrical, bearing the name, title and the year of e reign in which the stone was set up. The itinerary milestones were Terent. On the road from Cologne to Boulogne at the *mansio* of Tongres ere was an eight-sided pillar each side of which gave information about e distance to various cities.

Roads proliferated on both sides of the Rhine. *Mansiones* attracted *ponae* and taverns, and around these various trades developed. In time *icus* grew up, then a municipality and finally a city. There is scarcely a y in Germania that did not originate in this fashion. Way-stops and verns appeared every eighteen miles; some cities have even retained the me of tavern, such as Saverne or Rheinzabern.

ipposite : The museum at Regensburg preserves this impressive lapidus and Roman columns
iove : Roman milestone on the road to Salzburg

VI · GAUL

Rome, was very early made aware of a power called 'Gaul'. In Northe[r]
Italy beyond the Apennines, and along the foothills of the mountains
Cisalpine and beyond, lived diverse tribes, all known to the Romans [as]
Gauls. In 396 BC these tribes led by Brennus converged on Rome, sack[ed]
it, burned it and retired with booty.

The Greeks were already in Gaul when the first Roman trade missio[n]
arrived there. Massilia (Marseilles), set within a large natural harbo[ur]
near the mouth of the Rhone, had been a Greek trading post for centuri[es].
A common fear of Gallic invasions by land and Punic raids by sea dr[ew]
Roman and Greek together. Hannibal, coming out of Spain, used Gaul [as]
a base, then passed over the Alps into Italia. While Hannibal remained [on]
Italian soil, the Roman incursions into the lands beyond the Alps alm[ost]
ceased, but when the Punic Wars ended in a Roman victory, the Roma[ns]
decided to neutralise Gaul.

Conquest and road
building

As Rome began the conquest of Gaul, so it began the construction of [a]
road system. The first road to be built was a coastal road. The Via Aureli[a,]
built in 177 BC, went out of Rome north to Luna; between Luna a[nd]
Genoa the road was known as the Via Aemilia Scauri; after it crossed t[he]
Alpes Maritimae at the point where they tumble close to the sea, the sam[e]
road was called the Via Julia Augusta; when skirting coastal Gaul it w[as]
known as the Via Domitia, but when it entered Spain the road was call[ed]
the Via Herculea, since it was believed that Hercules, after clearing t[he]
Straits of Gibraltar to allow the Mediterranean to flow into the Atlant[ic,]
opened up the coastal trail on his journey to the Hesperides. That co[n]-
tinuous road from Gades (Cadiz) to Rome is 1,700 miles in continuo[us]
length, one of Rome's longest roads.

Nero's grandfather, the Consul Gnaeus Domitius Ahenobarbus, was t[he]
first to build a road beyond the Alps; called the Via Domitia after him, t[he]
road extended from the river Rhône to the Pyrenees.

The Gauls in that part which the Romans called Provincia at fi[rst]
showed themselves fully willing to become Romanised so as to av[ail]
themselves of Roman prosperity. A certain M Fonteius was ma[de]
propraetor of the province by the Senate, and he began to organise a[n]

At Carpentras in the Rhône Valley are the remains of an arch
with a relief depicting enchained Gallic prisoners

ax; *tributum* was levied, and so effectively that Gallia Narbonensis was yielding annually as much as fourteen million sesterces, and, rumour suggested, a few million more for Fonteius. Although he enlarged the roads – the work was done by *corvée*, which was a further *tributum* put upon the inhabitants – it did not prevent denunciations against Fonteius. Cicero defended him, referring to his great efforts at road-building: 'All Gaul is filled with traders and is full of Roman citizens, yet let the accusers produce one witness hostile to Fonteius.'

In 58 BC Caesar was allotted the governorship of the remainder of Gaul. The Senate enabling act had scarcely been signed and Caesar's trip to Gaul scarcely organised when he received news that the Helvetii were attempting to move through Gaul. He set off from Rome travelling by a *reda* – a two-wheeled gig pulled by one horse – covering in relays 100 miles a day. He arrived at Geneva, where the Rhône is crossed by a bridge. Of it Caesar said: 'I gave orders for general mobilisation and had that bridge destroyed.' The war on Gaul was enjoined.

The three Gauls of Caesar – Lugdunensis, Aquitania, and Belgica – comprised over 10,000,000 people grouped into tribes within what is now all of France, Belgium, part of Switzerland and Holland, and Germany west of the Rhine. The Romans found that the Gauls had already developed river-roads as well as folk-ways, which were mainly dirt-tracks. Pompey, in 77 BC during his campaigns in Gaul, had built the first road across the Alpes Cotticae; this road went from Turin in Italy over the Alps and down to Vienne (on the river Rhône). Now Julius Caesar provided a third route to Gaul, by rebuilding the old route from Aosta, across the Great St Bernard Pass to Geneva; in time this road was extended to the city of Lyon. *The three Gauls*

Caesar marched his legions over these routes in search of a total victory. Within six years he had slaughtered a million people of the the three Gauls in battle or in reprisals, but by 50 BC he had begun the Romanisation of the area as well. His engineers started by building causeways over the marshes about Avaricum (now Bourges) and further north.

Archaeologists have found the remains of Caesar's two bridges which he had built across the swamps of Breuil-le-Sec (Oise) in the forest of the Compiègne. They were parallel bridges, each 600 metres in length, 3·30 metres in width. They started from one point and then diverged for tactical reasons so that troops could cross the swamps in two groups and make a less linear approach to an enemy. First the engineers surfaced the marsh with layers of fascines – bundles of brushwood; where the peat bog was deeper, entire logs were sunk into it. On this prepared bed a framework of planks was laid horizontally. Long wooden pegs skewered the planking into the fascines and the peat; upon this frame, smaller planking was laid (this being the fundamental road-bed), and over it a thick mass of foliage and finally gravel-sand. No metal was used in the construction. Structurally the bridge was divided into units 3·3 metres wide and 3 metres long; each

The Roman bridge of St Julien in Provence carried the road from Arles to Apt

section, like each section of a modern Bailey bridge, was prefabricated, so that the bridges could be widened, narrowed, extended and shortened a needed. The 680-metre *Pons Longus* was composed of more than 200 such sections.

Victories of engineering skill Although superior in numbers, the Gauls were unable to withstand such engineering skill. Plutarch records that in his eight years in Gaul Julius Caesar '... had taken by storm above eight hundred towns, subdued three hundred tribes, and of the three millions of men, who made up the gross sum of those with whom at several times he was engaged, he had killed one million, and taken captive a second.'

During the reign of Augustus, the Rhône valley was settled with cities – Nîmes, Arles, St Rémy, Avignon, Carpentras, Orange, Vaison, Valence Vienne, Lyon – and soon serviced by roads. Strabo himself travelled over them and tells of the difficulties of making the Alpine passage:

'At some places the Alpine road is so narrow that it makes one dizzy, not only for men, but also for beasts of burden ... Then there are avalanches of snow which are capable of intercepting a whole caravan ... Among the passes that led over from Italy to Gaul ... [one] leads through the country of the Salassi [tribe] on its way to Lyon; it is practical for wagons through the greater part of its length.'

A much-used pass into Gaul – or to the Trans-alpine Celti, as Strabo called them – was the Cottian Pass. The road began in Turin, passed through the great arch of Susa – erected by Augustus to himself and recording the Alpine tribes he had conquered and the road-agents he had sent out – climbed the Cottian Alps down to Chambéry, and continued by an easy route to Vienne in the Rhone Valley.

The Via Julia Augusta, the Tyrrhenian coastal road and prolongation of the Via Aurelia, was the easiest route into Gaul, but the longest, since it followed the coast. The road passed through Monaco on the hills above Monte Carlo. At what is now the village of La Turbie, Augustus (to commemorate both the road and his legions' victories over the forty-four tribes who had disputed his passage) built an immense *trophaeum*, a monument fifty metres high. This monument has been in large part restored; even the inscription once copied by Pliny has been recovered. The road then proceeded along the coast, it was very narrow in places, and as Strabo complained 'it squeezes the strip altogether towards the sea and leaves the road impassable'.

One of the first cities in coastal Gaul – Forum Julii, now called Fréjus – was established by Augustus as a colony for veterans of the Legio VII Augusta. The place was known for its benign climate and for its naval station (part of Cleopatra's fleet defeated at Actium was berthed there), a harbour which functioned until the Middle Ages, with quays, shipyards, a lighthouse and a large garrison.

The Via Aurelia (also called the Via Augusta in this part) ran through Fréjus and on to the city of the hot thermal baths Aix-en-Provence. This

The Dodekatheron at Arles, built by Augustus. Julius Caesar settled veterans of the Gallic campaigns in the Roman colony he founded at Arles

was the first colony in all Gaul, having been founded in 125 BC, when Fluvius Flaccus led his legions across the Alpes Maritimae, dispersed the 'Long-hairs' and erected a fort and city which he called Aquae Sextiae. From here the road passed further inland to avoid the bays and marshes before the way-stop of Mastrabala. At St Chamas the road crossed a small river, the Touloubre, by means of a charming single-span bridge, the Pont Flavien, decorated at either end by arches. Built at the time of Claudius, it was donated by a resident whose name is inscribed on the cornice as L Donnius Flavius, *Flamen Romae* – priest of Rome.

Agrippa the builder In 19 BC Agrippa became proconsul of all Gaul. The greatest builder the world has ever known, he was to set his stamp on Provincia. It was Agrippa who rebuilt most of Rome so as to allow Augustus, in ingenuous self-praise, to state, 'I found a capital of brick, I left it one of marble.' He built two aqueducts in Rome, the Aqua Julia and the Virgo. Agrippa repaired the entire sewage system of Rome, enlarging it so that it could be inspected from a boat; he directed the rebuilding of the Via Flaminia, planned its fifteen bridges, constructed the great bridge over the river Nar. Mérida in Spain was his inspiration, and the superb aqueduct in Segovia that still conveys water was also his work. He was a general who won wars in Spain, the admiral who defeated Anthony and Cleopatra at Actium, the architect who built the Pantheon.

On the day – June 9, 19 BC – that Rome was celebrating the arrival of water through his Aqueduct Virgo, Agrippa arrived in Gaul armed with consular and tribunicial powers. He began at once to set down the pattern of roads and cities.

Agrippa's road began at Arles (Arelate) and is now the much travelled Route Nationale 7. The Rhône valley was one of the granaries of the Gauls; wheat, millet, oats were grown as well as barley (which was used mostly by the *cervesarii* – beer makers). At Arles goods were brought down the swift-flowing Rhone by barge and were transferred to ocean-going ships. Arles outstripped Massilia (Marseilles) as a commercial city but had no schools of medicine and philosophy. Caesar founded Arles in 46 BC and settled veterans of the Legio VI there. As a para-military colony Arles was supplied with walls and gateways, and those sections which still stand include the gateway through which the Via Domitia passed between theatre and ampitheatre, both of which stand. Foundations still exist of parts of the thermal bath and a circus, and the semi-circular court of the Dodekatheon has been preserved. Roman columns and stonework are found in the walls of convents and churches; an arch guides one to the rows of sarcophagi at the church of Saint-Césaire-aux-Aliscamps.

Agrippa's road made its way through what was then the centre of the city, moved north following more or less what is now the *rue du 4 Septembre*, and then bifurcated. The Via Aurelia-Augusta (it is still known locally as Camin Aurelian) passed through a large gateway; as the Via Domitia it crossed the Rhône on a large permanent pontoon bridge. The stone

The Roman amphitheatre at Nîmes, another colony of veterans, established by Augustus

abutments wedged into the river bank have resisted time and show where the pontoons were attached and held.

Nîmes was one of the larger cities of Gaul. Named Colonia Augusta Nemausus after Augustus, it was built largely by Agrippa. Its Tour Magne – an immense tower – is one of Gaul's oldest monuments; over seventy-five feet in height, its observation post is reached by a winding staircase, and the sea can be seen from it. Other structures were built beside a lake developed from a natural spring; the Temple of Diana, close to where the Roman road passed, survived only because it was taken over as a convent in the tenth century. Almost all the official buildings were built and given by Agrippa to the city which he created. The most famed is the capitolium called the Maison Carrée. It is in such a good state of preservation that Thomas Jefferson, in his tour of Provence, had a scale drawing made of it and used it as a model for the building of the House of Burgess in Virginia.

To provide Nîmes with water Agrippa designed and directed the building of an aqueduct that carried water from the river springs – the

The Maison Carrée in Nîmes, a Roman temple 82 feet long,
was dedicated to the adopted sons of Augustus

Fontaines d'Eure at d'Airan – near Uzès and conveyed it for fifty kilometres. At the river Gardon the aqueduct had to cross the deep ravine of Bornègre. A purely functional bridge aqueduct 160 feet high and 884 feet long, the bottom part composed of six arches which in turn support ten arches carrying across the conduit, the Pont du Gard rises above mere engineering to become a work of art. After it leaves the river the aqueduct winds in and about hills, crossing ravines and canyons; no less than six additional bridges had to be built to convey water into Nîmes.

Agrippa's road (the northern route) left the wall at the Porte de la Cavalerie for its push northward. Within six Roman miles it came to Saint Gabriel (anc. Ernagina), where there was a lateral road. One of the three Alpine roads bifurcated here to climb the Alps. The first station was Glanum, which guarded the throughway to the Alpilles, the sharply chiselled foothills of the Alps. The road passed under a triumphal arch erected in the time of Augustus at what is now St-Rémy-de-Provence. By it stands a tomb, a towering structure of Corinthian columns with sculptural reliefs on all four sides. The road moved toward Cavaillon (Cavalline), where there are remains of a forum. The road crossed the river Durance over a graceful one-arch bridge, now called St Julien and still in use, and continued toward the Alpine pass.

Secondary roads led to cities which were far from secondary. A road parallel to the Rhône highway led north to Carpentras, famous for its woodwork and for the wagon called *carpentum*, a light, two-wheeled vehicle used by women and highly popular in Rome.

The secondary road then led north to Vasio (now Vaison-la-Romaine), a compact town, typically Roman, although on a small scale; the graceful theatre did not seat more than five-hundred people. The streets were paved, and the remains of Vasio included luxurious accommodations; the house of the 'Silver Bust' (so called because the excavators found a silver bust – presumably of the owner – within it) had the usual stores facing the street and the usual amenities of a complete villa.

The main road, laid down by Agrippa and redone by Claudius, passed through Avignon and then arrived at Orange. A triumphal arch stands at the entry to Orange; a gigantic pile with three passageways, it impresses more by its size than by the quality of its sculpture. Orange is best known for its theatre, the entire façade of which has been preserved.

After leaving Orange, the road slowly climbed the valley of the Rhône. In twenty Roman miles it arrived at Vallentia (Valence), which was once an important city, although little remains of it today. Here yet another lateral road broke off from the main route to meander through the valleys of the lower Alps.

Milestones put up in the time of the Emperor Claudius have been found all along the road north to Vienne, indicating that the original road is buried under the Route Nationale 7. The road was excavated by the eighteenth-century French road engineer Sieur H. Gautier, who found that

This military stele, dating from the first century, was found in Strasbourg

it had been an *agger viae*, that is, a road raised several feet above the ground. Gautier made several stratigraphical cuts of the road and found that the prepared road was three feet deep; local stones the size of human heads were placed at the bottom, and over this was superimposed a layer of stones the size of eggs. The road material was contained by lines of kerb-stones, between which the fill was rammed down and rolled by a heavy stone roller. The final layer was produced by watering clay, sand or hoggin into the gaps between the stone-fill. As the road entered Vienne, it was solidly paved, and a section of Agrippa's Way can still be seen in the public park; five metres wide, it is set with high kerbstones and has deep wheel-ruts made by iron-shod wagons, proof that it was in use for a long time. Originally called Colonia Julia Vienna, Vienne was a communications centre and a rival of Lyon, and one of the best known Gallic cities; its theatre, odeon and circus had few rivals. It had a university and a famous spa, and was a gathering place for exiles and retired officials.

Parts of the Roman road at Vienne have survived for almost 2,000 years

Archelaus, son of Herod of Judaea, was exiled there as well as Pontius Pilate, who retired to Vienne sometime after AD 36.

The remains at Vienne include the base of a bridge as well as parts of the encircling Augustan wall and its gateways. There is a magnificent Temple to Augustus and his wife Livia. The Temple of Cybele is slowly being unearthed, and a well-laid street, complete with curbing and drainage, have been found below the present street level.

The importance of Vienne – and its cultural and economic feud with Lyon – stemmed from its roads. Three issued from its gateways, two of which led to the Alpine passes.

The roads that followed the curve of the Alpine hills were naturally constructed differently from the lowland routes. Emphasis was put upon drainage, since water is the destroyer of roads. That part of the road which faced the hill had a heavy stone drain to intercept the water and dispose of it. These mountain roads were narrower than the flatland roads – often

The remains of a Roman bridge at Narbonne
provide the foundation of French dwellings

Remains of the original Roman vaulting
survive in this bridge at Narbonne

Remains of a Roman tower at Nîmes. The walls erected by
Augustus boasted ninety towers and ten gates

s narrow as 1·65 metres – and the side facing the valley was heavily erraced. Such roads had to be reconstructed constantly. Ammianus Marcellinus, the fourth-century Antiochene Greek soldier and historian, ells of the sensation of going over these Alpine roads: '. . . as for the one hat comes from Gaul, the ridge falls off with a sheer incline; terrible to ook on because of the overhanging cliffs on every side. Especially in the eason of spring, when the ice melts; then over precipitous ravines on ither side and chasms rendered treacherous through the accumulation of ce, men and animals descending with hesitating step slid forward . . ., vagons as well. They bind together a number of vehicles with rope and old them back from behind with powerful efforts of men and oxen and proceed at a snail's pace. But when the road is caked with ice . . . travellers oft-times are swallowed up. They drive stakes at the outer edge in order hat their line can guide the traveller.'

The first road proceeding from Vienne went eastward to Turin. The oad passes particularly precipitous terrain when it goes through the area known as Les Deux Alpes to Brigantio (Briançon) on the upper Durance iver where three roads met; those from Arles, Valence and Vienne.

A large fortress stood at this important road junction, as well as the omb of King Cottius, a Gaul, after whom the Cottian pass was named. At he highest point was the *Matrona*, Mont Genèvre. The curator of the road maintained a post-house named after Mars, *Mansio Martis*, which was built by Caligula. It is generally believed that Hannibal had taken this oute through the country of the Taurini; that he '. . . hewed a road out of he cliff which rose to a vast height by burning it with flames of immense heat and crumbling it by pouring vinegar on the heated rock'. Then he marched down the valley and captured Etruria.

The Cottian Pass

The second Alpine highway, the Vienne-Aosta road, went through the Alps Graiae and the Little St Bernard. Although two roads leave Aosta (Augusta Praetoria), they separate and go over the Alps in different directions. 'It is a double pass', as Strabo explains it, 'the one that leads to Lugdunum (by way of the St Julian Pass and Geneva) being practical for wagons through the greater part of the year.' A *mansio* stood at the top of the Great St Bernard Pass. Among the inscriptions was one to the *genius stationis* – the spirit of the way-stop – set up there in AD 222 by one Marcus Suplicius, Marcellus of Cologne, a military policeman; he was doubtless happy to be alive after the crossing.

The other branch was the Poeninus; as Strabo says, it was 'steep and narrow', but a short cut. However, both of these first led to the Rhône just below where the river Saône joins it, crossed on a ferry or bridge and converged on Lugdunum, the capital of southern Gaul.

'Lyon (Lugdunum) is the acropolis of Gaul, 'wrote Strabo. 'It is not only important because two rivers meet here [the Rhône and the Saône] but because of its central position . . .' It is on this account also that Agrippa began at Lyon when he built his road. Lyon was the hub of four great

Overleaf left: St Remy-de-Provence, Roman tomb with Corinthian columns and reliefs
Right: Among the antiquities preserved at Vienne are the remains of the *spina* of the Roman circus. The *spina*, topped by an obelisk, pillars and shrines, ran the full length of the circus

roads. The first Rhône valley road which now followed the Saône through Autun, to Metz and Trier branching to both Mainz and Cologne on the Rhine; from Arles to the Rhine this route was 825 kilometres long.

Lyon had first been called after Lug, a Celtic god, and was founded as a Roman colony in 43 BC by the same Lucius Munatius Plancus who had founded another city (Augst) on the upper reaches of the Rhine. There are few remains in Lyon to reveal its importance in ancient times – a small section of the theatre, suggestions of the forum, a fragment of an aqueduct – but there are many coins, medals and inscriptions, as it was the seat of the governor and a shipping centre, as well as headquarters of an urban cohort, protectors of the mint. Lyon began as early as 16 BC to strike its own coinage. It was, wrote Strabo, 'the most populous of all cities of Celtica (except Narbo) for not only do people use it as an emporium, but the Roman governors coin their money there.'

Two emperors were born in Lyon. Claudius was born there in 10 BC. His partiality to Gaul is revealed by the many milestones set beside the roads which he remade or extended. Marcus Aurelius Antonius Bassianus, better known as Caracalla, was born there in AD 176. His nickname is a reference to the *caracalla*, the Gallic cloaks dyed in vivid colours which Antonius Bassianus liked.

Although Lyon was primarily a commercial centre – as it has remained through thousands of years – it was also known for its villas and private libraries. The younger Pliny writing to a friend said: 'I didn't think there were any booksellers in Lugudunum, so I was all the more pleased to learn from your letter that my efforts are being sold.'

From Lyon the main axial road followed the west bank of the river Saône to Cabillonum (modern Chalon-sur-Saône), a *civitas*, a river-port and the guardian of three roads. One of the three crossed the Saône by bridge or ferry and, keeping to the river bank of the river Doubse (*Dubis* in Latin) passed through Vesontio to reach the Upper Rhine fortress of Augusta Rauricorum.

The second great highway to the Rhine left Cabillonum from what was the forum and followed the present-day avenue de Paris toward Beaune; it continued to Dijon – even then famous for its mustard – and then by stages to Metz and Trier, where it split in two.

The important road that led to the Channel ports broke off before Dijon and turned westward to Autun. Autun, fifty-two kilometres from the river Saône, was settled and became a city in the time of Augustus and took as its name Augustodunum. One gateway still stands, the Porte Saint André, still preserving its two great central arches for the passage of vehicular traffic (the upper story consists of a loggia), and a temple of Janus, although battered by time, still survives. Autun was famous for its schools; some Gallic chieftains sent their sons there, and one school, the Maenianum, lasted until the third century.

Autun was on the direct route to the Channel ports and one of the most used, especially in the fifth decade of the Common Era, when the Emperor Claudius began his invasion and conquest of Britannia. The small island-city of Lutetia, the *civitas Parisiorum* (the nucleus of Paris) was on one of the routes. Lutetia was of importance even during Roman times, for its two bridges across the Seine carried a road to St Denis, then to Beauvais and the large centre of Samarobriva (Amiens) on the way to the Channel ports.

To prepare for the invasion of Britannia the Emperor Claudius repaired – so say the milestones – the Cologne-Namur-Bavai-Boulogne route, over which the Legio Valeria marched from Cologne and the Legio XI Gemina from Mainz. To do so they had to pass over the swampy marshes of the river Maas, and over this the Roman engineers had to construct a cause-way, in other places a deep road bed. This is the Via Mansuerisca, which endured as the main artery of communication well into the Middle Ages. It then became known as the 'Devil's Causeway' and the 'Ironways', since the black basalt paving stones taken from the Eifel country resembled iron.

In AD 43 the legions were tramping over this road to the Channel ports. The Legio X was withdrawn from the Danube and walked 1,000 miles to Gaul, while the Legiones II, XIV and XX were coming up from the various Rhine stations. The roads of the four Gauls had not seen as much movement since Julius Caesar's conquest one hundred and eight years before. The Emperor Claudius took up residence in Lyon in July, AD 43, to direct personally the arms and men that were flowing toward the Channel. Camels and elephants were to be used as surprise weapons; they were brought over the longer way through Narbonne. The elephant had long since lost its tactical value so far as the legions were concerned, but it was felt that since the Britons had never seen elephants, the animals might affect their fighting morale. Most commanders agreed with the historian Livy that 'More of the elephants were killed by their own riders than by the enemy. The riders used to carry a mallet and a carpenter's chisel and when one of the creatures began to run amok and attack its own people the keeper would put the chisel between head and neck and drive it in with a heavy blow.'

The legions marching with their caravan of elephants and camels continued along what is now Route 113 to Carcassonne, which has retained its Latin name. The road crossed over the site of the Pont Vieux and went directly into the little town. Carcassonne is followed by Badera, a *mansio* and *tabernae*, which grew to be the present-day village of Avignonet. From here the road continued to Tolosa (present-day Toulouse). Toulouse was said to have been founded before Rome. It was a natural granary and a market town situated on the river Garonne.

The road followed the Garonne valley through present-day Agen to Bordeaux (then known as Burdigala). The position of Bordeaux (famous for its wine before Roman times) on the river sixty miles from the sea, to which it had access, made it a natural communication centre of roads.

Bordeaux had two aqueducts, a temple existing almost intact up to the seventeenth century, and an amphitheatre. Nothing of the walls still stands visible, but we know of them from the writings of Decius Magnus Ausonius, who sings that 'goodly walls foursquare raise lofty towers where the channel divides the town, soon as the Ocean has filled it with his flowing tide'. The foremost poet and letter-writer of his time, Ausonius was born in Bordeaux in AD 309. His poems and epistles give an idea of Gaul during the time of the decline of Roman authority.

From Bordeaux, the road continued through Poitiers into Tours.

This was a Roman fortress called Caesarodunum which guarded the passage over the river Loire and is of special interest to gourmet travellers, since a monk at Tours in the ninth century made a copy of an original Roman cook-book, *Apicii Artis Magiricae*, the only one that has survived.

The road passed the stone bridge on the Loire and moved on to Le Mans (formerly Suidunum), which had a certain fame for being the finest fortified town in Gaul; part of its wall is still preserved. From there, the route led through Rouen to Amiens and finally to the Channel ports and the staging area for the invasion.

Bononia (Boulogne) had in July AD 43 all the sinews of war: four legions, the ships to carry them, siege machines, horses for the cavalry as well as Claudius' elephants and the camels (these were quartered some distance away as horses cannot tolerate their odour). Boulogne was also the port for the Channel fleet, *Classis Britannica*, and the terminus of the two great Roman roads, the one that led up through Amiens from the south, and the other that led through Bavai from the Rhineland.

Thus by July 15 AD 41, the Roman roads through Gaul had conveyed all that was deemed necessary for the conquest of Britain.

Bononia and the invasion of Britain

VII · BRITANNIA

Roman invasion of Britain

'I thought that it would be of considerable advantage to visit the islands to see what the inhabitants were like and to make myself acquainted with the lie of the land, so I sent a warship in command of Volusenus.' Thus Julius Caesar records his curiosity to see the land of the Britons whom he had encountered as allies of the Gauls. Eighty transports were placed at the disposition of two legions, and on August 25, 55 BC, they landed at Dover 'Keep Caesar safe', the poet pleaded with the gods, 'when he marches on Britain at the end of the earth.' There was scarcely need for divine intervention; Caesar fought, won and obtained hostages, then as the 'equinox was close at hand' he returned to the mainland. In the spring of 54 BC he was back again. The ships assembled at Portus Itius, which is next to Boulogne, transported his five legions across the Channel and landed unopposed. The tribes attacked, but the end, as always, was Roman victory.

Julius Caesar had come, seen, but had not conquered; 'For though he hinted to posterity,' said Tacitus, 'how the island might be won, Britannia was not his to bequeath.'

Claudius, ninety-seven years after Caesar, was well-supplied through merchants, exiles and spies, with the intelligence needed for the conquest of the isle. Four legions under Aulus Plautius, plus cavalry and auxiliaries, were to disembark at three beachheads at the widely separated ports of Lympne, Dover and Richborough. These spearheads then converged on what is now Canterbury, then as a unified striking force they began the thrust towards London along a well-used Celtic track-way.

The active preparations of the Romans were noted and the invasion came as no surprise. The Britons gave fierce battle, then retired to the river Medway. Here, under the dual leadership of Caratacus and Togodumnus, the Britons disputed the passage of the river. The Batavian contingent, however, used to swimming icy waters with full military equipment, managed to cross and set up a bridge-head, the legions passed over and battle was enjoined. When Togodumnus was killed the Britons fell back on Londinium on the other side of the Thames.

The pioneer road-builders then laid down the first road, Watling Street. It was to be the most used and most important in the isle. It is possible that

Hadrian's Wall, Walltown Crags, Haltswhistle, Northumberland.
The wall was more than 73 miles long

t was originally a Celtic track, but the layout is Roman. On the dampened
earth was set down the road-bed 'with 2 feet of gravel above it coated with
mortar'. From Richborough to Canterbury and beyond, it moved more or
ess in a straight alignment; there is no evidence that it was paved. How-
ver, Stone Street, one of the first three roads, was paved between Lympne
and Canterbury.

Two months after the initial victory, the legions of Aulus Plautius were
bogged down near Woolwich, since the Britons had withdrawn across the
Thames and attempted crossings of the river had been repulsed. Suddenly
the war had developed into a siege. As prearranged, Plautius sent a
message to the Emperor, who waited in Rome.

Roman mosaics in Britain. *Above:* 'Bellerophon', from Lullingstone Villa
Opposite, above: Dove, from Woodchester *Below:* Tiger, from Woodchester

Claudius made rapid journey by ship and road, arrived in Boulogne and arranged to have elephants and camels, along with additional reinforcements, transported to Britain. The ship, wide-beamed and two hundred feet long, which Caligula had had built to transport an eighty-foot-long red granite obelisk from Heliopolis to Rome, was used to transport the elephants and camels. Claudius landed at Pegwell Bay, where the engineers had built the provisional port of Rutupiae (Richborough), and proceeded to join the main force before Londinium.

The second road to be built went from London to Colchester. It was the 'Great Road.' built 57 feet wide, an unprecedented width, and explicable only by the fact that it was laid down as a strictly military route for the 40,000 troops, siege apparatus, elephants and camels which travelled along it. The central part of the road, however, was made only 27 feet wide. Timber uprights were sunk along the edge to provide a curbing while the road-bed consisted of a thick layer of red gravels serving as drainage for the moist subsoil; over this thick layers of pebbles were 'firmly grouted into its surface'; then layers of marble-sized pebbles were rolled and grouted into a rock-sand conglomerate. Such was the

manner in which the Roman engineer handled the marsh-bogs of East Anglia.

A decisive battle was building up in these marshlands of the Trinovantes around their capital Colchester, which was defended by a natural moat; between the interstices of bottomless bog and myriads of rills and rivers Caratacus had established formidable defences. These the Romans infiltrated, then they bridged the river and brought their forces up for attack. Defeated in battle, Caratacus escaped; the tribal capital was captured and in time became the Colonia Victricensis. The Emperor Claudius, after spending only 16 days in the conquest of Britain, and being assured of eventual victory, returned to the continent with his circus of elephants, camels and Nubian spearmen, leaving it to his legions to consolidate East Anglia.

Out from Colchester the Roman network of roads was being built so as to spread like a spider's web throughout the Trinovantian lands. The Romans settled veterans in the new Colonia – as insurance against any future uprisings.

Within months of the conquest, the legion, with prisoners and slaves serving as navvies, began to construct at Camulodumum (Colchester) a theatre, a Forum and a Temple to Claudius. But they forgot 'the wall', the cardinal basis of their defence; the city later was attacked by a coalition of tribes and its inhabitants butchered. The half-built Temple to Claudius, hated by the Britons as *arx aeternae dominationis*, was destroyed, as well as the Legio IX hurrying down to its aid; only a squadron of cavalry escaped the ambush. But under Roman persistence the tribes were again beaten back and roads were extended north. The Peddlars Way went up north to the Wash; and that way which is called the Via Devana was sent across the marshes and heath toward Durolipons (Cambridge). The last of the four roads to issue from Colchester was Stane Street, which moved due west. At Braughling it had its junction with Ermine Street moving north out of Londinium.

By the time the ageing Aulus Plautius had retired in AD 46 Roman occupation, and roads, extended from Colchester to Chichester. New thrusts had been sent out north towards Lincoln and extended to Isca, the future site of Exeter, doubtless in hopes of reaching the tin deposits which had been exploited by the Phoenicians in the fifth century BC. The ruggedness of the country, and the indomitable Dumnonii must have been too much for the famed Legio II Augusta, for the road went no farther than Exeter.

First, however, the road moved down from Londinium to Staines, where it crossed the upper Thames. Forty-four miles from Londinium the road entered the weald of Calleva. A tribal capital (mod. Silchester) was built up and walled; it had a forum, an amphitheatre outside, and baths, work-shops and dwellings within its wall. The city was widely known for its dye-works, as well as for goat-hair cloth, the *birrus Britannicus*, which, being shipped out over the Roman road, was sufficiently well known to find a place in the third century on Diocletian's price-list. In return, Calleva (Silchester) imported luxury items over the same route, some buildings even being faced with porphyry brought all the way from Egypt.

The 'Port Way' conducted legions and travellers alike over 36 *milia passuum* from Silchester to Old Sarum. All along the route the *agger* of the road was raised to at least two feet above the surface. The 'Ackling Dyke' section of the road ran out of Sorviodunum, as it was then known, down 23 miles to Badbury, entered the town and went along that which even today retains the name of 'Roman Road'. From this Vindocladia the engineers ran one section of the road to the sea-bay of Hamworthy. The road then went to Dorchester, passed through Charmouth, and where the river Axe was bridged the Fosse Way began. Thence it was then only a day's walk – twenty-one miles – to Isca, where the 196-mile road from London ended.

Continued threat of Caratacus

Rome's conquests in Britain were threatened continuously by the men of Caratacus, so it was to contain them that Ostorius Scapula began the Fosse Way after AD 47. To guard that which Rome held, he drew an imaginary line from South Devon to Lincoln and legions and prisoners alike dug a trench 220 miles in length; it was at once frontier and road. On his *limes* the legions and native-trained auxiliaries were stationed to hold all else in check. The Fosse Way itself was anchored in the south to the mouth of the River Axe (Axemouth), whence it went twenty-six miles northeast; an 18-foot-wide road, moving through heath and weald, it was raised as a causeway two feet above the ground. It arrived at the place known as Lindinis (Ilchester), located at the source of the River Parrett, thirty Roman miles from Bath.

But of all things in Britain, the most Roman is Bath. The Aquae Sulis drew the Romans as a lodestone, for it wafted warmer climes into the damp and eternal drizzle. The baths of Sulis Minerva, the largest in Western Europe, bubbled up at 120°F and offered warming solace as well as a curative for rheumatism, chilblains and scrofula. The Romans walled the city and brought over their best architects to put up a structure to make it worthy of the baths. The bath proper was set with stone ashlar, made into a piscina and roofed by a graceful building with columns and tasteful decoration. It ranks with some of the finest architecture in Gaul.

On and on went the Fosse Way. Passing Cirencester (Corinium), crossing the Silchester-Gloucester road, it moved northeast to High Cross (Venonae), which was the road junction with Watling Street coming up from Londinium. Thence the road continued to Leicester (Ratae Coritanorum) and to Lindum, where the *colonia* occupied the fortress evacuated by the unfortunate Legio IX.

With the Fosse Way completed as *limes* and road to give limited protection to their first occupancy, the Romans now made ready to finish Caratacus.

The first Roman fort at Corbridge, ancient Corstopitum, was built
under Agricola. Surviving remains date from the third century

Caratacus was beaten and his family fell into Roman hands, but he
again escaped only to be handed over to the Romans by Cartimandua
queen of the Brigantes. Caratacus in chains was the high-point of the
general's triumph in Rome. He had held off the Romans for nine winters
and 'the people', wrote Tacitus, 'wanted to see the man who had defied
their power for so many years.' Caratacus made a speech to Claudius
which Tacitus put down, perhaps verbatim: 'Had my lineage and rank
been accompanied by only moderate success, I should have come to this
city as friend rather than prisoner, and you would not have disdained to
ally yourself peacefully with one so nobly born . . . As it is, humiliation is
my lot, glory yours. I had horses, men, arms, wealth. Are you surprised
that I am sorry to lose them? If you want to rule the world, does it follow
that everyone else welcomes enslavement?' Claudius, who was always
responsive to eloquence, thereupon gave Caratacus freedom to live with
his family in Italy; he asked, upon seeing the splendours of Rome, 'Why
do you, who have got so many and so fine possessions, covet our poor
tents?'

The legions in Britain by this time were not only coveting, they were
destroying; for now it was the sacred groves of the Druids in Anglesey that
were to be eradicated. The Senate, wearying over the great length of time
it had taken the legions to subdue the Britons, sent out Suetonius Paulinus

Hadrian's Wall, near Walltown Crags. Originally the wall was
about 15 feet high and topped by a parapet

a general who, as Tacitus said, 'enjoyed two years of success, conquering
tribes and establishing forts, and was emboldened thereby to attack the
island of Anglesey.'

The island of Anglesey had welcomed refugees and nurtured warriors; it
also had a large community of Druids, fanatically opposed to Rome. To
reach the island the legions put their prisoners to work extending Watling
Street, which ultimately reached from Londinium to Deva (Chester), a
distance of 180 miles. In its march to 'earth's end', Watling Street went up
and out from Londinium from what is now Marble Arch along the
Edgeware road, where, during recent pipe-laying, workmen found the
road; a foot of rammed gravel, a foot of carefully laid, large nodular flints
set in lime grouting, and, holding them in, a kerb wall of gravel concrete –
Roman road construction at its best.

Watling Street then proceeded to Verulamium (St Albans) 19 miles
distant, then on past Dunstable (Durocobrivae) to Towcester (Tripontium),
where three bridges must have conducted the road across three con-
secutive tributaries of the river Avon. At High Cross, Watling Street
bisected the Fosse Way and moved into the city of Wall (Letocetum).
After their conquest of the Druids of Anglesey, the Romans proceeded to
'land's end.' And beyond the water lay Hibernia.

But the Romans however showed great wisdom, for they never set foot in Hibernia. A fortress, however, was built at Caernarvon on the strait that separate it from Anglesey.

Brigantes and the Romans

The Brigantes tribe in central Britain were made aware that their tur had come when the pioneer-corps, who were in advance of the legions began to extend the roads; troops under Petilius Cerealis had began th invasion of the north country along its two extreme flanks.

Chester, called Deva, the terminus of Watling Street, had been mad into a fortress-city, the new base of the Twentieth Legion, which ha moved out of Viroconium (Wroxeter). The army was poised to pus forward and the road to the north was now to be extended out of Deva s as to pass through Northwich, where there were extensive salt works. Th road moving generally in a north-easterly direction approached Man chester. Thence the main road, the direct route to the north, left fo Ribchester, to pass on to Overborough.

On the eastern flank the push northward was along Ermine Stree After Watling Street, Ermine Street was to become the most importan road in Roman Britain. It began directly at the first Thames bridge, wen through Bishopsgate along the high road to Tottenham and on to Hertfor Heath.

At Braughing, twenty-six miles from London, there were radial-roads t Colchester and Cambridge, but the main route, 20 feet wide on a 4 foo bed, with slight deviation went over Alconbury Hill. After passing what i now Godmanchester the Roman *agger* was widened to 45 feet and raised a a causeway four feet above the ground, and in this measured width i strode into Durobrivae.

North from here to Lincoln (Lindum) there were two routes for th marching legions; one road branched to reach the iron-mines beyon Great Casterton; the other road continued in a more or less straigh alignment, until both converged upon Ancaster (Causennae). From thi point the road is prominently visible, since it is 42 feet broad and five fee above the surface of the land, a veritable causeway. Before it enters th old Roman *colonia*, Ermine Street joins with the Fosse Way, the strategi road-frontier that was built up from Devon, so that both roads as on continue up Steep Street to enter the walls of Lindum.

Between AD 71 and 74, the Legio IX Hispana from the banks of th Danube, weaned on hard-fighting in Pannonia, moved to the site; an under Petilius Cerealis Lindum was enlarged. In AD 90 it was made colonia. A rigidly planned city, it originally comprised only forty acres, bu by the fourth century it had, according to archaeologists, 'handsome, eve lavish buildings.' The city was provided with an elaborate sewerag system, for cleanliness was a Roman cult. Clean water flowed into an city when it became Roman. Lincoln also had a watermill and a bee (*cervesa*) factory, for a fourth-century chronicler writes of the 'twofold us of grain; for bread and beer'. It imported Egyptian marble as well a the blood-red marble from Italy, and trade made it prosperous.

In the years AD 71–74, the legions continued to build two roughly parallel roads on the edges of Brigantian territory. The military road, Ermine Street, was pushed on to York: the road was laid thirty-three miles straight to the river Humber. The Roman road between Lincoln and Winteringham to the ferry-port on the Humber has been rightly described as one of the most magnificent in Britain. Forty-five feet wide throughout its length, the road has an embankment as high as six feet in places.

At the river Humber, too wide to bridge, there was a ferry, and on the other side lay Petuaria (Brough). Thence the road made a half-moon turn and reached York in thirty-two miles. This was the direct route, sixty-one miles in length. Later engineers laid down a longer and drier route 71 miles to York. This road took off from the main road outside Lincoln and moved towards Doncaster. There were two way-stops en route: Littleborough, which guarded the bridge over the *Trisantona flumen* (Trent), and Bawtry, also erected to guard a river bridge. Doncaster (Danum) was doubly important, since a radial broke off here to go to the other Baths, whose tepid waters still flow in the town of Buxton. The route, called 'The Great North Road', had to cross seven rivers and numerous rills, which meant of course extensive bridging to bring the forty-two foot wide road into the *colonia* and legionary fortress of Eburacum.

York (Eburacum) was founded by the Legio IX Hispana and occupied later by the II Adiutrix. In time the luxuries arrived: linen from Asia, cotton cloth from Egypt so thin as to be pulled through a ring, papyrus for writing-paper, and such ultra-luxuries as marble, glass and wine. 'And so the Britons,' wrote Tacitus, 'were gradually led on to the amenities that make vice agreeable – arcades, baths and sumptious banquets. They spoke of such novelties as "civilisation" when really they were only a feature of enslavement.'

York was destined to be the residence and death-place of emperors. Hadrian would be there during the building of the Wall; Septimius Severus, far from his native shore, would die there; Constantius, father of Constantine, was to succumb to the climate.

By the time that Agricola arrived in Britain as governor in AD 78, the Brigantian threat had been disposed of by the embracing roads; Agricola's effort was to be the final conquest of the farthest north.

As usual the roads were laid down in advance, auxiliaries working with war-prisoners and slaves doing the digging and hauling. Two parallel roads moved up beyond York: the one called 'The Street', proceeding up from the Humber, kept to the drier ground at Thornton-le-Street. Here-after the road had to cross a morass of rivers and marsh, probably on a causeway, to arrive at Chester-le-Street (called Concangium by its conquerors), where the 17-foot-wide road ran upon a high causeway which led directly to one of the well-known Roman bridges, the Pons Aelius, built across the River Tyne to Newcastle. The other road, Dere Street, running on the left or west bank of the river Swale cut through

York, the Roman Eburacum

The Roman fort at Chesters, ancient Cilurnum, was the station of a cavalry regiment

Aldborough, Heale-on-Bridge up to Catterick, where the upper river Swale was bridged. At the edge of Carkin Moor near Scotch Corner the Roman engineers built a branch road and fortified it at ten mile intervals to link up with the western axial road. Meanwhile the main road was pushed northward until it descended on Corbridge, which in a later century would be one of the key-forts of the defensive wall.

The roads having been rapidly built, Agricola's legions massed for his drive into the lands of the Picts, as the Scottish tribes came to be called. By AD 81 the first advance had reached the line of the Forth and the Clyde by means of the roads, still running parallel on the two extremes of the island, which had been gradually built up to head the line of advance. The Roman fleet cooperated with the land-troops, and with them Agricola started his final assault on the Caledonians. A single road was built north of Camelon and a wooden bridge was put across the river Forth. Then the road was pushed to Strageath on the Earn. Beyond here a fort was built at Bertha, at the highpoint of the river, to protect supplies coming by sea. From that point the road is last seen going up near Inchtuthil (Pinnata Castra) to the most northern fort. These were the northernmost *milia passum* of the entire Roman road system.

Agricola's victories

Victorious over the Caledonians, Agricola marched his legions 'into the territory of the Boresti, and when there was nothing to see any longer' he turned back and placed his men in winter-quarters. Then all Britain settled down under the yoke of peace.

After Agricola's term as governor (AD 81–85) there was relative peace in the land and the process of Romanisation continued. The total lack of record during the thirty years following the departure of Agricola 'was not due,' observed R. H. Barrow, 'to the prevalence of peace'. Yet while disturbances were not enough to bring Trajan, that well-travelled soldier-emperor, to Britain to maintain the peace the government had been severely shaken by revolts which, it was claimed, took as many lives as those lost in the Jewish rebellion. The day that Trajan died the Legio IX Hispana, stationed at York, was decimated in mysterious circumstances; like the legions destroyed by Hermann in Germania, it never appeared again in the army lists. It was this event, then, that brought Hadrian to Britain and caused the wall to be built that was to be the finest frontier boundary in any land. And it was under Hadrian that the last and most important programme of road building was to be undertaken.

The new governor arrived before Hadrian in AD 119 and to replace the IX he brought the newly-activated Legio VI Victrix. There was no doubt about the quality of Hadrian's choice of governor; A. Platorius Nepos had been *curator* of four of the important roads in Italy, the Viae Cassia, Clodia, Cimina, and the Nova Traiana, which climbed up from Lake Bolsena into Tuscany.

In AD 122 Hadrian arrived in Britain. On arrival he ordered that Londinium, which had been destroyed by fire, be quickly restored, then following the well-serviced roads, he went with Nepos to the troublesome border country. Hadrian drew a line between the Tyne and the Solway Firth and ordered the building of a wall to be financed out of the imperial purse. The frontier was to be permanent. The engineers under Nepos' supervision were first to excavate a *vallum*, a military ditch thirty feet wide and seven feet deep, extending across the full 71 miles. Next, the wall: the core was concrete and following the dictates of a good *architectus*, the builders worked potsherds into it – only the facing was to be of stone. When finished, the wall was 13 feet high and it stretched from Bowness on the Solway Firth to Wallsend on the east.

It was not a static defence, but a complex of *vallum*, forts, milecastles, turrets, supply depots, outposts and roads.

At Newcastle-upon-Tyne, where the road called Dere Street came up from York, the engineers erected a bridge. The Pons Aelius, called after Hadrian's family name, was 735 feet long and designed to accommodate the 20-foot-wide-road; stone piers 50 feet apart held the wooden super-structure. Bede mentions bridges among the visible remains of things Roman surviving in the eighth century, and some were still being used in the twelfth.

The Stanegate The Stanegate which ran along the Wall began at Corbridge, and since it was primarily a military road it was built solidly and carefully; it was twenty-two feet wide and laid upon a foundation of stone six inches deep and a cambered layer of gravel, with heavy stones buttressing the sides. At the fortress of Vindolanda (Chesterholm), a massive milestone (without inscription) stands in its original position. Farther on, at Magnis (Carvoran), the Stanegate connected with another road coming from the south, doubtless a supply-line to this important fortress; at this junction another milestone was found. Most of the milestones that have been recovered date from the time of the Severan Dynasty and later: from the times of Probus (d. 282), who finished the walls of Rome; Constantius, who died at York in 306; Maximus; and Constantine the Great. All these milestones reveal the continued Roman interest, right up to the grim finale of the Empire.

Septimius Severus and his son Caracalla arrived in York in 208 to oversee and extend the Wall and to restore the roads that led to 'the other Wall', that erected by Lollius Urbicus between the Firths of Clyde and Forth under the orders of Antoninus Pius in the years 139–142. Septimius Severus was the last great road builder of the Roman Empire. The Via Severiana, which was constructed along the marsh-edge from Terracina to Ostia, the port of Rome, can still be seen.

Roman road techniques varied greatly, depending on the soil, and swamps presented varied problems to the engineers. One road that ran through the Medway valley near Rochester was constructed on top of pile-driven oak logs four feet long which were hammered into the marsh; on these was laid a rock-based road. Another one in Eastcheap, London,

Hadrian's Wall, near Housesteads Roman fort in Northumberland

was actually mounted on a concrete base on which stone walls eight feet high held in the stone-fill that supported the road. One of the most remarkable roads in Britain is the stone-laid section that crosses the moors between Manchester and Ilkley. The entire surface of the road is paved with stones set sixteen feet wide and framed by kerbstones.

Severus did not finish his work in Britain. He had long been ill and was an easy victim to the climate of York. His notorious son Caracalla continued the road and defence work in Britain and elsewhere.

And though the barracks-emperors did keep up the roads (there are milestones in Britain recording road construction down to the last) the Wall could not contain the thrust of the growing strength of the people beyond it. Constantius Chlorus came to Britain with his son Constantine in hopes of re-establishing Roman power, but he died in York in 306. In 367 the Picts swept over the Wall and raided as far south as Kent. Rome herself was raided by Alaric and the Huns in 408, and she could now no longer send aid. In 410 there went out the fatal message: Honorius told the *civitates* of Britain to arrange their own affairs: they could no longer rely on Rome. Britannia was being set free again.

VIII · HISPANIA

According to Strabo, it was 'the second city of the world,' this Gades, the mythical site of one of the Pillars of Hercules, left by that hero when he split open the rock walls that bound the Spanish peninsula to Africa and allowed the waters of the Mediterranean to flow into the Ocean-Sea.

An ancient trading-post, Gades was the most active market in the ancient world. What is now Cadiz had been Gadir to the Phoenicians, who founded it before 1500 BC, and it became Gades to the Romans.

Like Tyre of Lebanon, Gades was a half-island, a narrow peninsula defensible by land; yet its ships were protected from the frightening moods of the Atlantic by a deep-throated harbour. The persistent fame of Gades was such that it drew Julius Caesar to its sanctuary. There in 68 BC he gazed at the statue of Alexander the Great.

From that long-necked peninsula ran the Way of Hercules, the route that the god had taken and opened up on his journey to the gardens of the Hesperides. In time it was to be Rome's longest continuous route, 1,700 miles from Gades to Rome and so well-known that silver mugs, shaped like milestones and etched with an itinerarium of all cities on that route to Rome – the Itineraria Gaditana – were made for those who took the long overland journey.

Few European countries have kept their Roman heritage as intact as Spain. From the Pyrenees to the Pillars of Hercules, from Lusitania to the Costa Brava, there are remains of roads, bridges, triumphal arches, quarries, aqueducts and amphitheatres, all evidence of the six-hundred-year-long Roman occupation of Hispania. Roman emperors from Augustus to Gratian have left records on milestones and bridges, self-praising mementoes to cheer the path to oblivion. The names of almost all the cities owe their origin to Roman colonisation.

Famous Romans in Spain   Many great names of Roman history are connected with Spain; the Scipios, those 'two thunderbolts', made the first test with the Carthaginians, and Hannibal began his odyssey there; Cato – 'red-haired and green-eyed, snapping at all comers, even in Hades' – made his first political mark in Spain, as did Metellus and Pompey and many others; Julius Caesar fought two grim battles there. Augustus built roads and planted cities; the

The Via Argenta, the Silver Road, ran between Salamanca and Mérida.
It was begun in 24 BC under Tiberius

There are remarkable reminders of the Roman presence throughout
the Iberian peninsula, like the remaining wall of this fine tomb of the Attilii

The Roman Arch of Bara, Tarragona, is a structure of classic simplicity

maligned Tiberius gave generously to Spain and built its most famed road, the Via Argenta. Rome's two greatest emperors, Trajan and Hadrian, were Spanish, and the last effective ruler of the Empire, Theodosius, was a native of Cauca near Segovia. There were other titans – the two Senecas were born in Cordoba, as was the poet Lucan. The geographer Pomponius Mela lived there in Claudian times; Martial was born at Bilbilis as were other writers, such as Columella and Quintilian – all these and more travelled the high roads, built by Roman genius and Spanish brawn, walking and riding over them to distant lands.

The Punic Wars brought Rome and its roads to Spain. First Rome acquired Sicily and Sardinia, then Corsica, and by 225 BC they had occupied a part of northern Spain, the boundaries being set by the Rio Ebro (Iberus), which poured its silt-laden waters into the Mediterranean.

The Punic Wars and the Romans

Carthage had no intention to suffer continued defeats, so the Carthaginians came in force to Gades, fortified it, enlarged that ancient land-track, the Via Herculea, then moved to the other coast, where there was an immense natural harbour. Here they built New Carthage. When queried by the Romans as to their real purpose, they answered that all this was being done to obtain silver bullion to pay off Carthage's indemnity.

'This', said a historian, 'was the sort of reply the Romans could appreciate and they allowed themselves to believe it.'

It was at this point that Hannibal appeared on the stage of history. He had taken his oath to avenge Carthage and never make a Roman peace. First he moved his armies up to Saguntum, a fortress and trading-centre below the Rio Ebro boundary. The Roman Senate replied by warning that Saguntum was under its protection. Believing that Roman policy was expansive, hypocritical and untrustworthy, Hannibal ignored the ultimatum and attacked Saguntum. The second Punic War had begun.

In May 218 BC Hannibal crossed the Ebro with forty thousand men and a corps of war elephants to carry out a predetermined war policy, for Rome could, he rightly concluded, only be defeated through the destruction of her legions in Italy; all victories on the periphery were empty victories.

The legions of Publius Cornelius Scipio set off to Spain in the belief that Hannibal would attack Massilia in Gaul. Hannibal had by-passed it, and realising now that he was making for Cisalpine Gaul, Scipio sent his brother Gnaeus on to Spain with two legions to cut Hannibal off from Spain. Meanwhile Scipio returned to Italy.

As long as Hannibal remained in Italy the plans for extending the Roman highway system came to a halt. But not in Spain, for over the primitive tracks Publius and Gnaeus Scipio marched with their legions in order to contain Hasdrubal and prevent him from joining his brother. Hannibal was ravishing Italy, defeating every Roman legion put up against him. 'Nought is accomplished,' the poet Juvenal had Hannibal say, 'until my host breaks down the city gates and I plant my standard in the midst of the Subura of Rome.' But while Hannibal lay waste Italy, the two Scipios defeated the Carthaginians in almost every battle; they relieved Saguntum in 212 BC and rapidly pushed down the coastal track from the north.

In the same year, in separate engagements, these two Scipios were silenced, but another appeared. Scipio Africanus was to be the greatest of Rome's generals, and his duel with Hannibal was only to end on a distant Pontian shore. In the spring of 290 BC, after a forced march over a terrible road from Tarragona, Scipio Africanus surprised the garrison of New Carthage, seized ships and military stores, preventing them from being sent to Italy to supply Hannibal. Hasdrubal then moved into Italy with two thousand men, planning to reinforce his brother; while this force moved along the newly built Via Flaminia it was cornered by Claudius Nero at the Metaurus river.

In Spain, Scipio Africanus, following up his victory, moved on to Cádiz, took it by assault and then granted it the status of a free city. Then he moved his troops toward Seville, twenty-four miles northwest, and founded Italica as the first Roman *colonia*.

The beginning of Roman roads in Spain

It was in 206 BC that the history of Roman road-building began in

An assemblage of antiquities found in Tarragona (from an engraving in Alexander de Laborde, *Voyage Pittoresque et historique de l'Espagne*, 1806)

CLAVI
DVLAR

Spain; it would not end until 600 years later, after the building of 34 distinct highways with an over-all length of 6,953 miles.

Since Cádiz was then the most important city of Farther Spain and located at the terminus of the fragmented coastal route (and that single highway the most important route in Spain) the full completion of it became one of the first concerns of road-planners; work was begun at both ends about the same time.

In 195 BC Cato arrived in Spain with two legions at Emporium (Ampurias), near the borderlands of Gaul at the far end of the Via Maxima. Cato arrived at Emporium to attempt to crush native Celtiberian resistance, which during the hiatus of the Hannibalic wars had taken on new ferocity.

The Romans had come to exploit the famed mines that lay in the remote Cantabrian Mountains, but they were checked by the determined and skilled defence of the Celtiberians, the best fighting men in Spain. 'The Iberians . . . wore light armour . . . using javelins, sling and dirk . . . Their horses were trained to climb mountains and, whenever there was a need for it, to kneel down at the word of command.'

Cato shifted his attack to the Catalonian hills, and to get his fighting men into position roads were built, not formal, well-organised roads, but makeshift ways. By 120 BC, however, according to Polybius, the road known as the Via Maxima, from Cádiz to Le Perthus, 980 miles in length, was complete to the last milestone. This in time would become the Via Augusta, the most used road in all of Spain. The road was repaired over and over again for six hundred years.

Via Maxima and Via Augusta

In November of 46 BC, memorable for its prematurely cold winter, Julius Caesar with his legions marched all the way from Rome to Obulco in 27 days to crush revolt. The Romans had a natural distaste for the sea and Caesar proudly pointed out that he had brought a whole army to Spain without once wetting their feet. On the way Julius Caesar wrote an essay, long since lost, entitled 'The Journey'. And that 'journey', explains the geographer Strabo, 'went over the heights of the Pyrenees where runs the road from Italy to what is called Farther Spain (Gades). This road, the Via Augusta, sometimes approaches the sea and sometimes it stands off at a distance from it . . . It runs toward Tarraco.'

Over a lateral road, already marked with *miliaria* set up by the Gracchi in 120 BC, the road ran from Tarraco (Tarragona) inland. Here, during his first visit to Spain, in June 49 BC, Caesar turned off the main route and taking this lateral moved his legions on to Lérida. Ilerda (Lérida) stood on a rocky hill which rose abruptly from the right bank of the Rio Segre; even then it was spanned by a Roman stone bridge.

Julius Caesar moved on Obulco (Porcuna), which lay on the Baetis River (Guadalquivir) thirty-five miles east of Cordoba on the main Via Maxima route, there to give final battle to the last of the Pompeians. The Cordoba-Linares section of the road must have already been built, for

The Roman bridge at Salamanca. The city was captured by Hannibal in 222 BC, before it was subject to Rome

The ruins of the four-way triumphal arch of Capera on the Silver Road

Caesar, in trying to capture the several bridges that had already been built across the Baetis, found roads sufficiently well laid to withstand the weight of siege weapons. The main battle took place below Munda on the Llanos de Vanda, and by September the war was over.

The Romanisation of Spain

Caesar had begun the Romanisation of Spain, but Augustus, who arrived in Spain in 26 BC, achieved it. By 21 BC he had made, for administrative purposes, three Spains: Hither, later Tarraconensis, with Tarragona as its capital; Lusitania, with Mérida to be its capital; and finally, the southernmost, Baetica (named after the Baetis river), with Gades as its sea-port and Cordoba as its capital. Lusitania and Baetica corresponded roughly to what had previously been known as Farther Spain. The principal network of roads was laid down so as to get Rome's fighting men into the silver-bearing regions of the Cantabrian Hills, but first the great coastal road was completely relaid and given new mile-stones. And the ancient way was now the Via Augusta.

From it two lateral roads broke off to the north to move into the interior. The first was at Barcino (Barcelona), a latter-day metropolis which still retains the name of its founder, Barca, a reminder of the Carthaginian presence. Roman remains include some fluted columns of a temple

A view of the magnificent aqueduct bridge of Lladenet, six leagues from Barcelona

fragments of defensive walls with two half-circular towers, and the main gateway, which still stands in the Plaza Nueva; and Barcelona's museums abound with things Roman. Out from Barcelona the road passed over a single arched bridge at Martorell, Puente del Diablo, and led to Lérida. The second lateral came out of Tarragona.

The road to Lérida from Tarragona goes first to Vallis, where the deep valley is spanned by an aqueduct carrying water into Tarragona. Now called the Puente de las Ferreras, it was built in the time of Trajan of unmortared ashlar with eleven arches, which in turn hold sixteen more on the higher level, and these support the conduit.

This Tarragona lateral joined the Barcelona-Lérida road and they move as one road toward Zaragoza (Saragossa). This city, which lay 69 *milia passuum* from Lérida, was the meeting place of three rivers and four roads. It had been named Caesar Augusta after its founder. One of its four roads led due north to the Pyrenees into Gaul and northwest to Bordeaux, and another went to the Cantabrian hills. The northern route followed the Ebro valley and passed through Calahorra. Known as Calaguris, it was the birthplace in AD 35 of the famed orator and rhetorician Marcus Fabius Quintilian. The throughway leaving Quintilian's country continued through present-day Logroña, and to the north the road is still remembered and actually to be seen in the little town of St Domingo de la Calzada through which it passes on the way to Burgos.

The other branch followed the valley of the Rio Jalón and veered off at Calatayud, known as Bilbilis and famed for its hot baths. Marcus Valerius Martial was born there in AD 40, and it was in the theatre of Bilbilis that he first tried out his biting wit. The road from Bilbilis passed close to Soria and the ruins of Numantia. The road then followed the foothills of the Sierra de Urbion toward Osma. El Burgo de Osma had begun its history as 'Uxama', a Celtiberian stronghold that had been stormed by the Romans in the time of the Numantian siege.

The next halting-place was Clunia (Coruña del Conde), bare and forbidding. Here lived the aged Galba, who at Nero's death was proconsul of Hispania Tarraconensis and was then proclaimed Emperor. At the Rio Duero, the road broke off into several laterals, but the main road, over which the legions led by Augustus himself marched, went on to Segisamo (Sasamón) near Burgos. Agrippa arrived in 25 BC to carry out the Romanisation of Spain, which meant founding colonies and building roads. With this old war-horse on hand, the fragile Augustus went into winter-quarters in warmer Tarragona, leaving it to Agrippa to direct the armies, build the roads and create colonies in his Augustan name.

The first was Léon. The Legio VII Gemina, as the Antonine Itinerary shows, was established there and out of it grew the city Legio (León); the streets of the old part of the town still preserve their Roman form, and more than half of its estimated 70 towers still exist. The next was Lugo on the road to the sea. The glory of Lugo, founded as Lucus-Augustus, was its great Roman wall which still runs 7,000 feet around the old town. Vitruvius, one of Augustus's architects, laid down the plan and it was presumably well-followed, for it is one of the most complete walled Roman cities extant. Astorga was another; founded as Asturica-Augusta, it lay on the main road midway between Burgos and the sea, and from it issued three important roads.

To hold this still rebellious region in check Agrippa had worked out a master-plan for the road communications. The coastal road to Lusitania (Portugal) ran down to the Cape of Finisterre. There, at the 'end of the earth', Agrippa erected a monument, *Ara Augusti*, the Altar of Augustus. The Lusitania road proceeded along the coast to Bracara Augusta, modern Braga, which still is a hub of communications. The road that connected Braga in Lusitania with Astorga was built, as the milestones testify, by Augustus in the years 11–12 BC and was the shortest route to the mines, yet the most difficult, since it followed the tortuous windings of the Rio Minho. Later generations called the road the Camino de Geira because of its many curves. It was repaired by Claudius and Trajan, and entirely rebuilt by Hadrian in AD 135, and again rebuilt by Caracalla. Diocletian repaired it. The last living act of Gratian, in AD 380, was to effect its repair.

The immense Roman aqueduct of Segovia was built at the direct order of Augustus. The construction is granite ashlar

once more. Until the nineteenth century the road retained many of its milestones, and examples are still to be seen today, an extraordinary record of the upkeep of a single road for 400 years.

Agrippa began another road from Braga to the *colonia* on the Rio Tamega; the milestones state that it was built in 32–33 BC. Later, in the time of Vespasian, the city by the river was refounded as Aquae Flaviae and the bridge across the Rio Chaves was erected in the reign of the Flavians. The 18 arches (of which 12 are original) span the river in a graceful, 116-metres-long bridge. The importance of the route is attested by the fact that during the years AD 77–80 Vespasian ordered the building of yet another Braga-Astorga route. Called the Via Nova on the milestones, it was completed on the same day that the Colosseum in Rome was begun in AD 80. Hadrian rebuilt the road in AD 125, and Caracalla did so again in AD 214.

Extent of roads under Augustus By the time of Augustus' death, Strabo estimated that Rome was operating 2,000 miles of land roads and 1,500 miles of river roads in Spain. Most of the roads in the northwest concentrated on the mining regions and had been laid by the Emperor Vespasian. To find their way among the northwest road complex, the soldiers had ceramic itinerary tablets which were shaped like a bread-board with a hole at the top. They list the way stops on the roads leading to and about Léon and Astorga and are interesting for their confirmation of the route given by the third-century Antonine Itinerary.

Tiberius appeared in Spain in AD 24. He began the Via Argenta in the years AD 24–25. One of the great roads of Spain, it was designed to go from the mining districts of the Cantabrian hills down through the heart of Spain to Cádiz. It began at the source of silver shipments, Astorga, and moved south to Brigecium (Benavente), where it joined another road coming down from León. It continued down through Zamora to Salmantica (Salamanca), where the road was conveyed across the seasonally rampant Rio Tormes by a massive bridge of 12 arches. The 124-mile-long Via Argenta had a roadbed of some depth, and on it was placed the familiar mosaic of massive stones similar to roads in Italy but rarely found outside Italy. The road with an invariable width of 5.50 metres preserves some sections intact. It was repaired by Claudius in the year AD 45–50 and again by Trajan. Hadrian, too, restored the road. And so well did Caracalla rebuild the entire road in AD 214–17 that it was never repaired again by an emperor.

The *via* was well known in the Middle Ages as the 'Camino de la Plata' by which time it had become rutted and gutted. Its surface dislodged and broken, it is used today by mules that pick their way between the once nobly laid stones. But in its heyday the noble road followed the valley and river of the Alagon, went on to Caparra, crossed a bridge over the Rio Ambroz, still in use, and passed under the well-known four-way arch of Capera. This had been an important way-stop on the Silver Road, with a

Remains of an arched fourth-century Roman bridge that spanned a gorge of the Foz de Lumbier

The Via Augusta crossed the Martorell bridge outside Barcelona.
Parts of the original Roman structure survive

small theatre, many villas and paved streets. The arch alone is intact.

Colonia Norba (Carceres), the next city of importance on the Via Argenta, has preserved nothing of its Roman heritage, but out of it ran a road, built by Trajan in AD 104 to link up this highway with the road, which he had previously built (AD 100) in Lusitania, that went from Lisbon (Olisipo) north to the important road centre of Braga. The lateral was designed to go due westward, cross the deep gorge of the river Tagus and connect at Conimbriga (Coimbra in Portuguese) to serve the road that ran from Faro, in the Gulf of Cádiz, up the coast through Lisbon and Braga, past the Ara Augusti, to the great lighthouse at La Coruña.

Two great bridges were built across the river Tagus. The first bridge was built across the Upper Tagus by none other than Apollodorus of Damascus, the same architect who, at Trajan's orders, constructed the great bridge across the Danube. The Tagus bridge, which the Arabs called Alcónetar, was built entirely of stone, had 18 arches and an over-all length of 220 metres. What is notable in this bridge is that Apollodorus used the same technique in stone in Alcónetar that he had employed in wood in the earlier Danube bridge. Only three arches, and some tumbled piers in the river, are now to be seen of the Tagus bridge, which was destroyed in the eighth century by the Moors.

Bridges on the Tagus

The other bridge on the Tagus, the greatest not only in Spain but in the Roman world, is the Alcántara. Its six gigantic arches, built of carefully hewn ashlar set together without mortar, rise 150 feet above the water with an over-all length of six hundred feet. Near the western end of the bridge, on the Portuguese side, is a small almost perfectly preserved temple supported by two Tuscan columns in front.

Mérida, 50 kilometres south of the road that led to Alcántara, was founded by Augustus himself in 25 BC, as Colonia Emerita Augusta, capital of the province of Lusitania and a colony for his legions, the v and the x, retired from the Cantabrian Wars. It was designed by Agrippa to be the centre of all communications; seven roads converged on Mérida, which still preserves some notable monuments of its Roman past.

Of the seven roads that issued from Emerita Augusta according to the Antonine Itinerary, two entered what is now Portugal in widely separated areas; one went to join the coastal road; the more northern route entered that main artery above Santarem. The north-eastern route passed through Trujillo to enter Toledo (Toletum) by a roundabout route. Another went directly to that city, which stands in a tight bend of the river Tagus. The ancient tribal centre of the Oretani, Toledo was civilised even before the arrival of the Carthaginians in 500 BC. It was not a leading city in Roman times, yet it had a circus, a theatre and two bridges. From Toledo the Mérida-Zaragoza road went on to Titulcia, near Morata de Tunaja.

Before reaching Seville, the Via Argenta passes through Santiponce (Italica). The oldest *colonia* of Spain, Italica, was founded in 206 BC by Scipio Africanus. First a frontier fortress, then a *colonia*, in time it became

Overleaf, *left:* The Roman aqueduct of Tarragona. The city was captured by the Scipios in 218 BC *Right:* The Bridge at Alcántara spanning the Tagus river was built about AD 105 in honour of Trajan

a thriving city. Marcus Ulpius Traianus was born there in AD 53; Trajan's
son, he became emperor in AD 98. His cousin Publius Aelius Hadrianus
was also born in Italica, in AD 76. To glorify this birthplace of emperors,
Antoninus Pius, successor to Hadrian, erected an amphitheatre at Italica,
the largest in all Spain and the fourth largest in the whole Empire, but it
was used as a quarry in the Middle Ages, leaving the amphitheatre like a
tree in winter, stripped of all its majestic foliage.

Sevilla, which has come to us through the Arabic 'Ishbiliya', was
known in Roman times as Hispalis. It lay on the River Baetis in one of the
most beautiful and fructuous regions in all Spain. Wheat was so plenteous
that Baetica was listed officially as one of the granaries of Rome; its oil-
and eating-olives were then, as now, of the best; to few Roman provinces
was the triad of wheat, vine and olive so appropriate as in Baetica. There
is, however, little of the Roman past that has survived. There are remains
of walls and fragments of an aqueduct. Although Hispalis was itself a
seaport, the Via Argenta branched off to two other seaboard cities,
Málaga and Cádiz.

From Cádiz the road led to Almeria and then went briefly inland,
skirting the Sierra Nevada to Acca (Guadix), and then descended again

Left: An entrance to the Roman theatre at Mérida, founded in 25 BC as Augusta Emerita
Right: The bridge near Andujar, the ancient Isturgi

247

The Los Malagros aqueduct of Mérida. The forms were adapted
as decorative motifs by the medieval Mozarabs

through Lorca to emerge at Carthago Nova. Thence northward the road
went on to meet the Via Augusta coming from Córdoba (Corduba).

Corduba, the highest point of river navigation on the River Baetis, was
the capital of the province of Baetica. Corduba is entered on the south by
the Via Augusta over a sixteen-arch pontoon-like bridge. The supporting
piers are all that is left of things Roman in Corduba. It was famed for its
hides and the leather made from them – Cordovan leather with a high
sheen. The Senecas were natives of Corduba, as was Lucan the poet.

From Corduba the Via Augusta, the ancient Way of Hercules, given
new lustre almost every half-century, completely rebuilt three times in
three hundred years, moved over the gentle hills following the high ground
above the Tagus valley to Linares on its way to the coast.

At coastal Saetabis (Jativa) the Via Augusta made junction with the
southern coastal road from Carthago Nova and absorbed it completely. At
Valentina (Valencia) the traveller could begin to use the second column
of the Itineraria Gaditana which starts with 'Valentiam'. The traveller on
the Via Augusta from Spain to Rome needed no other guide or *itinerarium*
for these four silver beakers, made in Gades, had the names of all the cities
and the distances between them carefully etched. Each was eight inches in
height and cylindrically shaped like a *miliarium*. The beakers were found

Roman sanctuary sepulchre at Fabara

When Rome destroyed the Carthaginian power in the Iberian peninsula Portugal was part of Hispania. Portugal preserves remains of its Roman past

in 1852 by workmen digging in the sacred baths of Aquae Apollinares at Vicarello by Lake Bracciano north of Rome.

From Valentia it was 20 Roman miles' distance to Saguntum; after crossing the wide Ebro, either by bridge or ferry, the traveller reached Tarraco. Here, one by one, the larger roads and the feeder roads flowed into the one mighty artery that led to Rome. One by one the 34 roads of Spain crossed, emerged, and amalgamated like rail lines converging on the central route. At Gerundam (Gerona) the last of the roads comes into the Via Augusta, then after passing through Emporium the swollen highway mounts the hills of the Pyrenees among the scented pines. It now crosses the heights on which was set the Trophaeum of Pompey, testifying to 876 towns between the Alps and Farther Spain subjugated by him. The mile-cups announce 'Juncariam xv – fifteen miles to the Juncarian Plain,' and then the descent.

The aqueduct of Segovia, which was erected during the Augustan period

The road, albeit still the Augusta, is now in Gaul. As Narbo is passed, more roads flow into the larger one on its way to Rome. Nîmes is reached, and the river Rhône is crossed at Arles. Then all of Gaul's roads begin to converge on the coastal Via Augusta.

The principal route to Rome, however, into which all the roads of Spain, France and Britain coalesced, was this one that guided travellers towards the Alps. After Arles the silver *Itinerarium* states 'Glanum XVI' and so we know, as did they, that the road is going through the Alpilles. This road joins other roads at Brigantio (Briançon). By this time the silver cups, which led from the Silver Road, have gathered in most of the northern routes into one large road, and its traffic passes through and over the Cottian Alps.

As soon as the traveller reads 'Durantium', he knows that he is leaving Gaul at last. Henceforth all roads lead to Rome.

IX · ALL ROADS LED TO ROME

The roads of Spain, France, Britain, Germany, Austria, Hungary and Yugoslavia were compressed by the Antonine Itinerary into the ten routes which crossed the Alps into Italy on the way to Rome. Once over the Alps, all the roads of the north began to coalesce.

The Cottian Highway, having gathered hundreds of miles into its corporate body, reached the Alpes Cottiae, which had been opened up to vehicular traffic by Pompey in 77 BC. Here the Alps are overwhelming, commanding empty spaces, while all about is a dreadful nothingness and silence. The highway, following the curve of the precipitous slopes, is welded into the bedrock so firmly that it seems part of the rock-hard surface itself, with its ample gutters facing the incline to catch the ever-present water, the destroyer of mountain roads. According to Ammianus Marcellinus, a fourth-century Antiochene Greek soldier, the crossing of the Cottian Alps could be a terrifying experience. The road 'follows the ridge that falls off with a sheer incline; terrible to look on because of the overhanging cliffs on every side. Especially in the season of spring, when the ice melts; then over precipitous ravines on either side and chasms rendered treacherous through the accumulation of ice, men and animals descending with hestitating step slide forward . . . , wagons as well. They bind together a number of these vehicles with rope and hold them back from behind with men and oxen and proceed at a snail's pace. But when the road is caked with ice . . . travellers ofttimes are swallowed up. They drive in stakes along the outer edge so that their line can guide the traveller.'

The descent toward Italy is rapid. By the time the traveller had consulted his silver guide-cups he had arrived at Segusio (Susa), where the road passes under a triumphal arch to Augustus, built by King Cottius in 8 BC.

Augusta Taurinorum (Turin) received that part of the Alpine traffic which had come down from the two passes of St Bernard. One road coming out of Gaul crosses the Alpes Graiae by way of the Little St Bernard and approaches that coming through the Alpes Poeninae over the Great St Bernard at Aosta (Augusta Praetoria). This city was founded by Augustus on a scale so vast that neither time nor man has destroyed the Arch to Augustus, the huge Praetorian Gates, the theatre or the bridge that carries

The first-century Arch of Augustus at Aosta, the Roman Augusta
Praetoria, was erected to commemorate Varro's victory

he road on its way south. The highway that Agrippa built along the River
Dora Beltea keeps to the left bank; at Donnaz, several miles south of
Aosta, his engineers, in order to avoid water, cut the road out of the living
rock, a 200-metre-long vertical cut to a height of fifty feet, recorded by
numbers and circles as well as by the name of one of its masons, left in the
wall. The whole unit includes an arch, completely tunnelled, a set of
formal steps also cut out of the rock, and the milestone XXXVI, thirty-six
miles from Aosta, in the bold lettering of the early Empire. Deep ruts of
wagons 3 feet wide are cut into the surface, a memento of the immense
traffic that came down through the towns of Eporedia and Vercellae. Into
the latter town pours a lateral road running from Bergomum (Bergamo)
through Milan into the main route. At Cuttiae the road from the St
Bernard passes met this main route.

Many of these towns along the route began as *mansiones*, then surrounded
by taverns they became *vici*, villages; then towns and in time they evolved
into *civitates*. But Cuttiae was not one of them; although placed at the
strategic meeting of three Alpine roads it has disappeared and its location
is known only by its appearance on the various itineraries. This is not true
of Ticinum (mod. Pavia), which lay on the River Ticino. The cups of
Cádiz record the site as, a municipium in the second century BC. The long
Cádiz-Rome road entered Ticinum from the west, there to meet the road
coming from Como through Milan. Pavia's streets still preserve the Roman
grid and the *cardo maximus* is aligned with the bridge that carried the road
across the river.

Milan, the Roman Mediolanum, was in the earlier part of the Empire a
municipium. The road went through Milan and followed the course of the
River Lambrus on the way to Piacenza (Placentia), the earliest Roman
colony in the Po valley. Placentia was founded in 218 BC, thirty years
before the Via Aemilia was constructed. It was on the front line of the battle
which Rome was about to launch against the whole of Cisalpine Gaul.

Placentia, more or less in the centre of the immense Po valley, had no
sooner been founded when Hannibal, reinforced by Gallic troops, overwhelmed the Roman army, and Placentia became the shelter for legionaries
fleeing the battlefield of Trebbia.

By 187 BC Aemilius Lepidus's legions had swept into the Po valley, and as
they conquered they built a wide and straight road. It was doubtless
quickly finished, since the road was straight and there were neither
terraces nor retaining walls to be built. Aemilius Lepidus capped it with
his name. The Via Aemilia began at Placentia and proceeded in a straight
alignment $170\frac{1}{4}$ miles to Ariminum (Rimini), which lay where the rugged
foothills of the Apennines meet the Adriatic Sea. In addition to the
Aemilia, three other roads met at Placentia there; the road coming down
from Milano, the third Via Julia Augusta on its east–west axis from
Genua, and the Via Postumia connecting all the northern towns along the
foothills of the Alps – Altinum, Patavium, Verona and Brixia.

*The junction at
Placentia*

The St Bernard Pass. The Roman road, remains of which
can still be seen, runs below the modern highway

Parmam (Parma), the next large city on the flow of the Aemilian Way to the sea, had been founded in 183 BC.

Verona was equally important because of its strategic position on river and roads. The Via Claudia Augusta and the Via Postumia passed through Verona. All traffic that emanated from Verona moved down to the Via Aemilia. Aside from strategic river-port cities, towns were built about every twenty miles along the road: Reggia, Modena, Bologna, Forli, Rimini. There are few towns along the Via Aemilia which did not begin either as a *mansio*, a *taberna* or a *vicus*. This great highway, though only 170 miles in length from Placentia to Rimini, carried all the traffic from the roads from the northern Empire.

Ravenna was connected to Rimini by the Via Popillia as well as by the Po, thanks to a canal that Augustus built from Ravenna.

From Rimini the Via Flaminia leads to Rome.

Along the coastal part of the road several bridges still survive, lonely skeleton arches precariously suspended over rivers. The road proceeds to the Augustan city of Fanum Fortunae (mod. Fano). Thence the road proceeds to Forum Semproni (mod. Fossombrome), where in 207 BC a Roman force under general Claudius Nero met 20,000 Carthaginians led by Hasdrubal, marching to reinforce his brother Hannibal in southern

Above: The Roman bridge at Canosa, the ancient Canusium, in Apulia
Opposite: Roman road at Donnaz. The archway, the milestone and the road were cut from the living rock

Italy. Beyond the Passo del Furlo, the town of Scheggia, and the remains of Tadinum the road came to Nuceriam (mod. Nocera Umbra). It proceeded to Mevanium (mod. Bevagna) and then to Otricoli. It was now only twenty miles from Rome.

At the ruins of the villa of Livia Augusta, Augustus' wife, overlooking the Tiber, the Flaminia turns to Ad Rubras, now Prima Porta, where Constantine battled Maxentius for the rule of the Empire and had his vision of the cross. Then, absorbing the little Via Tiberina, the Flaminia runs sinuously down the valley of the Tiber, making its way between empty cores of tombs long since stripped. There this impatient giant stops and waits at the edge of the river for the other *viae consulares* to join it so that it can move majestically into Rome to the Golden Milestone.

The northern roads   The seven northern roads that provided the communications for all Umbria and Etruria – the Cassia, the Clodia, the old Veientana, which once entered the Etruscan 'capital' of Veii, the Annia, the Cimina, the Amerina, the oldest of them all, and the Tres Traianae (only one of which has been found) – came down to join the Flaminia before its final entry into Rome.

Via Cassia   But of these, the Cassian Way is perhaps the most interesting. The construction of the original road began about 300 BC, when the long struggle between Rome and Etruria ended. The Romans called the Etruscans 'Tusci', a people of mysterious origin who were long thought to have come out of Lydia in Asia Minor. In time they evolved a League of Twelve Cities of Etruria, a loose confederation held together by blood ties and culture along the natural lines of communication, the valleys of the Tiber and the Arno and the vale of Chiana. The Etruscans had advanced agricultural methods, and they were skilled in metallurgy (gold, silver, copper and bronze), in modelling terra cotta, and fresco painting. They trafficked in ores, developing mines in Elba, Corsica and Sardinia. Some of their engineering projects were of considerable scale: they began the Cloaca Maxima in Rome, and their extant bridges show good construction. This heritage was passed on to those wonderful appliers, the Romans.

Sometime after 180 BC, at least ten years after the Via Aemilia was completed, L Cassius Longinus Ravilla, during his term as censor, had a paved road laid down which when completed went from Rome to Florentia. It was named the Via Cassia. This road left Florentia Tuscorum and followed the west side of the Arno toward Arezzo. Another branch followed the east side under Pratomagno and crossed the Arno by the Ponte il Romito, of which one arch, mostly medieval, still stands like a sentinel. Thence the traveller moved through the shadow of the vine to the head of the Val di Chiana.

At the junction of the two valleys lay Arezzo (anc. Arretium), originally one of the Twelve but sufficiently Romanised by 217 BC for Gaius Flaminius to use it as a base when, as consul, he marched up the old road, before Cassius paved it, in pursuit of Hannibal.

Overleaf: Ruins of a bridge at Aeclanum. Hadrian made the town a colony when he repaired the Via Appia from Beneventum

Next came Chiusi (anc. Clusium) the homeland of Lars Porsenna. South of Città del Pieve, near Fabro, one of the alternative roads of the Cassia left the valley and moved over higher and safer ground toward Lake Bolsena. At Bolsena this road made connection with the Via Cassia itself. This then veered away from Viterbo, and made its way across the Plain of Baths, where sulphur water boils up in springs from the earth. Out of twelve-gated Viterbo a by-pass called the Via Cimina moved east around Lago di Vico and joined the Cassia proper near Monterosi. The Cassian Way, however, kept to its southeastern route and crossed the River Arcione on what was then called Pons Quinquagesimus, the fiftieth bridge from Rome. Further south is Sutri, known for its medicinal waters, amphitheatre, Etruscan rock-tombs and Roman walls.

Via Amerina

At the dry crater of Baccano (level with Lake Bracciano) the Via Amerina, named for the city of Armeria (mod. Amelia), joined the Cassia. The capital city of the region, Città Castellana (Falerii Veteres), was destroyed by the Romans in 241 BC who built Falerii Novi on the flat lands across which the Via Amerina was then directed. The Via Amerina joined the Cassia at Baccano and swelled the stream of traffic straining up the long incline before the last descent to the Tiber crossing.

Via Clodia

The last of the three *viae* was the Clodia. Its mission was to traverse the classic ground of Etruria from Rusellae to Rome, and like theViae Cassia and Amerina, the Via Clodia was laid down on an original Etruscan way, a narrow dirt-gravel road running between the volcanic lakes and the sea and linking the Etruscan urban centres and necropoleis.

The Clodia's record begins at Saturnia, a small spa located on the Upper Albegna River, midway between the lake of Bolsena and the sea.

On the River Marta, half-way between Bolsena and Tarquinia, the road went through the town of Tuscania (Toscanella). The road then passed on to Norchia. The Via Clodia followed the old Etruscan track into Bieda, and beyond, around Barbarano Romano, one can see the only visible sections of the Via Clodia with a bridge. Nearing the Lake of of Bracciano the road bifurcated. The smaller road moved east, routed to follow the north shore of the lake to the Cassia, passing the Bagni di Vicarello. It was in the ruins of these Baths of Apollo that workmen in 1852 uncovered a hoard which included the famous silver cups, the Itineraria Gaditana, which guided travellers all the way from Cádiz to Rome.

Swollen with traffic from the Viae Annia, Cimina, and Amerina, the Cassia passes Veii and at La Storta, where it makes a bend, unites with the Via Clodia. The Cassia meets the Flaminia and both come to the Milvian Bridge.

Via Aurelia

The Via Aurelia was the other great arterial road from the north, and it absorbed all the roads that the Flaminia did not. The Aurelia began in Genua and followed the Tyrrhenian coast to Rome. Begun in 241 BC, the Via Aurelia had been planned to go only as far as Luna, the most distant of coastal Etruscan cities, but a century and a half later, in 109 BC, it was

The Ponte Grosso, which carries the main branch of the Via
Flaminia across the Furlo Pass

The ruins of Aeclanum. Hundreds of inscriptions have been
found which provide information about the site in Roman times

extended to Genua. This road, when extended further by Augustus, became known as the Via Augusta when it reached Gaul, and under various names it ran from Rome to Cádiz, the longest continuous road.

The Via Aurelia began its long movement southward continued down past Livorno to Vadis Volterris (mod. Volterra), and then to Populonia by the sea. The next stop, Cosa, is situated on a promontory only eighty-six miles from Rome.

While the Aurelia continued along the coast, withdrawing up to a mile or two back from the sea, laterals led inland to the defeated cities, such as Castro Nova (mod. Montalto di Castro), where a road, plainly seen with its fine paving of flintstone, led to the Roman-Etruscan city of Vulci. Farther down the Aurelian Way, at the official way-stop at Gravisca-Tabellaria, a similar road led inland to Tarquinia. At Cetumcellae (mod. Civitavecchia) the road led to Trajan's port of embarkation to Sardinia, an island well traversed by Roman roads after it became a province in 241 BC, with the defeat of Carthage in the First Punic War.

Then came Cerveteri (anc. Caere) with its fabulous round Etruscan tombs.

Turning off the coast at Alsium (mod. Palo) the Via Aurelia took its time-honoured route to Rome, going over the gentle rolling hills. It passed through the Porta Aurelia in the walls erected by Aurelian in between AD 270 and 275, and came down the sloping Janiculum Hill to halt at the Tiber, where the Pons Aemilius, standing just upstream from the older Sublicius and dating originally from the third century, carried traffic across into the Forum Boarium. Meanwhile, the shorter Via Cornelia descended past Nero's circus on the Vatican slopes and waited at the river.

Via Triumphalis

Here it was joined by the Via Triumphalis, which cut across Monte Mario from the thirteenth kilometre of the Cassia and bore general and carter alike over the Pons Neronianus and into the city.

To bring their burden of traffic to Rome from the rugged lands of Apulia, the Abruzzi and Sabine country, roads were superimposed over two of the oldest ways, the Viae Salaria and Valeria.

Via Salaria

The Salaria, older as a primitive road than the Appia, existed as a much-used track even before 450 BC. The Sabine people used the Salt Road, following it down from their mountainous land along the Tiber's left bank. Where there was a ford at that river the Salt Road met the other ancient paths, the Latina and the Veientana. At this nodal point Rome developed. Here the Salaria crossed the river and went down to the Tiber estuary on the right bank. At first the Via Salaria went only as far as Reate, sixty miles from Rome, but after 16 BC Augustus extended the track to the Adriatic.

Via Tiburtina

The thrice-named road, Tiburtina-Valeria-Claudia, was laid down as far as the fine white travertine quarries on the River Anio near Tibur (mod. Tivoli) as early as 307 BC. It got no farther than midway to the sea until AD 58, when the Emperor Claudius pushed it through the mountains to emerge, as does the Salaria, on the road which in effect is the 'Via

Adriatica'. This long coastal road ran from Brindisi to Rimini, both cities having been made Roman *coloniae* at the same time (297 BC). This road is in effect only a prolongation of the Via Flaminia. It worked its way up the limestone-bound coast, through the greener Apulian lands and after 300 miles came to the port created by Claudius as Ostia Aterni (mod. Pescara). The road known as the Via Claudia-Valeria following the River Pescara had no difficulty in its first miles. The easy gradient carried it on the left bank past Chieti (anc. Interpronium) to Corfinio and beyond. At Forca Carusa, 1,107 metres above sea level, that part of the road built by Claudius ends, and the older section, the Via Valeria, built by the consul Valerius in 307 BC, begins.

The early road had made a wide encircling movement to avoid the large Lago Fucino, until Claudius undertook the Fucine drainage scheme in AD 46. Only then were engineers able to lay down the Via Valeria in a straight alignment. The Via Valeria was sent along the lake shore and continued down to Carsulis and Lamnas. Near Lamnas (mod. Arsoli), the Via Valeria connected with yet another road, the Via Sublacensis. Frontinus says that it was first paved by Nero, and it was important because it led to Subiaco (anc. Sublacium).

Subiaco was also the end of the Via Praenestina, which led next to Treblis (mod. Tervi) and then Praeneste (mod. Palestrina), where Sulla, in 83 BC began the immense sanctuary of Fortuna Primigenia.

Via Praenestina

At Rome the Praenestina shares the famous Porta Claudia (Port Maggiore) with the Via Labicana, going through the immense opening that is at once gateway and aqueduct. Two conduits pass over the arches into the city at this point, the Aquae Claudia and Anio Novus.

The Valeria became the Tiburtina at Tivoli, below which Hadrian erected his villa. The Via Tiburtina then came into Rome under an arch first erected to Augustus, but this was later incorporated into the walls of Rome as the Porta Tiburtina.

The Via Salaria, pushed to the Adriatic by Augustus at the end of 16 BC ended on the coastal Flaminia 'Adriatica' and had its terminus and port at Castrum Trentinum (mod. Porto d'Ascoli). The road then climbed the valley to Asculum (mod. Ascoli Piceno). Then it ran to Acquasanta (anc. Ad Aquas), Surpicano (Accumoli), Palacrinis (Falacrino, near Città Reale), then Interocrio (Antodroco) and Reate (mod. Rieti), the tribal centre of the Sabines. Next appears Ad Novas, called Osteria Nuova, from which a lateral proceeded west to join the Via Flaminia. Thereafter the Salaria turns to the edge of the Tiber, which it follows southward to Rome. At Eretum, it had its junction with the Via Nomentana. A short road, it led from Nomentum (mod. Mentana, whence a lateral road proceeded to Tibur) fourteen miles into Rome. Martial, Seneca and Ovid had estates at Nomentum, and today the large baronial castle is incrusted with tomb fragments and inscriptions worked into its walls.

At the Achilles heel of the Italian boot, Brundisium (mod. Brindisi) –

An arch near Canosa on the Via Traiana Nova

One of the columns that Trajan had erected at Brindisi to
commemorate the building of the Via Appia Traiana

the focal point of all southward communications to Greece, Asia Minor,
Persia, India, Egypt – had been a natural harbour since the nineth
century BC for ships bent on trade or mischief. The Via Appia, begun in
312 BC, was extended in slow stages to Brindisi, which it reached in 264 BC,
thirty years after that city had been made a Roman colony. Four roads
ended at Brindisi; that one which came from Reggio at the toe of the
Italian boot followed the 'instep' and merged at Tarentum (mod. Taranto)
with the Appia. The old Appia came down to Tarentum, then went
directly on a straight alignment to Brundisium. The 'Via Adriatica' met
with the Via Appia Traiana coming into Bari from Benevento in the
interior, and these marched into Brundisium with the others. The four
roads went through the principal street to the roadstead, where ships
rested at anchor. To commemorate the completion of his road, Trajan had
columns erected in AD 117 at the terminus.

Via Appia

The old Via Appia went to Tarentum, a Greek port dating back to 707
BC, which had been used as a Spartan base in the wars against Italy.
Then the Via Appia turned inland into 'sirocco-scorched' Apulia; a long

Detail of Trajan's column at Brindisi

and dusty route, generally avoided, it led through Venusio, Ponte Aufidi, Aquilonia, and Aeclanum to the great centre of Benevento.

The first stop north of Brindisi was Gnatie (Egnatia), an exposed port cut out of the limestone lying in direct line with the Via Egnatia. Barium (mod. Bari) next, the large port-city already famed for its sea fauna. Beyond this the Via Traiana leaves the coastal road and turns inland to Canusium (mod. Canosa) where still stands a much-used Roman bridge.

Beneventum (mod. Benevento), high on a windy hill, was the crosspoint for six roads and the junction of the old Via Appia coming up from Calabria as well as beginning point of the Via Traiana. Benevento has one of the best triumphal arches extant, set up in honour of Trajan in AD 114 to commemorate the completion of the Via Traiana. Capua, the second largest city in ancient Italy, appears as the next and most important stop.

Via Popilia The whole of southern Italy, from the instep and the toe, was serviced by a single – albeit bifurcating – road, the Via Popilia. It was, and still is, an important coastal road, meandering along the southern Apennines,

Head of Trajan excavated in the theatre at Ostia

which hang at places directly over the sea. At Reggio, at the very tip of the toe of the foot of the Italian boot, the Romans constructed on the ruins of a Magna Graecian city this Regium Julium. Into Reggio and onto the Via Popilia poured all the land traffic from Sicily, which had roads as early as its conquest. After the first Punic War the paved Via Valeria (begun in 210 BC) encircled the island, from Messina to Palermo, then on to Agrigents, Syracuse Catania (whence depart two laterals that cross the island's centre close on the flanks of Mt Etna past the Villa of Piazza Armerina, with its late Roman mosaics), then back again to Messina. Here a well-developed ferry service carried goods, people and wagons to the Via Popilia on the mainland to make its way along the coast to Rome.

At Vibona, fifty-four miles from Reggio, where Monteleone now stands among the ruins, a lateral took off across the instep of the Italian boot and made for Taranto. At the next way-stop, Annicia, the Via Popilia split into two sections. One went inland to Lucania. This road was probably built by the Samnites before 321 BC and only after the Romans had secured final

Overleaf: Relic of Augustus' Golden Milestone in the Roman Forum

victory made into a paved highway. The other section of the Popilia, the coastal, continued along the tortured landscape to Terusa (mod. Tirrena), Clampeia (mod. Amantea), and then on to Lavinium (mod. Scalea). Beyond this it enters the region of Bruttium. At Ascea Marina are the ruins of Elea (Velia), the birthplace of Zeno, founder of Stoicism, once a compact Greek port-city with harbour and lighthouse and a templed acropolis at the edge of a high promontory.

The Via Popilia now moves into the large flat marsh-like lands – the Piana del Sele – where the great walled Greco-Roman city of Paestum lies between the sea and the mountains. Paestum was settled by the Sibarites in the seventh century BC. In 273 BC, when Rome had subdued the Samnites and the Greeks, a Roman colony was founded there.

The road went on to Salerno and Nuceria, the most important junction point of the whole area. The Via Popilia, the high road, went to Nola, where the Emperor Augustus died. The second road out of Nuceria went out to the promontory of Sorrento, where the Peutinger Tablum has painted the Temple of Mercury, which overlooked both the gulfs of Salerno and Naples. The third road out of Nuceria, the coastal route to Naples, passed under the shadow of Mt Vesuvius, which sent up its perennial white-black plume of smoke, and proceeded between Pompeii and sea-girt Herculaneum.

The route through Naples was the Via Antiniana, which went through *Viae Antinina and* the hill of Posillipo to get to Puteoli (mod. Pozzuoli) and the immense *Domitiana* natural bay of Baia. Puteoli, the entrance to the Phlegraean Fields, had been a Greek port-city in the sixth century BC and was continuously enlarged after the Roman conquest of Campania after 338 BC. It also became the starting place of a short route toward Rome, the Via Domitiana. The Via Domitiana, only forty-nine miles long, was rapidly finished at the direct order of the Emperor Domitian in AD 95, the plan being to connect the coast from Puteoli to Sinuessa, where the old Via Appia arrived from Capua.

The Via Appia crossed the River Garigliano on the bridge, Pons Tirenus, remembered by Cicero in his letter to Atticus, to enter the city of Minturnae, which was built at the river's edge and established as a Roman colony in 296 BC. Then it went to Formia and through Itri, where, narrowly confined by a compressed canyon, modern and ancient road, separated by a ravine, continue together for several miles. It is one of the finest and best preserved sections of the road, showing a retaining wall, paving, ruins of a way-side *taberna*, remains of a bridge, and nearby, a tomb. Then the road continues to Fondi (anc. Fundi).

Water is the keynote of the road beyond Fondi. The Appia went inland so as to avoid the large Lago di Fondi. Along the road there are massive dikes made of huge stone blocks held together by bronze clamps, intended no doubt to prevent the agitated lake from eating into the roadbed. At Monte Biagio, the old Via Appia climbs the hill to Anxur, the site of the

A Roman tomb on the Via Flaminia. The brick structure was faced with marble

Temple of Jupiter Anxur. Built in the times of Sulla, it was set upon the heights overlooking Terracina.

Via Severiana

Terracina is the starting point of the Via Severiana, which Septimius Severus built in AD 198, the last of the great imperial roads. It goes for 100 kilometres along the edge of the Pontine marshes to connect Terracina with Portus, the harbour of Rome. The Via Severiana passed Anzio (anc. Antium), then Ardea, from which the Via Ardeatina went toward Rome; it also went through Laurentum, whence the Via Laurentina likewise led to Rome. Then the Via Severiana entered Ostia from the south and there it has been uncovered, under several feet of detritus, moving towards the Forum past a first-century synagogue.

Ostia was linked to the capital by a very old road, the Via Ostiensis, that followed the river bank. The Severiana, meanwhile, by means of two ferries, continued across the Isola Sacra at the mouth of the Tiber and reached Portus, the newer harbour started by Claudius and finished by Trajan, whence another road left for Rome.

Via Latina

The Via Latina was one of the first principal roads, and Strabo places it with the Appia and the Valeria as the most famous. Traces of the road can still be seen beyond the Pass of Algidus (as far as which it was certainly built by 389 BC, when the pass was first secured), and soon after it merges with the Via Labicana, the laternate road in the valley which eventually took its place. The Via Latina continues close to Frascati – a watering place for well-heeled Romans – and passes near Tusculum, famed among other reasons as the birthplace of the Elder Cato. On it goes across the Campagna, under aqueducts and past many ruins, until it arrives at the Porta Latina, beyond which it converges with the Appia.

Curiously enough there is no monument to the builder of the Appia, but there are numerous references to Appius Claudius. Livy recalls that 'the year 312 BC was renowned . . . for the censorship of Appius Claudius and Gaius Plautius, but the name of Appius was of happier memory with succeding generations because he built a road'.

Nineteen roads entered Rome

Nineteen roads entered Rome. Nineteen roads had absorbed all of the 372 distinct roads of the world, 53,000 miles of roads from Hadrian's Wall in Scotland through the fertile plains to India, from the Pillars of the God Terminus on the Euphrates to the Pillars of Hercules, from the sand-bound Fezzan to the gloomy forests of Germany.

All those who had travelled by conveyance had to leave these outside the city limits and proceed on foot. There were no exceptions to this order. The iron hand of the dictator held firm for 400 years, and no emperor changed that law imposed by Julius Caesar. He decreed that from sunrise until dusk no transport, cart, wagon or chariot of any form would be allowed within the precincts of Rome.

The roads went through two different sets of walls and gates: the Aurelian walls, built in the years AD 270–5, which had thirty-seven gates, and the so-called Servian walls within, built in 368 BC. The Viae Salaria

A detail of Trajan's Column. The column itself is 98 feet
high (not including the base) and was erected in AD 113

and Nomentana used different gates in the Aurelian wall but met at the ancient Colline Gate and trafficked together to the Forum, passing down the Vicus Longus by the Forum of Nerva and then past the Senate House directly to the Golden Milestone.

The Tiburtina was directed through the gate of the same name and was joined by the Via Collatina, a local road only ten miles long. Within the walls these *viae* entered the Servian Porta Esquilina, where lordly Maecenas, the patron of Horace and wayfarer of the Appia, had built his sumptuous gardens. The Viae Praenestina and Labicana joined the other two at this gate, and then the four proceeded as one through the quarter known as the Subura, the thickly populated, noisy and odoriferous district whose streets swarmed with the mobs of Remus; blacksmiths lying cheek and jowl with hairdressers, woolmakers, fullers, and barbers who cut their clients' hair in the streets. Slaves and servants did their shopping there, the more affluent could also buy pickled flamingo tongues, stuffed humming-bird wings, ostrich neck and unrepentant dormice. There were gang brawls about the Subura, and it was thought inadvisable for a boy to be sent there until he was old enough to wear a toga. Loose women beckoned to the users of the four roads from the windows, and yet people of some quality had also lived there. Julius Caesar, until he was elected Pontifex Maximus, lived there in inelegant surroundings. The sloping street (*clivus*) came to the back of the huge complex of Trajan's markets and entered the Forum with the Salarian traffic along the street known as the Argiletum.

The Latina and the Appia passed through the wall by their own gateways, coalesced shortly thereafter, passed near the Thermae Antoninianae, known as the Baths of Caracalla, and either carried their traffic alongside the Circus Maximus to the Forum Boarium and the Tiber, or headed towards the Colosseum and followed the Via Sacra through the arch of Titus down the Forum to the Severan arch, the Rostra and the Golden Milestone, the pillar marking the centre of Rome.

Litters (*lecticae*) were permitted to use the streets, or one might be borne in a carrying chair (*sella*), such as matrons were wont to use, or again one might be content with a sort of wheelbarrow like the one Trimalchio had presented to his favourite. The taverns offered sleeping quarters of questionable quality, and the inns, where *caupones* served cooling draughts of watered wine, had back rooms for gaming and seductive parties with prostitutes as barmaids.

When night fell, two-wheeled wagons carried building materials, wagons picked up the filth of the day, and young fops drove their chariots about at a fierce pace. 'Where is sleep possible?' Juvenal asks. 'The wagons crossing in the narrow winding streets, the swearing of drovers brought to a standstill would snatch sleep from a seacow or the Emperor Claudius himself.'

The Via Ardeatina followed the Via Appia for a few miles but then struck off on its own and entered the Porta Ardeatina. It passed to the rear

The Via Flaminia about 25 miles outside Rome. The ancient
and modern roads generally follow the same alignment. The Via
Flaminia was repaved by Augustus in 30 BC

of Carcalla's Baths, joined the Via Ostiensis coming up from the port of Rome, and both continued along the Vicus Piscinae Publicae – the Public Bath Street – along the Septizonium with the Appia and Latina to the Colosseum, and thence into the Forum Romanum by the Via Sacra.

The Via Portuensis, as its name suggests, the 'Port Way', came up on the other side of the Tiber directly from the Claudio-Trajanic port across from Ostia. Along the banks of the Tiber, on both sides, are the remains of *horrea*, warehouses, of the Empire. Barges pulled by oxen brought the produce up the Tiber, wagons weighted down with the material for Rome's sustenance used the Via Portuensis to bring this to the storage bins; wheat from Africa and Egypt, the famed olive oil of Spain and as well its lead, silver and gold; wood, marinated venison and wools from Gaul, dates from the oases and *liquamen* sauce from Libya, along with ostrich feathers, hides, elephant skins and ivory. Delivered to Rome were the cured meats of Baetica, dried fish and salted fish from Gades, the marbles of Tuscany, Greece and Numidia, gold from Dalmatia and Dacia, amber, 'that precious act of God', from remote Baltica, the glass of Phoenicia, papyrus from Egypt, parchment from Pergomena in Hither Asia, silks from China by way of the Parthian route, incense from Arabia, the *purpura* dye from the Levant and pepper, which was so highly esteemed that Alaric the Hun would not open negotiations with fallen Rome in AD 408 until he had been delivered 30,000 pounds of the stuff.

The Via Aurelia, which joined the Portuensis, led past the Theatrum Marcelli, parts of which were incorporated into a fifteenth-century palazzo, then directly to the Forum, the Rostra and the Golden Milestone.

The regionaries, compiled in the fourth century under the aegis of Constantine, give a description of the city of Rome as well as a list of the number of bridges, hills, forums, etc. The city had then 11 public and 856 private baths, 37 gates, 423 parishes (*vici*), 29 main roads from the centre to the outskirts, to which must be added an enormous number of minor streets, alleys and *areae*, small squares scattered among the network of streets; 25 suburban roads, 8 bridges; 2 Capitols; 190 granaries; 2 large markets (*macella*); 254 mills; 8 large parks (all the open land that was left); 11 forums; 10 basilicas; 37 marble arches; 1,352 fountains; 28 libraries; 2 circuses; 2 amphitheatres; 2 *naumachiae* for naval shows; and 4 gladiatorial barracks (*ludi*). All this brought people to Rome, to conduct business, to enter school, to start a trade, to enter a legion, to file a complaint, to argue a law case, to plead with the Senate or emperor, or to die came thousands of diverse people from diverse lands.

The Via Flaminia brought in the last roads to Rome. It had joined all those north of the Alps, beyond the Pyrenees and the Alpine regions of Noricum, the serrated lands of Dalmatia and beyond. As a mighty stream it gathered in all these roads. Now within the city itself the Flaminia made common cause with the Aurelia as it marched along. Beyond the Milvian Bridge it moved directly to the heart of Rome. It passed under its own gateway into and out of what is now Piazza del Popolo, down what is now Via del Corso, then passed the tomb of Augustus and the Ara Pacis. The altar erected by the Senate was dedicated on January 30, 9 BC, on the occasion of the emperor's return from Spain and Gaul, to the peace he had wrought. The Via Flaminia passed the Column of Marcus Aurelius, raised in 176 AD to honour that emperor's campaigns against the Sarmatians and the Marcomanni, a frank imitation of Trajan's Column.

The Via Flaminia was conducted on its last journey by the Vicus Argentarius past Julius Caesar's Forum toward the Golden Milestone. The wayfarer on the way to the Miliarium Aureum could lay aside his silver cups and stay his path to see, like the finger of God, Trajan's great column projected 38 metres into the Roman heavens. After that, within 100 metres the Via Flaminia, the last of the nineteen roads, crossed the flank of the Capitoline and moves down to Severus's arch in the Forum.

The Miliarium Aureum was well known in history. The carved pillar, covered with gilded bronze, was set up beside the Rostra by Augustus in 20 BC. It bore the engraved names of the principal cities of the Empire and their distances from Rome. And here those great lifelines of civilisation, coming from every edge of the horizon, met in the heart of Rome. These are not the *disjecta membra* of the past but part of its living body and the construction, extension and maintenance of the Roman road system had a continuity of purpose that has never been equalled.

This road building went on for eight hundred years until the end, as it must for all empires, finally came.

By that time Rome had paved the world.

CHRONOLOGICAL TABLE

DATE	POLITICAL EVENT	ROAD BUILDING
BC 753	Legendary founding of Rome	
ca. 450		Roads existing, at least as dirt tracks: Salaria, Latina, Norbon (Appia), Tiberina (Flaminia), Cornelia (Aurelia), Veientana (Cassia), Clodia and Ardeatina
ca. 350		Via Latina goes to Mt Algidus and to Liri Valley as a *via vicina*
350	Campania becomes part of Rome	
327	Second Samnite War	Lime mortar, cement, introduced into Magna Graecia
312		Appius Claudius begins Via Appia on top of Via Norbona
ca. 300	Etruria absorbed by Rome	
267	Brindisi captured by Rome	
241	Sicily ceded to Rome at end of First Punic War	Via Aurelia built from Rome to Pisa
220	Gaius Flaminius censor	Via Flaminia: Rome, Fano and Rimini
218	Hannibal crosses the Alps: victor over the Romans at the River Trebbia	
187		M. Aemilius Lepidus builds the Via Aemilia from Rimini to Piacenza. Old track from Rome to Arezzo rebuilt
177		
149–146	Third Punic War; Carthage destroyed	Via Postumia built to serve Genoa, Piacenza, Cremona, and Aquileia; Via Aemilia extended to Piacenza and Tortona
148–132		Via Flaminia extended along the Adriatic to Brindisi
ca. 145		Via Egnatia built from Albania to Greece. First stone bridge built across the Tiber
ca. 140–125		Via Cassia in slow stages reaches Florence and Pisa
132		Old gravel track rebuilt and named Via Popilia, goes from Capua to Reggio (Rhegium)
130	Cn. Manlius Aquilius	Builds first roads in Asia Minor: milestones
123	Gaius Gracchus; social revolution	Milestones on all roads become general
109		Via Aemilia Scauri built to continue Via Aurelia
77		Pompey builds road over Cottian Alps (Alpes Cottiae) from Turin to Vienne in France
60	First Triumvirate: Caesar, Pompey, Crassus	
58	Caesar begins conquest of Gaul	
49	Caesar crosses the Rubicon	
44	Caesar murdered; Octavian consul	Law forbidding wheeled traffic in Rome
27	Octavian emperor	Repairs whole of Via Flaminia
15	Campaign of Tiberius and Drusus in the Alps	Drusus builds new road over Reschen Scheideck Pass
I		Via Augusta in Spain rebuilt between Narbonne and Cadiz
AD 3		Via Sebaste (Augusta) built in Turkey
5	Conquest of Rhaetia and Noricum	Agrippa builds roads in Lower Rhine
11–16	Germanicus' campaign against Germans	Tiberius builds road between Gabes and Tebessa
12–15		Via Gemina built; Via Julia Augusta built over the Plöckenpass–Aguntum–Junavum (Salzburg)
24–5		Via Argenta built from Mèrida to Salamanca (Tiberius)
41–54	Claudius emperor	Repairs Via Augusta in Spain
43	Britain conquered by Claudius	Work begun on Rome port opposite Ostia
44		Watling Street in Britain extended to St Albans
53		Claudius completes Via Claudia Augusta through the Brenner Pass, Altino (Adriatic) to Donauworth (Germania)
54	Claudius murdered; Nero emperor	

DATE	POLITICAL EVENT	ROAD BUILDING
54–9		Nero repairs the Via Augusta and the Via Argenta in Spain
64	Great fire in Rome; first persecutions of Christians	
69	Vespasian emperor	Via Flavia built on Dalmatian coast
75		Road built in Africa from Bône (Hippo) to Tebessa
77–9		Vespasian builds the Via Nova from Astorga to Braga
79	Eruption of Vesuvius; Pompeii and Herculaneum buried	
ca. 80		Via Domitiana built from Sinuessa to Naples
81	Colosseum completed in Rome	
86		Road built along entire Dalmatian coast as the Via Gabrina
98	Nerva dies; Trajan emperor	Via Nerva begun in North Africa (Tripoli–Alexandria)
98–117		New Road built by Trajan from Qift (Coptos) to Berenice
ca. 100	Greatest extent of Roman Empire	
104		Bridge over Danube built by Apollodorus of Damascus
104–106	Conquest of Dacia; becomes Roman province	
113–6		Trajan's engineers repair the Via Egnatia
114		Via Traiana, from Benevento to Canosa and Brindisi, begun;
115		Trajan builds the Via Traiana Nova from Lake Bolsena to Chiusi; by-pass of Via Cassia
117	Trajan dies (August 8) at Selinous (Turkey); Hadrian emperor	
121		Hadrian reinforces the *limes* in Germania: improves roads
125		Hadrian overhauls the Via Cassia
122–7		Hadrian's Wall built in Britain
123		New road built in Africa from Tebessa to Carthage
128		Special Via built between quarries of Simmitthus (Tunisia) and sea-port of Thabraca
137–8		Via Hadriana Nova joins Antinöopolis (on the Nile) and Berenice (Red Sea)
138	Hadrian dies; Antoninus Pius emperor	
180	Marcus Aurelius dies; Commodus emperor	
193	Septimius Severus emperor	
197		Via Severiana built to connect Terracina with Ostia
211	Death of Septimius Severus; Caracalla emperor	
214		Caracalla rebuilds all principal roads in Spain
271	Aurelian emperor; begins wall of Rome	
284–378	Diocletian emperor	Repairs roads in Spain. Desert road, Vallum Diocletianum, Damascus–Palmyra. Builds Strata Diocletiana, Sura (on the Euphrates) to Resafa
306–37	Constantine emperor	Constantine rebuilds Via Nova in Spain
317–23		
330	Constantinople second capital	
346–78	Valens emperor	
375		Repairs and erects last dated milestone on the Via Egnatia (Salonika–Durazzo)
410	Britain is cut loose from the Roman empire	Repair of roads left to provinces. General decline of Roman road system

SELECTED BIBLIOGRAPHY

GENERAL

Bergier, Nicolas, *Histoire des Grands Chemins de l'Empire Romain*, 1st ed., 1626; 2nd ed., Bruxelles, 1728; 3rd ed., 2 vols., with engraved Peutinger Table, Bruxelles, 1736; *A General History of the Highways*, 4 vols., London, 1712 (trans.). *The Cambridge Ancient History*; De Camp, J. Sprague, *The Ancient Engineers*, London, 1963; Charlesworth, M.P., *Trade Routes and Commerce of the Roman Empire*, Cambridge, 1924; Forbes, R.J., 'Notes on the History of Ancient Roads and their Construction', *University of Amsterdam, Archaeol. Hist. Bijdr. A*, No. 3, Amsterdam, 1934. Reprint 1964, Hakkert, Amsterdam; Gregory, A.H., *The Story of the Road*, London, 1938; *Itinerarium Provinciarum Antonini Augusti*; *Itinerarium Hierosolymitanum* (Burdigalense), first published by Wesseling, 1736; Miller, Konrad, *Weltkarte des Castorius gennant Die Peutingersche Tafel*, text and map, Ravensburg, 1888; *Die Peutingersche Tafel (der Weltkarte des Castorius)*, Stuttgart, 1962; *Itineraria Romana: Römische Reiswege an der hand der Tabula Peutingeriana*, Stuttgart, 1916; Mommsen, T., *The Provinces of the Roman Empire*, London, 1886; Rostovtzeff, M., *Caravan Cities*, Oxford, 1932; *Social and Economic History of the Roman Empire*, Oxford, 1938; Singer, Charles, ed., *A History of Technology*, 5 vols., Oxford, 1954–7; *Tabula Peutingeriana*, first published by Marcus Welser, Leyden, 1591; Tenny, Frank, ed., *Economic Survey of Ancient Rome*, 6 vols., Baltimore, 1937; Warmington, E.H., *The Commerce between the Roman Empire and India*, Cambridge, 1928; Wells, J., and Barrow, R.H., *A Short History of the Roman Empire*, London, 1950; Wheeler, Sir Mortimer, *Rome Beyond the Imperial Frontier*, London, 1954.

NORTH AFRICA

Aurigemma, S., 'Pietre Miliari Tripolitane', *Rivista della Tripolitania*, Anno II (1924), Nos. 1–11; Baradez, Jean, *Fossatum Africae: Vue Aérienne de l'Organisation Romaine dans le Sud-Algérien*, Arts et Métiers Graphiques, Paris, 1949; Corò, F., 'Le antiche strade romane della Tripolitania Occidentale', *Rivista delle colonie italiane*, Jan.–Feb., 1931; Goodchild, R.G., *Roman Roads and Milestones in Tripolitania*, British Military Admin., Dept. of Antiquities, Tripoli, 1947; Gsell, Stéphane, *Les Monuments Antiques de l'Algérie*, 2 vols., Paris, 1901; *Histoire Ancienne de l'Afrique du Nord*, Paris, 1913; Haynes, D.E.L., *The Antiquities of Tripolitania*, Tripoli, 1955; Poinssot, Claude, *Les Ruines de Dougga*, Institut National d'Archéologie et Arts, Tunis, 1958; Romanelli, P., *Le grandi strade romane nell'Africa Settentrionale*, Istituto di Studi Romani, Rome, 1937; Salama, P., *Les Voies Romaines de l'Afrique du Nord*, Imprimerie Officielle du Gouvernement Général de l'Algérie, Algiers, 1951; Warmington, B.H., *The North African Provinces*, Cambridge, 1954.

MIDDLE EAST

Dinand, Maurice, 'La Strata Diocletiana', *Revue Biblique*, 1 April, 1931, pp. 227–8; Fedden, Robin, *Syria and Lebanon*, London, 1966; Harding, G. Lankester, *The Antiquities of Jordan*, London, 1959; Isidorus of Charax, *The Parthian Stations*, Philadelphia, 1914 (trans.); Meredith, David, 'Roman Remains in the Eastern Desert of Egypt', *J. of Egyptian Archaeol.*, XXXVIII (1952), pp. 94–111; XXXIX (1953), 95–105; Monterde, R., and Poidebard, A., *Le Limes de Chalcis*, Paris, 1945; Murray, G.W., 'Roman Roads and Stations in the Eastern Desert of Egypt', *J. of Egyptian Archaeol.*, XI (1925), pp. 138–150; Poidebard, A., 'Coupes de la Chaussée Romaine Antioche-Chalcis', *Syria*, X, 1929, p. 22ff.; *La Trace de Rome dans le Désert de Syrie*, Paris, 1934; *Periplus Maris Erythraei*, New York, 1912 (trans.); Stark, Freya, *Rome on the Euphrates*, London, 1966; Treganza, L.A., *The Red Sea Mountains of Egypt*, Oxford, 1955.

ASIA MINOR

Bean, George W., *Aegean Turkey: an Archaeological Guide*, London, 1966; Calder, W. M., and Bean, George W., *Classical Map of Asia Minor*, British Institute of Archaeology, Ankara, 1957; Fahrner, Prof. R., *Die Brücken und Höhlen in Anatolia*, Berlin, 1967; Magie, D., *Roman Rule in Asia Minor to the End of the Third Century after Christ*, Princeton, 1950; Mollinary, A., *Die Römerstrassen in der Europaische Turkei*, Zagreb, 1941; Munro, S. A. R., 'Roads in Pontus, Royal and Roman', *J. of Hellenic Studies*, XXI, 1901; Stark, Freya, *Alexander's Path*, London, 1958; Talip, S., *Le strade romane nell' Anatolia*, Rome, 1938.

THE BALKANS

Ballif, F., *Römische Strassen in Bosniën und Hercegovina*, Vienna, 1893; *Das Strassenwesen in Bosniën und der Hercegovina*, Vienna, 1903; Collaert, Paul, 'Une Réfection de la Via Egnatia', *Bulletin de Correspondance Hellenique*, LIX (1935), pp. 395–416; Domaszewski, A. von, 'Beneiziarposten und das Römischen Strassennetz', *Westdeutsche Zeitschrift für Geschichte und Kunst*, Trier, 1902; Evans, A., *Antiquarian Researches in Illyricum*, I–IV, Westminster, 1883–5; Makaronas, Char. I., 'Via Egnatia and Thessalonike', *Studies Presented to David Moore Robinson*, pp. 350–8; Mengeringhausen, J., 'Die Trajanstrasse am unteren Donau', *Technikgeschichte Bd. 22*, 1933, 136; Panaitescu, Emil, *Le grandi strade romane nella Romania*, Istituto di Studi Romani, Rome, 1938; Petsas, Photios M., *Pella, Studies in Medit. Archaeol.*, Vol. XIV, Lund, 1964; Vulič, Nicola, *Le strade romane in Jugoslavia*, Istituto di Studi Romani, Rome, 1938; Zippel, G., *Die Römische Herrschaft in Illyrien bis auf Augustus*, Leipzig, 1877.

RAETIA, NORICUM AND GERMANIA

Cartellieri, W., 'Die Römischen Alpenstrassen', *Philologus*, Supplementband XVIII, Heft I, Leipzig, 1926; Deringer, H., 'Die Römische Reichsstrasse Aquilei Lauriacum', *Carinthia*, Klagenfurt, 139 (1949), 140 (1950); Hagen, Joseph, *Die Römerstrassen in der Rheinprovinz*, Bonn, 1932; Janderek, H., *Die Strassen der Römer*, Wels, 1951; Koban, Heinrich, 'Die Veneter- und Römerstrasse bei Mauthen', '*Carinthia 1*,' *Mitt. des Geschichtsvereines für Kärnten*, Klagenfurt, 1948, pp. 247–66; Meyer, H., 'Die Römischen Alpenstrassen', *Schweiz. Mitt. Antiq. Ges. Zurich*, XIII, 1861, Zurich; Meysels, Theodor F., *Auf Römerstrassen durch Österreich*, Vienna, 1960; Paulus, E., 'Die Römerstrassen', *Schriften des Wurttemb. Althert. Ver.* 1863, Heft 6; Polaschek, E., *Die Römische Vergangheit*, Vienna, 1952.

GAUL

Blanchet, J. A., with Grenier, A., *Carte Archéologique de la Gaule Romaine (Forma Orbis Romani)*, Paris, 1931–60; Breuer, J., *La Belgique Romaine*, Bruxelles, 1946; *Le strade romane nel Belgio*, Istituto di Studi Romani, Rome, 1938; Brogan, Olwen, *Roman Gaul*, London, 1953; Byvanck, A. W., *Nederland in den Romeinischen Tijd*, 2 vols., Leiden, 1945; Carnoy, A., 'Toponymie des Chaussées Romaines en Belgique et dans les Régions Avoisinantes, Essai d'Hodonymie', *L'Antiquité Classique*, Bruxelles, XXIII, 1954, fasc. 1, pp. 18–25; Cumont, F. V. M., *Comment la Belgique fut Romanisée*, Bruxelles, 1914; Grenier, A., *Manuel d'Archéologie Gallo-Romaine*, 2 vols., Paris, 1931, 1934; *Le strade romane nella Gallia*, Istituto di Studi Romani, Roma, 1937; Lefebvre des Noëttes, 'Le Tracé des Voies Romaines', *Bull. Antiqu. de France*, 1924, 85; 'Comparaison entre la Voie Romaine et la Route Moderne', *Bull. Antiqu. de France*, 1924, 253; Wuilleumier, P., and Sautel, J., *Les Voies Axiales de Lugdunum*, Lyon, 1943.

BRITANNIA

Boughery, G. M., *Along the Roman Roads*, London, 1935; Codrington, Thomas, *Roman Roads in Britain*, London, 1918; Cotterell, Leonard, *The Great Invasion*, London, 1958; Margary,

Ivan, *Roman Roads in Britain*, 2 vols., London, 1955, 1957; Mothersole, Jessie, *Agricola Road into Scotland*, London, 1927; Ordnance Survey, *Map of Roman Britain*, 3rd edition, Chessington, 1956; Richmond, Sir Ian A., *Roman Britain*, London, 1963.

SPAIN

Arias, Gonzalo, ed., 'El Miliario Extravagante', *Boletín intermitente de Geografía Histórica*, Ris-Orangis (S-O), France, 1963; Bardón, P.C.M., and Román, B.O., 'La Calzada Romana "La Plata" en la Provincia de Salamanca', *Min. de Obras Publicas*, Serie B, No. 2, Madrid, 1949; Menéndez Pidál, Gonzalo, 'Los Caminos en la Historia de España', *Cultura Hispanica*, Madrid, 1951; Menéndez Pidál, Rámon, *Historia de España*, vol. 11: *España Romana*, Madrid, 1962; Van Sickle, W.W., 'The Repair of the Roman Roads in Spain under the Roman Empire', *Classical Philology*, XXIV (1929), pp. 77–88; Wiseman, F.J., *Roman Spain*, London, 1956.

ITALY

Ashby, Thomas, *The Roman Campagna in Classical Times*, London, 1927; 'Via Collatina Praenestina, and Labicana', *Papers of the Brit. Sch. at Rome*, I, p. 121ff.; 'Via Salaria Nomentana and Tiburtina', *Papers of the Brit. Sch. at Rome*, III, p. 1ff.; 'Via Latina', *Papers of the Brit. Sch. at Rome*, IV, p. 1ff.; (with Fell, R.A.L.), 'Via Flaminia', *Jor. of Roman Studies*, XI, p. 125ff.; 'Via Tiberina', *Memorie dell'Accademia Pontificia*, Rome, I, 2, p. 129ff. Bartoli, Pietro Santi, *Colonna Traiana*, Rome, 1673; Canina, Luigi, *La prima parte della Via Appia dalla Porta Capena a Boville*, Rome, 1853; Gardner, Robert, 'Via Claudia Valeria (Collarmele – Pescara)', *Papers of the Brit. Sch. at Rome*, IX (1920), p. 75ff.; Harris, William, 'The Via Cassia and the Via Traiana Nova between Bolsena and Chiusi', *Papers of the Brit. Sch. at Rome*, XXXIII (1965), pp. 113–33; Hofmann, A.von, 'Via Flaminia', *Neue Schweiz. Rundschau*, XX, 8, 797; Labruzzi, C., *Via Appia illustrata ab Urbe Roma ad Capuam*, Rome, 1790; Martinori, Edouardo, *Via Flaminia, Studio Storico-Topografico*, Rome, 1929; Martinori, Edouardo, *Via Cassia e sue deviazioni, Studio Storico-Topografico*, Rome, 1930; *Via Salaria, Studio Storico-Topografico*, Rome, 1931; *Via Nomentana, Via Patinaria, e Via Tiburtina, Studio Storico-Topografico*, Rome, 1932; Pratilli, F.M., *Della Via Appia riconosciuta e descritta da Roma a Brindisi*, Naples, 1745; Van Essen, C.C., 'Via Valeria from Tivoli to Collarmele', *Papers of the Brit. Sch. at Rome*, XXV (1957), pp. 22–38; Ward Perkins, J.B., and Fredericksen, M.W., 'The Ancient Road Systems of the Central and Northern Ager Faliscus (Notes on Southern Etruria, 2)', *Papers of the Brit. Sch. at Rome*, XXV (1957), pp. 67–203.

TABULA IMPERII ROMANI

Published under the auspices of the Union Academique Internationale, Brussels by the efforts of the Unione Accademica Nazionale Italiana in Rome.

Sheets issued so far
H.I.33, *Lepcis Magna*, compiled by Goodchild, R.G., Society of Antiquaries of London, 1954; H.I.34, *Cyrene*, compiled by Goodchild, R.G., Society of Antiquaries of London, 1954; L.32, *Milano* (*Mediolanum – Aventicum – Brigantium*), Unione Accademica Nazionale, Rome, 1966; L.33, *Trieste* (*Tergeste*), Unione Accademica Nazionale, Rome, 1966; L.34/5, *Drobeta – Romula – Sucidava* (*Dacia Inferior*), compiled by Tudor, D., Rumanian Academy, Bucharest, 1965; M.32, *Moguntiacum* (*Mainz*), compiled by Goessler, P., Archäologischer Institut des Deutschen Reiches, Römisch-Germanische Kommission, Frankfurt-Main, 1940; (N.)F.36, *Wadi Halfa*, Survey of Egypt, Giza, July, 1934; (N.)G.36, *Coptos*, compiled by Meredith, David; Society of Antiquaries of London, 1958. This was the Aswan sheet of the Survey of Egypt series; (N.)H.35, *Alexandria*, Survey of Egypt, Giza, June, 1934; (N.)H.36, *Cairo*, Survey of Egypt, Giza, July, 1934.

INDEX